The Foe We Face

THE FOE WE FACE

BY PIERRE J. HUSS

GARDEN CITY, NEW YORK   1942

DOUBLEDAY, DORAN & CO., INC.

I dedicate this book to
JOSEPH V. CONNOLLY
and
BARRY FARIS,
the bosses.

Prelude to Hitlerland

INSIDE HITLER'S GERMANY there are three component parts which make the Third Reich tick: the military, the Nazi party, and behind all that, like an unseen hand, the Gestapo. It is a dread word, abbreviated from the German for Secret State Police: Geheime Staats Polizei.

It is scarcely possible for anyone to live there nowadays without being keenly aware of the existence of that far-spread web headed by Heinrich Himmler, the cold and calculating master of the fixed tiger smile. He is everywhere, looking into your heart and home. This without ever perhaps having the Gestapo come right at you in the open to take you away or raid your apartment; no, it is just the fact that when living in Germany you must live and breathe from the secret lung of the land.

As the years under Nazi rule went by and restriction

after restriction piled up to narrow personal liberties, the average German knuckled down and played safe by withdrawing more and more into his shell. Month by month I watched with trepidation as those German faces became harder with a look of suspicion in the eyes for every second man. Soon enough it became useless to arrange for a luncheon chat with more than one German at the table. Two together would talk to you, but in reality they would talk for the other German in the company, displaying the patterned Nazi viewpoints to the bitter end. For, by force of habit, they were playing safe and thinking of the Gestapo. Over the years, a great many of these Germans actually came to believe their own hypocrisies until they now take for granted all the Nazis tell them.

Herein lies the basic barrier to the Germany of days gone by, when Heidelberg students dueled and drank beer between songs and forty-eight political parties fought for seats in the Reichstag. There was always that military spirit, but not the deadly weight of the Nazi machine with its ruthless subjugation of the individual to the state.

As a foreigner living inside the Reich, you may circumvent or even escape some of the greater hardships of Nazi life such as the irksome pressure of overzealous party minions, but the whole background weighs heavily on you. Go shopping, and in the welter of Hitler pictures and swastikas you find on almost every store and display window the ominous sign: Not for Jews. Read a foreign newspaper on the streetcar, and people stare. Get food packages from the outside—coffee, butter, eggs, ducks—and immediately you become an object of suspicion. Sooner or later jealousy and distrust draw you within the shadow of the Gestapo.

I lived eight years inside this Hitler Reich, pounding away at the job of covering Central Europe for the hot wires of International News Service. Everything under the sun happened out of Berlin in those eight years, in peace and war. You had to work hard and long, frequently taking your food and sleep on the wing to keep up with Hitler. You had your hands full, which may be why the few of us who stayed from Hitler's rise to power to his war on America were able to stand it, Gestapo and all. But our break had to come, and it is just as well that it did come before 1942.

If the German and the foreigner within the Reich walked constantly in an atmosphere pervaded by fear, then the foreign correspondent of important outlets across the borders was the focal point of special attention from official Nazidom and the silent target of the ever-watchful Gestapo. Until the middle of 1941 the American key correspondents —chiefs of the news agencies and the big papers—were the hottest game of the Nazis. The merry-go-round of official propaganda centered everlastingly around them. I had good times and bad, with the constant strain and stress of getting the news and the feeling at all times of being utterly out of place.

It got on your nerves, this life with the Nazis. Yet they tried to be pleasant and courteous, although tempers slipped occasionally and then a lot of pent-up steam came out. The barrier to a less restless existence in Germany lay in your heart, deep and unmistakably so, where you felt the curious unreality of Hitler's kingdom and misgivings for the future. At times, when visiting firemen from home or fellow correspondents from New York on transient assignment said the wrong thing or implied it without intending to, you began to resent your lot. Many correspondents went out of Berlin back to America a year or more ago. That made it still harder, for you felt like a sucker and worried lest folks at home wondered why you, too, didn't leave the Nazis behind. In the end you kept your mouth shut and went on with your work.

When Hitler attacked Russia and Roosevelt began to make it clear in the middle of 1941 that the world is too small for Hitler and America, things really got tough for the American correspondents in Berlin. Day by day we expected the end. In fact, in the maelstrom of Nazi politics we became the football of clashing interests and rivalries. You had to watch your step, keeping in mind that every German official who mixed with you as he used to was simply being foolhardy. The "verboten" sign hung all over us, and over in the Gestapo headquarters I suppose they dusted off those thick dossiers on our histories.

For the last four months of 1941 it was amply clear to me that to continue my work as it should be done was no longer possible. Official communiqués and the military announcements, with speeches and tirades on the part of the controlled press against America in general and President Roosevelt in particular, just about completed the allotted freedom from censorship. Everything else was taboo. The outlook for 1942 was even blacker. I had had enough, and decided to go, a task in itself an uncertain and difficult one. But it worked, and three months after laying my plans I landed in Lisbon en route for home. Japan's attack on America and Hitler's declaration of war came shortly thereafter, blacking out the last of the Americans corresponding from most of the Continent.

In the busy years before we were able to observe and absorb much for future reference, storing up the facts and sidelights on a fanatic and his people. There is much to be told. I lived through eight years of Hitler and his Nazis and got to know them at first hand. The facts as I remember them—and I remember them vividly—show Hitler and his minions at work, at play, and as nearly as possible as they act under given circumstances. In the attitudes and actions, which I have recorded in this book, of the human spawn in brown shirts whom I came to know so well in their first eight years of power, may be found perhaps some part of the key to the strange character of the greatest foe we have ever faced.

It goes without saying that eight years in a man's life cannot be lived out in a country hostile to his every ideal of political and private conduct without either inuring or embittering him deeply. When I closed my desk up in the Dorotheenstrasse on a murky November day in 1941, I knew that my task and my life in Berlin were over. I glanced through the window into the Wilhelmstrasse below me, and a feeling of relief came surging up. The Nazis and their false showmanship, their insincerities, and their pretexts of being a super-race would soon be gone. But gone, too, would be those German men and women who helped make it possible for me to endure those hectic eight years in Hitlerland, years of my life which can never be repeated or forgotten. They are all there today, a few among millions but nevertheless representative of many minds other than those cracking the whip on top. They are the Germans waiting for salvation, waiting for Hitler and his Nazis to fall, waiting for escape into the ideals and principles we are fighting for.

In these eight years, of course, I had the rare pleasure of rubbing elbows with colleagues from the four corners of the earth. I could name them by the dozen, scattered today on all the fronts of the world, the cream of the foreign correspondents, men of courage and ability who need not take their hats off to any Richard Harding Davis. They were a privilege to know and to work with, and wherever they are, I greet them from the pages of this book. They are recording the history of today, in many cases at the risk of their lives or at least at the cost of great personal sacrifice.

I said good-by to Berlin in a November dawn and flew off from Templehof with scarcely a regret. We came down in Stuttgart for final inspection by the Gestapo, and there they stripped me of money and letters; this despite the official requests to the contrary I had wangled out of the Foreign Office in Berlin. The Gestapo in Stuttgart obviously had taken to heart the new Nazi lessons of hatred against all Americans, and acted accordingly. That was my farewell to Germany.

In Barcelona, where I spent the night, I found hunger

and dangerous undercurrents of dissatisfaction. Rifled guards from Madrid patrolled all streets and stood in groups of six on street corners; in Madrid I found the same thing, except that the guards were from Catalonia. They would just as soon shoot a Madrileno as eat. That was evident on their faces, and the same sentiment was reflected on the faces of the natives of Madrid.

In Lisbon I encountered the Gestapo. I walked into the York Bar with Lynn Heinzerling of the Associated Press and found myself staring into the face of Grosse, chief of the foreign liaison section of the Gestapo's International Police in Berlin. That rather took my appetite away, and I sailed off a couple of days later on the American ship *Excambion* without a word of farewell for Europe. It was my good fortune to find Alexander Woollcott aboard, who gave the sound advice and encouragement I needed for the subsequent writings for *Cosmopolitan* and this book. The Lisbon lights still shone on the Tagus as we moved quietly down the river to the sea, leaving the spreading black-out and Hitler to their inevitable fate. I have no fear that we shall master both.

PIERRE J. HUSS

Contents

xv

The Foe We Face

CHAPTER 1

The Foe We Face

IN JANUARY OF 1935 Adolf Hitler was sitting out the winter in his alpine chalet on the Obersalzberg, above Berchtesgaden, somewhat tensely awaiting the outcome of the plebiscite. A vote in his favor for the return of the Saar to the Fatherland meant success and the go-ahead signal for his revolutionary program of twenty-five points drafted in the Nazi party political platform; a lost plebiscite would have spelled doom and bitter disappointment for his ambitious future plans as master of Europe. He let Goebbels and others loudly beat the drum while he sat up there in the snow and went walking with the huge white Hungarian shepherd dog always at his side.

At such times the German Fuehrer strictly forbade his guards to follow; he relied entirely on the dog at his side, the heavy walking stick of knotted wood, and the rapid-fire lueger automatic in his pocket. He wore a gray golf suit with heavy woolen socks stuck into snow boots and an old felt hat drawn down over his right eye, and on days when the wind whistled sharply or snow whipped through the air, a gray mackintosh with a muffler around his neck. He'd crunch the snow with a slow step and proceed by a short cut over the hill back of his chalet toward a somewhat forsaken Bavarian-style café. It was built of wood and had rocks on the roof to hold it down. There, sitting on the hard chairs hewn by peasant hands, Hitler drank hot milk and chatted about mountains and weather and cows with the bearded mountain men who might be having their daily restoratives of schnapps at that moment. Now and then they'd delve into politics but only if Hitler led the way, as occasionally he did. For this was his own close circle of alpine neighbors, a surviving fraction of private life still dear to him then but shortly to vanish entirely in the rush of power and glory that came with new conquests.

I had arranged through Karl Boemer and Alfred Rosenberg for an interview with Hitler on the day of the Saar plebiscite returns, on the assumption that it would be an opportune moment sure to find him in the best of moods, provided everything went in his favor. I arrived there to find him in high glee, with Goering on hand in a huge white sweater to help celebrate the victory in the Saar with its overwhelming majority in favor of immediate return to Germany. Hitler was in his golf suit, studying the latest returns, and his eyes were alight with joy. Without wasting time on ceremonies, he got his hat and stick and insisted that I accompany him on his usual walk before lunch. The big Hungarian dog plowed ahead of us through the snow, cavorting and barking with delight. But he seldom rushed further than ten yards away, turning back to see that his lord and master was following in good order. Later I was told that this dog could be relied upon to rip to pieces any stranger approaching Hitler unannounced.

We reached the crest of the hill at the edge of the pine woods and looked back. I was breathing hard, for this was not my customary daily routine. Hitler grinned slyly and said it was good exercise, this walking through the deep snow, the only kind of exercise, he said, he had time or inclination to take. He pointed with his stick to his chalet below and to the sweeping hills around it.

"A good rifle shot, aiming through telescopic sights, could easily pick me off from here while I am sitting on the porch or in that back room there," Hitler said in a matter-of-fact way. "I am buying up all these hills and making it forbidden property so that Himmler can quit worrying. I have also had the road you came up on commandeered, closing it to public traffic so that in effect this whole section of the mountain will now be closed off to any but authorized persons."

His walking stick pointed far across the valley to the distant city of Salzburg we could just make out under the clouds over in Austria. "Himmler and the army people got together sometime ago and figured out that a few well-directed cannon shots from over there some dark night could blow us out of bed," the Nazi Fuehrer said with something of a forced laugh. He resumed the walk and added: "I told Himmler he'd have to worry a while longer over that problem; I cannot just walk over the border and take a piece out of Austria, and I will not move this house away or abandon it just to get out from under the range of Austrian cannons. I am a fatalist and all those things take care of themselves."

I thought to myself that Hitler was taking chances walking by himself in these lonely mountains, even if he did buy them by the mile in order to keep strangers at a distance. A legion of people would gladly have knocked him off. With this in mind, I pointed to two woodchoppers making their way some hundreds of yards ahead of us toward the lonely Bavarian café and boldly said they could easily overpower him before he'd have a chance to defend himself or call for help. I wanted to hear what he'd say.

He nodded and whistled for the dog and held him by the collar, while he told me to press a hard snowball together and throw it high and afar. I did this, and the snowball went sailing off into the air.

Hitler whipped an automatic out of his pocket and with deliberate aim fired at my snowball. A split second after his shot rang out the snowball burst apart in midair, obviously torn by the passing bullet. I suppose I looked a bit skeptical, for Hitler asked me to throw a second snowball. He shot leisurely, and, it seemed to me, almost without aiming. The snowball broke violently to pieces in midair.

Hitler replaced the pistol in his pocket and tapped me on the arm. "*Sehen sie*, I am not entirely defenseless," he smiled. "It is generally conceded in the S.S. and the army that I am a better pistol shot than most of their best ones. I also make it a point to know more about guns and weapons and bullets of all kinds than those who come to me to explain the intricacies of a new rifle bore or a cannon's mechanism. I have read and studied many technical books on those subjects, including one or two by your American experts. I believe I can say with justification that I am one of the few all-around ballistic experts in the world today."

I checked up in German army circles on that claim and found it generally substantiated. He has a standing order out for every book on that subject and frequently reads deep into the night to absorb a new experiment with shells or bullets. He can draw a blueprint on the involved mechanism of German or foreign large- and small-caliber guns and do it from memory. That is one of those things about Hitler one shouldn't forget in sizing him up as the man we now are out to beat.

He is a fanatic, every inch of him, going into a passion or fury when the occasion demands. I touched him off on that walk in the snow with a hint that some of his twenty-five-point program would set the world afire if carried out to the letter. He stopped dead in his tracks and like a flash he changed from the Bavarian alpine rambler to Adolf Hitler, dictator of flaring temperament and rabble-rousing fanatic. He stamped the snow with his boot and waved his walking stick in fervid agitation.

"Sooner than give up one little point on my program," he shouted out, "I'd go over to that tree and hang myself. I have no need for political programs designed to fool the masses into voting for me; no, I created a program many years ago and today I stand on it. The Saar bore out my program in yesterday's plebiscite. Look at the results. I know my Germans. The twenty-five-point program cannot change or be changed; it can only be fulfilled to the letter because it expresses the will of Germany. I expressed the will of my people in it and therefore my people will follow me to its fulfillment. It will stand as the Third Reich will stand, and generations coming after us will point to it and say that there the new Germany and with it a new future was born."

More than a year later he marched into the demilitarized Rhineland, first step of a long series plotted out carefully in his mind to score the fulfillment of his program as recorded in *Mein Kampf*. He will never change, for in his mind is anchored the firm conviction that he is endowed with a Divine mission and guided and inspired by Providence, and that therefore he can do no wrong. He judges everything accordingly. He resents interference and makes it a point to pay back tenfold the grievances inflicted in the old days before he was taken seriously, and at the same time he likes to rub salt in the wounds of others by heaping gifts and favors on those who offered a kind word or fed him when hungry. In Naziland, if you were new there and apt to wonder, this sidelight on the Fuehrer would have explained many a puzzling thing. The reason, for example, why hunchbacked Heine Hoffmann today has unlimited monopoly on Hitler pictures and paintings and has become a multimillionaire. He invested his pennies wisely by feeding Hitler and providing a roof over his head.

I recall how mystified the curiosity-loving Viennese were in March of 1938 when, amid all the Nazi martial music and marching, Hitler arrived with his cavalcade of cars in the city he had known as a penniless youngster before World War I. He had failed there, and gone hungry, eventually turning a disgruntled back on its spires for the onion-topped towers of Munich. He came back in 1938 as Hitler, the dictator, and if Vienna didn't recall the young house painter and dabbler in art who wanted to be an architect, he remembered it very well. He swung off the main highway outside the city and directed his chauffeur through side streets away from the cordoned approaches to the inner heart of beautiful Vienna. Finally, proceeding down the Ring to the Imperial Hotel, Hitler stood up in his car and gazed around.

"*Ja, meine herren*, here we are!" he said for all to hear, although I doubt whether the Viennese and his own entourage caught the significance of that smirking smile. I had stood there in the crush, waiting for his arrival for nearly half an hour. He got out of the car and many a Vienna native who stood in front of the Imperial Hotel must be wondering to this day why the Nazi Fuehrer paid no attention to heils and cheers but paced up and down on the sidewalk there between the cordoned spectators mumbling something to himself. Now and then he'd look up at the eight-storied building, a decorated exterior obviously reminiscent of vanished days when the Hapsburgs and Metternichs dined and wined here and brought their most beautiful women to its white-and-gold ballroom to dance to Viennese waltzes.

Hitler, as he paced agitatedly up and down, remembered those days of imperial glitter and glamour, and the emotion which swelled within his breast showed plainly on his face. He had been a poor man, almost a beggar, with only a threadbare suit to his back and hunger in his stomach. The rich and titled who swept up to the entrance of the Imperial Hotel here and walked over the red carpet into its dazzling interior had on wonderful uniforms or evening clothes, escorting on their arms women with flashing jewels and ermine robes.

He, the mighty Fuehrer of Germany and new master of Austria, remembered all of that as he stood on the sidewalk before the Imperial Hotel on that memorable day. He stared for a moment at the red carpet, as if in a trance, with a vacant smile fleeting over his lips. Then, as the heils around him burst forth into clamorous shouting, he seemed to catch himself and recall that he was standing in the public eye on the main avenue of Vienna. He lifted his right hand in the Nazi salute and walked slowly over the red carpet into the Imperial Hotel. It was the first time in his life that he set foot in the lobby of faded glory, but for him it was a personal triumph beyond all imagination.

I had been sent to Vienna by Connolly and Faris to cover the story and to get our local correspondent there out of jail. He was a Jew, and it took some days and a lot of string-pulling with key men around Hitler to get him out and across the border to Italy. But it provided me with an opportunity also to keep a finger on Hitler's activity, and from talks with several of those always around him I pieced together his first night in Vienna.

He took over the royal suite, a high-ceilinged affair of three main rooms done up in much red drapery and furniture of white and gold. The bathroom was modernized, but not much else. The Imperial Hotel definitely had been coasting along on its reputation and made no attempt to rival the up-to-date Bristol and Grand across the way. But Hitler had his reason for coming to the Imperial, and that night he gathered a small circle of intimates around him and talked to them until the small hours of Vienna and his days there. He had Schaub, the personal adjutant, pull the glossy boots off his feet and occasionally bring him a glass of warm milk. Then he reclined in loose comfort on the sofa and delved into reminiscences, waxing excited enough to sit up straight and rumple his hair when telling of some of the hard times he had seen in that city.

"Even as a boy I knew inside of me that I could never reconcile myself to living for very long in a small Austrian village like Branau," he told the listeners around him, who were served all the food and drinks they wanted but did not smoke. "My father wanted me to enter government service but even in those days I had a horror of the *beamte* who carries his letters from house to house day by day or who sits for a fixed number of hours behind a desk and fills out the same papers until he can retire on pension. I left home when I was seventeen years old to escape this fearful future and came to Vienna to create my own life."

Hitler, as I recall being told by those who were present that night, then recounted some of the struggle for existence he went through during the next fourteen years, a period which covered his four years in the Flanders trenches. But in the royal suite he dwelled chiefly on his days in Vienna.

He told them: "In the old days the Viennese used to have a sentimental way of saying: 'And when I die, I want to go to Heaven and have a little hole among the stars to see my Vienna, my fair Vienna.' I didn't feel very much that way. The Hapsburgs and the spendthrifts may have looked at Vienna as a playground and paradise, but to me it was a city going to decay in its own grandeur. Only the Jews made money, and only those with Jewish friends or those willing to do the work for Jews made a decent living. I, and a lot of others like me, practically starved, and some went begging.

"I used to walk past the Imperial Hotel of nights when there was nothing else to do and I hadn't even enough money to buy a book. I'd watch the automobiles and the coaches drive up to the entrance and be received with a deep bow by the white-mustached porter out in front, who never talked to me if I came near him. I could see the glittering lights and chandeliers in the lobby but I knew it was impossible for me to set foot inside. One night, after a bad blizzard which piled up several feet of snow, I had a chance to make some money for food by shoveling snow. Ironically enough, the five or six of us in my group were sent to clean the street and sidewalk in front of the Imperial Hotel.

"That was the night the Hapsburgs were entertaining—old Josef was still alive but he didn't appear. I saw Karl and Zita step out of their imperial coach and grandly walk into this hotel over the red carpet. We poor devils shoveled the snow away on all sides and took our hats off every time the aristocrats arrived. They didn't even look at us, although I still smell the perfume that came to our noses. We were about as important to them, or for that matter to Vienna, as the snow that kept coming down all night, and this hotel did not even have the decency to send out a cup of hot coffee to us. We were kept there most of the night, and each time the wind blew hard it covered the red carpet with snow. Then I'd take a broom and brush it off, glancing at the same time into the brilliantly lit interior, which fascinated me. I heard the music and it made me wish to cry. It made me pretty angry, too, and feel the injustice of life. I resolved that night that someday I would come back to the Imperial Hotel and walk over the red carpet into that glittering interior where the Hapsburgs danced. I didn't know how or when, but I have waited for this day and tonight I am here.

"I shall have this hotel listed as our party hotel and I shall come here each time I am in Vienna. I shall have it renovated and modernized, but the name shall remain the same. And a red carpet shall be on the sidewalk every time I come so that I can walk over it into the hotel the same as those aristocrats did back in the days when I shoveled snow. I have never forgotten the resolution I made. Providence fulfilled my wish."

That is Hitler to the core. He can never forget or forgive, and everything he does has its motive. The conquest of Vienna and the Imperial Hotel in a way were to him the wiping of the slate, a settlement of scores.

He likes to gloat over his triumphs, and particularly to go back to places where he was spurned in the old days. Thus there is a hotel in almost every large city of Germany where he will stop and strut around because at one time or another he was boycotted and refused quarters in every hotel in that city except perhaps the one he now favors. Or he might have been given shelter and food by the individual who now owns the leading hotel in the city. All because that man did Hitler a favor in the days before he became a power in the land.

In Weimar, for example, there is the White Elephant Hotel, rebuilt by the party in lavish style with the reserved Fuehrer suite. In Nuremberg it is the Deutscher Hof, an expensively rebuilt edifice. In Godesberg on the Rhine, a little distance above the fabled rock of Lorelei, there is the Dreesen, where he held his famous conference with Neville Chamberlain a few days before the signing of the fatal Munich Pact.

The owner of the Dreesen Hotel is a provincial German who had sufficient money in the old days to allow himself the luxury of running an independent hotel. As a native Rhinelander, he watched the postwar pains of Germany with heavy heart and cursed himself purple in the face every time he looked at the black French troops standing guard on the banks of the Rhine. He hated people with communistic sympathies because, in a small way, he was a capitalist and property owner who saw only chaos and confusion under the red flag. He was fed up on the politicians in Berlin, who seemed to have time or inclination only for quarreling and for their own political gain; resigned on the whole to letting the country go to hell. When Hitler and his Nazis came crusading around, he gave them ready ear. The towns of Bonn and Godesberg and even the city of Cologne had no use for Hitler and practically slammed their doors in his face. The owner of the Dreesen snapped his fingers at the anti-Hitlers and offered him sanctuary free of cost in the Dreesen Hotel in Godesberg. That settled it, and whenever Hitler thereafter toured the Rhineland, he spent days and days in the Dreesen with the man who had done him a favor in the face of public disapproval.

Hitler, after assuming power, did with the Dreesen what he did with hotels he favored all over Germany. He took it under his official wing and partly remodeled it at the expense of the Nazi party for purposes of his own. He installed the usual Fuehrer suite of three rooms. That included a reception room of larger proportions, a sort of combination private office and sitting room, and a comfortable bedroom. I had a chance to go through his suite in the Dreesen a few hours before he arrived for his conference with Chamberlain and thus had a good opportunity to size up the arrangements.

In the Berlin chancellery and at Fuehrer headquarters he makes it a point during the war to sleep on a camp bed, but in the hotels and castles he picks on he has a comfortable, wide bed. In the Dreesen it is low and stands next to a window of bulletproof glass overlooking the Rhine. A blood-red silken bedspread enlivens the pink-colored room. There is an enameled white telephone on the night table. I was told that the hook on the side closest to the pillow is for a special pistol holster, which reminded me of the proverb that uneasy lies the head that wears a crown. I also remembered at that moment that he had demonstrated himself some years before to me as quick on the draw and a crack pistol shot.

There were flowers, chiefly chrysanthemums, all over the room in big vases. A freshly pressed uniform was laid out for him, along with a brown shirt fitted with special moisture-absorbing material around the collar. In the summer he changes underwear daily and shirts as often as three times, especially during days of strenuous speaking. He likes long underwear but nothing of silk. He likes to shave himself once in a while and always does so when there is a barber around he doesn't personally know.

I looked into his bathroom and in fact pulled the chain just to have the satisfaction of having done it in his bathroom. The bathtub and walls were done in pink, with shiny nickel fixtures and chairs with rubber cushions. The towels were initialed with a blue A. H. Altogether, he wasn't doing too badly by himself. Schaub, the personal adjutant, acted as his valet and general nursemaid, reportedly even washing his back. That is about all the beefy Schaub is good for anyhow, except for drinking and women.

Hitler also makes it a point to impress others with the vast background and varied information he claims to have accumulated. He tells everyone who comes near him that he knows every note and word of the Wagnerian operas by heart, an accomplishment not so astounding when one is aware of the fact that he has heard the score of *Die Meistersinger* at least one hundred and fifty times. He makes the opera his passion and before the war lavished money on opera houses and opera stars like a drunken sailor with a pot of gold. Some say it isn't real, this passion for music, but just another Hitler act.

He has the curious twist of mind which leads him to assume that he knows best of all how to impress the world, although he has never been outside the German borders except for official trips to Italy and rides through conquered countries. Yet he is apt to hatch out a melodramatic stunt in his mind for any given occasion and act on it without consulting anyone. He had a bunch of us foreign correspondents flown to the Warsaw airfield while the city was still a mass of smoke and flame in late September of 1939 and a few minutes later landed there himself, appropriately arriving in time to lecture us, against this fiery background, on the evils of mankind and the stupidity of England in encouraging the Poles to oppose him.

"A great crime has been committed," he said dolefully, and he gazed with a well-posed attitude of regret at the holocaust a short distance off. "*Ja*, the Polish military went mad and look at the crime committed against their own people. They were drunk with power and talked even of marching to Berlin. Then they barricaded themselves in the city and look at Warsaw now. You must tell the world of their callousness."

In Berlin, if he felt like it, he'd delight small circles of friends occasionally with mimicking men such as Goering or Himmler. I did not have to guess twice on the Warsaw airfield to know he was up to those tricks of his. He came there to be melodramatic and at the same time hide under false colors the awful horror he had visited upon a great European capital.

But his act was soon over, or forgotten. He came around to each one of us, as is customary, and shook hands as Press Chief Dietrich called off the name and outfit each one represented. Our little group included Bertil Svahnstroem, able correspondent for the newspaper *Politiken* in Stockholm.

"*Ach*, Svahnstroem," Hitler repeated slowly, and shook the correspondent's hand more heartily. "Are you related to the great Swedish actress and singer?"

"Only in a distant way," Svahnstroem replied. "But of course in Sweden she has become a sort of legend."

Oblivious to burning Warsaw, Hitler was off on the subject of Svahnstroem and her qualities, discoursing for at least ten minutes about her and his opinion of her renditions. He cited at length some high lights and criticisms of her career, in the same breath plunging deeper and deeper into an analytical oration on the respective values and merits of the Swedish and German stage and opera. He had decided opinions on the subject, none of which were challenged or questioned by those standing around in the smoke-tainted air. He was, in fact, showing off again, and everybody else had to listen. That is the advantage of being a dictator—especially a talkative one.

He used to tell people in all seriousness that he turned vegetarian because he couldn't bear the thought of animals and fowls being killed for human consumption. At other times he'd claim he had had to turn vegetarian because in the old days he couldn't afford the price of meat and fowl. He used to drink beer but gave it up when his figure showed bulges of fat. He has told Goering time and again that people will laugh at him or with him, but never take him seriously. That finally drove Goering to dieting for a few weeks, and he lost some fifty pounds.

Hitler likes to sneer at royalty and its trappings but he is not above a bow at its throne when the occasion calls for it. He went to Rome early in May 1938 on a state visit arranged for him by Mussolini, and he was eager as a little boy out to see the king and queen. He was nervous, too, and those around him told me he was edgy all through his stay at the Quirinal Palace, worrying about committing a *faux pas* of etiquette in front of the king and queen. He bawled out his adjutants on the least provocation, lining them up for a personal inspection and telling each one just what he must do. He forbade them to as much as touch wine or alcohol, lest their foot slip and give a black mark in royalty's eyes to the Nazi Fuehrer's entourage.

I watched him from the grandstand the Italians had built for the diplomats and foreign correspondents opposite the Colosseum, where the climax of the Roman spectacle came as Emmanuel's coach of six white horses rumbled up the Triumphal Way and passed the ancient ruins of Rome standing like ghosts in the searchlight flood. A slight hiss became audible over on the Colosseum as the imperial horses pranced past the great arch. As if by magic, lurid red smoke transformed the hitherto dark stadium of Caesar's days into a fiery caldron of color. Through my glasses I saw Hitler squirm around for a good look, and apparently he was so excited that he began tapping plumed little Emmanuel on the knee. Hitler had never seen anything like this, not even in the bawdiest Nazi shows Goebbels staged for him. Now the small boy was coming out in him. He forgot that he was sitting in a royal coach beside a real king, driving in state through imperial Rome. He bounced around and gaped at the show.

The spectacle of the Colosseum with the torches along the route was breathtaking and all of us in the grandstand watched in a sort of fascinated silence. But young Sulzberger of the New York *Times* had a dog with him, I believe a spaniel. The dog wasn't impressed by the show and yapped energetically. He was the only audible competition to the light clatter of horses' hoofs, for the wheels of the coach were rubber-tired. He sounded louder than a radio and drew the baleful stares of every Italian and German official near by. It was so funny, what with lanky Hitler bouncing along in the royal coach at the side of tiny Emmanuel, that one couldn't help laughing, and a silly ditty kept rolling through my head:

> *"Oh, give me a horse and buggy*
> *In a sun-browned Rome by day,*
> *And I'll go yapping down*
> *The Yap—App—Appian Way."*

Next day Frank Gervasi, now of *Collier's* but at that time the International News Service bureau manager in Rome, fixed it up through his Italian contacts to sneak me into the Capitol for the official reception of Hitler. I stood with a few dozen privileged diplomats in the ornate Roman chambers up in the Governor's palace on the hill. By reaching out I could touch with my hand paintings or statues of venerable age worth their weight in gold. They tell me the carpets and tapestries in that palace alone are worth an immense fortune.

Four buglers done up in mauve uniforms of the Middle Ages blew the royal signal of approach on silver trumpets as Hitler and the royal party walked in a procession through the Capitol chambers into the marble-and-gold reception room. He had on the usual brown uniform with a white shirt and brown tie. His boots shone like mirrors and his face above the white collar seemed unusually pinkish that day. His eyes moved nervously over the crowd touching his very elbows as he went by with slow step, leading Queen Helene on his arm. She was a little bit taller than he and did not look any happier than Hitler. He was plainly ill at ease, and evidently felt like a fish out of water. It was, after all, a far cry from the Bavarian beer halls and the hard-fisted Nazi ruffians he transformed into men of rank and title.

Behind him, looking like a white-haired dwarf in an emperor's uniform, came the frowning Emmanuel leading the Governor's tall wife on his arm. He stared straight before him into Hitler's back, and some of us afterward were agreed that Emmanuel was not a happy host at the time. On Capitoline Hill that day I did not notice any very hearty conversation between the royal house and Hitler, or maybe that was only because none could hold conversation with Hitler unless he or she talked German. They had interpreters present but Hitler stood around amid all this imperial splendor and folded and unfolded his arms. I had the impression that he just didn't know what to do with his hands. I imagine he was as glad to get away as I was.

Until a couple of years ago Mussolini, reverting back to his newspaper days, still liked to meet the foreign press and during the Hitler visit personally saw to it that we had all the opportunity and facilities in the world to be right up in front whenever or wherever he and Hitler appeared. Thus in Naples he had us stationed on a low balcony overlooking the square. The car with the two of them came driving slowly past us and Mussolini, in his vivacious manner of those days, yanked eagerly at Hitler's sleeve and pointed to us.

"There they are, the foreign press," Il Duce said in loud German. "I know practically every one of them." He waved in greeting and in not bad English called over that he hoped we were satisfied with arrangements.

Hitler scowled and glanced sourly up at us. He just couldn't understand Mussolini, for, on the whole, Hitler always has had a chip on his shoulder against the foreign press and in the past couple of years has come to hate us. He keenly resents all the slurs and insults he accuses the foreign press of manufacturing deliberately against him and in his mind is constantly groping about for a way to get even. Although that does not prevent him from inviting us around for his purposes when the situation or his mood calls for it. Only he doesn't care to have us crammed down his throat at every turn and in Naples he plainly showed that he was too busy with royalty to bother with the dirty foreign press.

In Florence he changed horses again and eagerly tried to impress on us that in his heart he is a born artist. He spent hours in this magnificent city of art, drinking in its soft beauty and gazing at the works of the immortal masters at the Uffizi. He talked to Mussolini and others by the hour of the genius and marvels of the Botticellis, the Titians, the Leonardos. He stood upon the heights of Fiesole, the ancient Etruscan town above Florence, and spread his arms toward heaven to eulogize the magnificence of the view at his feet.

"If I had my way, I'd go incognito to Florence for ten days," he remarked to several of us sometime later. "I'd put on a false beard, dark glasses and an old suit, and comb my hair a different way. Then I'd spend the ten days in those art galleries of Florence worshiping as an artist at the feet of the old masters."

He looked silliest on that night when he left for Germany by train from Rome. He came to the station straight from a farewell banquet, escorted by Emmanuel. I almost fell over, for on his head was a silk hat. It simply didn't go with him, and alongside of little Emmanuel he looked like a clown trying to be serious. The silk hat sat on his head as if he had carefully placed it on with both hands. He walked stiffly, and a glass of water could have stood on top of his lid without spilling a drop. He had pulled it down so hard, to make it stick on the ride to the station, that he had trouble getting if off when he said good-by to Emmanuel on the platform. As the train moved he stood at the window of the railway coach wearing his silk hat and with his right arm outstretched in the Nazi salute. That took the cake, and I would hardly have been surprised if Emmanuel and his entourage had burst forth into loud laughter.

I doubt very much whether he ever wore that silk hat again, for he himself must have been conscious of the ridiculous figure he cut in it. Most of his parties before the war required formal dress, but here again I have the feeling that it was all part of his personal window display. Like that crazy way of combing his hair, which is as much an affectation as his mustache and the double handshake he uses at times while staring deep into your eyes. This stare is what some people have called a mesmeric one, although I don't think much of it. It goes big with the women, and Hitler knows it.

In building around himself and the Fuehrer title a sort of halo designed to fasten his hold on the masses, he made it a special point to capitalize his bachelorhood by having himself quoted around town as saying repeatedly that he is wedded to Germany and as such must endure personal loneliness and sacrifice his desire for a normal family life. There has been much talk since the latter part of 1941 on the inside of the Nazi party that Hitler has decided to get married right after the war. It is known, of course, in those same circles, but never talked about with strangers, that for nearly a dozen years now Hitler has had his clandestine love affair with Fräulein Theresa von Thorn, one of the five daughters of an aristocratic Bavarian family. She is a petite brunette and likes to wear her hair in bangs. Her family was one of the first among the aristocrats to go Nazi and soon drew Hitler's attention by their unstinted activity on his behalf. The Von Thorns soon were invited to Berchtesgaden and silent romance blossomed between the Nazi leader and one of the younger girls shortly after. Since then the Von Thorn family have been the most frequent visitors up on the mountain, and the girl is always there when Hitler is in residence. Even the war has not kept him from her, and the girl, more than the Alps, is the reason he rushes off to Berchtesgaden at every opportunity. She hardly ever goes to Berlin, but when she does, she lives at the Kaiserhof Hotel under an assumed name, carefully guarded from intruding eyes. The Fuehrer would never forgive or forget the talkative one who'd spill the secret of the girl he sleeps with and intends to marry after the war. That is, if he is still around after the war.

I can't imagine him as much of a family man, for whenever any surviving members of his family got to him in the past several years, the fur would fly sooner or later. In 1935, for example, his half sister, Frau Raubal, appeared from nowhere and offered to keep house for him in Berchtesgaden. He agreed, and in fact he loved the sweet Viennese pastry she stuffed him with. A year later she walked out on him and married a professor of architecture in Dresden, who'd been up to the mountain a few times on public buildings Hitler had an interest in. Hitler was peeved when she broke the news to him and didn't even send her a wedding present. Some Nazis around him, I know, thought he was going to have that professor tossed into a concentration camp and Frau Raubal to boot. But he left them alone. In fact, two years later I saw the couple at the Nuremberg Party Congress as his invited guests, although I heard he never sent for them and they have not seen him to this day.

The same is true of his half brother, Alois Hitler, who came out of London some years ago and set up a beer shop on the Wittenbergplatz in the heart of Berlin. Hitler summoned him to the chancellery once, but instead of a brotherly meeting it turned out to be one of those lectures Hitler likes to hand other people on how to run their own affairs. Alois left with a red face and hasn't seen Hitler since. He went back to his beer shop and gave strict orders to the waiters and barmaids never to discuss Hitler with any guest. Then, in tiny black lettering, he painted his name on the windowpane looking into the street.

And thus I give you Hitler. He is not easy to dispose of with a snap of the finger or the contention that he is insane. He becomes dangerous when underestimated and will stop at nothing to gain his end. Crackpot or mad genius or a combination of all, he is the strange being of our times and the dark power we are at grips with. Superior force alone will conquer him.

CHAPTER 2

The Men around Hitler

ONCE UPON A TIME, in the days before 1933, Hitler and the brown-shirted minions always swirling around him like fireflies on a warm night were looked upon as crackpots in the best German circles.

Nobody cared a snap of the fingers whether a Nazi of the Hitler crowd was carried home on a stretcher after heated party rallies and clashes with Communists or sat around all night drinking himself into a stupor with schnapps and beer.

People lifted eyebrows or shrugged shoulders in exceptional cases of violence and scandal, and let it go at that. Rabble-rousing speeches, rowdyism, carousing, street brawls, and occasional fights among themselves were accepted and ignored in the public eye as part of the nature and earmark of the Nazis.

26

But when Hitler marched through the Brandenburg Gate as Reichschancellor and therewith cast the mantle of official dignity over his party and men, he found himself faced with the uneasy task of transforming a beer-hall machine into the machinery of state. Henchmen of his, adept at swinging a handy fist or heavy glass in free-for-all fights, were turned overnight into men of rank and position, the standard-bearers of the swastika regime of the Third Reich. They had to watch their step and acquire polish on the run, if only to impress the public at home and abroad.

The embassies were quick to gossip if you made a slip or forgot the black dirt beneath your fingernails; Hitler had a mania for being correct and on best behavior, repeatedly admonishing the inner circles of his Nazi party to show the world that they are made of the stuff of gentlemen. He had nasty scenes with men who forgot, and some who couldn't remember went down over the years and today sit in forgotten retirement.

But even eight years of carpeted offices and life in the aura of official dignity or the showmanship of Nazi-party functionings can hardly smooth off the rough exterior completely or hide forever the roughneck under the skin. Once in awhile there is again the sudden glimpse of the man who ate along the dives of the Hamburg water front, or of the original race-track tout, or of the officer gone to pot after 1918. It comes out on these Nazis, right down to this very day.

I remember so well the ludicrous Robert Ley, bullnecked head of the Nazi Labor Front, striving with might and main to act the polished host to the Duke and Duchess of Windsor. He nervously paced the lobby of the Kaiserhof Hotel while waiting for the couple to come down, and the first day of the visit twice commanded his stupid-looking adjutant to bring him another quick one of Pilsener accompanied by schnapps.

With a red-and-white handkerchief Ley wiped the moist triple folds of his neck and then his mouth. He turned to us foreign correspondents and said we must be sure to behave properly on this inspection trip to factories and institutions around Berlin. He wanted to be certain that in our dispatches we emphasized above all else the fact that Nazi Labor Front Leader Dr. Robert Ley had been appointed by Hitler as official host to the Duke and Duchess of Windsor.

The Duchess of Windsor stepped out of the elevator as graceful and self-controlled as the Queen of England, a set smile on the otherwise cold face and dressed in a trim dark suit for a tourist ride through Berlin. The Duke, trailing a step behind and yanking nervously at his collar and tie, seemed just a little startled when the heavy-set man in the brown Nazi uniform snapped his heels together and extended his right arm in salute. Ley tried to get some words of greeting across his lips but the nervous stutter again seized his tongue and he gave it up with a red face. He seized the hand of the Duchess, and, bending very far down, hiccuped just as his lips touched her forefinger. The Duke moved forward a little hastily and shook hands, greeting him in German.

Ley, after bellowing his adjutants into action, gallantly led the Duchess away on his arm, but complications ensued in the revolving door leading into the street and he had to back water and try again when an overzealous adjutant swung the door too energetically around and around for their exit.

I don't know how Ley's mental processes arrived at the program he had outlined so carefully, but the first thing on the bill was a visit to the Nazi headquarters for more and better babies, legitimate or otherwise, and the care of mothers.

Eyes somewhat reddened and watery, and thick of speech, Ley shouted earful after earful at the Duke and Duchess on the means and methods used to coax more babies out of the good folk of Germany and how the unwed mother can safely give birth to the children she wants without being censured. A few times, when Ley got a bit involved in hiccups and statistics, Hilgenfeldt, the director of the place, injected explanations in a vociferous voice, completely confusing our little circle of listeners.

The Duchess took it all in without batting an eye, while the Duke yanked at his collar and tie a little more often than usual. We remarked among ourselves that it was going to be a hard day, laying bets that the Duchess would duck the next day's rounds. She did.

At lunch time, in a model factory, Ley had a couple of opera singers on hand with the whole orchestra from the German State Opera House—a somewhat amazing stunt even to the distinguished pair—and Ley beamed with the pride of accomplishment. He told us aside later that he was willing to bet this beautiful surprise to the workers or the King never happened in England. Naturally, we must be sure to give an exact description and also tell the world of the wonderful paradise the Nazis were creating for the common workers of Germany.

Ley was full of these little surprises. Next day, with the Duchess remaining in the hotel, Ley took the Duke and those of us following around to a recreation resort for workers on the Baltic.

Outside of town he stopped the cars and in the pouring rain transferred us with a grand gesture of triumph to a huge, low-slung bus, fitted luxuriously with club chairs, a carpet, a radio, and, above all, an honest-to-goodness bar. Drinks were on Ley, with everything from champagne down to common beer and schnapps. He was chagrined to find that the Duke at the time was on the wagon and consoled himself with liberal portions of beer and schnapps.

Early in the afternoon it became clear that such a ponderous bus was chiefly a fine-weather vehicle for hard-surfaced highways and we decided to have lunch then and there and go back to Berlin. Nobody seemed to mind, the Duke least of all, and Ley slept it off with a rumbling snore. That night he made a bombastic speech to a mass meeting of railroad workers on the wonders of socialism and labor united in the Reich of Adolf Hitler.

Ley, a dock worker and water-front boss in the old days, has been publicly named the best Nazi of all by Hitler. It was Ley, they say, who coined the term "Mein Fuehrer" by which Hitler is now addressed, and Ley himself claims he sold Hitler the slogan compulsorily in use throughout the Reich of "Heil Hitler." Whatever the case, Ley is a favorite son around Der Fuehrer and can risk a few personal liberties. He married a sweet young German blonde half his age, parading her around in picture hats and white frocks at official occasions, and at banquets in the chancellery even wangled it so that more than once he seated her next to Hitler. Magda Goebbels and Emmy Goering handed out dirty looks and said he smelled of beer despite the young wife's perfumery, none of which fazed Ley a bit.

Near beautiful Lake Tegel he acquired the palatial villa of a vanished Jewish millionaire, and his prewar parties there were something to write home about. When aristocratic estate holders next door circulated the word around about the carousing in Ley's house, he tried to force those neighbors to sell out their property and land to him.

The court bucked this plan, but Ley didn't worry. He was the fair-haired boy of the Fuehrer and for the Fuehrer he had tamed 22,000,000 German workers. He had ruthlessly broken every union and labor organization and welded all hands in every walk of life into a single labor front run by him in the Nazi manner.

Indulgence in a few personal whims, such as covering the new villa roof with copper sheathing to make it glisten and glitter in the sun, surely was small reward for all he had done. He was slightly hurt when he got wind of unkind talk going around and he was miffed when a Hitler order came to take that copper off the roof and turn it into the war industry. I have been told he covered it up, convinced that the Fuehrer will understand.

One day in October of 1941 Ley set off from Berlin on an overnight journey to inspect the coal-mine areas. War restrictions on railway traffic have eliminated the private coach he and others like him used to have at their disposal and he stomped discontentedly into his reserved compartment. Ten minutes later, half undressed, Ley stuck his head out of the door and bawled loudly for his adjutant, the stupid-looking one named Kiel, who accompanies him everywhere.

"You, Kiel, come here," he shouted peremptorily. When Kiel came running, one boot off and one on, Ley handed him a small paper bag. "Here are my coffee beans for to-morrow's coffee. See to it that I get all that coffee and that this swine of a train porter doesn't steal half of the beans. You keep the bag with you and watch him closely tomorrow morning when he makes the coffee."

Ley got his coffee, every bean of it, and drank every last drop without wincing. The fact that coffee is a rare treasure in Europe, priced at fifty marks (twenty dollars) per pound on the black market of Germany, didn't bother him. It was all part of a day in life, and a Nazi big shot cannot waste time on trifles.

A couple of days later it was still the same thing when he staged a grand entrance with drums and flags into the main machine-shop hall of the vast Borsig plant in Berlin, where many thousands of workers keep the war wheels of production turning day and night. The workers were lined up

in semi-military formation, made aware properly beforehand that the head of the Labor Front, just a good fellow
with every workingman, was going to tell them about the
war they'd win and what vital part men in the shops must
play.

Ley, his round stomach sticking out a bit more than usual,
walked the length of the middle aisle between lined-up
thousands while a brass band played the "Horst Wessel
Lied." Somehow, there was something missing.

It took a minute to notice the lack of applause and of
welcoming cries of "Sieg Heil." Ley glanced around a little
nervously and climbed the speakers' platform based on half-
finished tanks. From up there, when the playing stopped
and raised arms came down, it didn't look so good. The
workers seemed to stand there in endless rows, arms folded
across chests, and definitely scowling. Ley may have
thought at first it was the seriousness of the occasion and
the war, particularly since Hitler a few days before had
announced the concluding offensive on the east front designed to sweep the remnants of the Russian armies into the
discard. He swung into action in his best oratorical style,
painting the wonders and beauty of life in the Fuehrer's
Reich, where the worker is a man of recognized importance.

There were moments when he got too excited and
his tongue twisted everything into a sputter, but Ley never
faltered in the flow of language and enthusiasm, wiping the
beads of sweat from his neck and brow whenever the dozen
shop directors and adjutants on the speakers' stand with
him applauded. The applause sounded strikingly thin in

that huge hall, although loud enough to serve as signal to the men below that now a spot of heiling would help things along. But they stood there with folded arms, as if listening to the reading of a military order. Ley tried again, baiting them with round condemnation of capitalistic slavery in the democracies and the German worker's elevated place in Hitler's postwar Reich. Red color began to heighten the flash in his eyes. His arms gesticulated more fiercely; the microphone shook from fist blows on the rostrum.

"We men from the ranks of labor whipped the red foe in shops and shipyards a decade ago, and today our armies are whipping the red foe on his own soil," Ley shouted with mounting vehemence.

His roving eye tried to fasten itself on the faces of those men below, to read them or make sense of their strange silence. Surely, surely, this wasn't organized, passive resistance, a new thing in Naziland. Ley continued: "You and I and all of us are helping here in the shops to whip the red foe and eradicate him from the face of the earth. All of us here are brothers, hard workers, German patriots, and faithful servants of our Fuehrer, to follow him wherever he commands. I am his appointed leader of you, and you are the soldiers of his home front. Together we march forward to glorious victory!"

He had touched a fine climax, built up in masterly Nazi style, for the tide of cheers and frantic heiling sure to follow. None came, except the feeble clapping and scared heils from the handful of men behind him. Ley of the bull-neck stood aghast in silence for a few seconds, wagging his head a little and his lower lip protruding.

Suddenly the right arm shot up to wave a warning finger at the massed men below. "If there are any Communists among you, let them step up to this platform and I, personally, will smash every one of them in the face with my fists. One by one I'll take on any dirty dog of a Communist among you and when I get done with each one I will wipe my boot on his face!"

Ley had lost his temper completely now and pranced agitatedly around the platform. Once he nearly fell off, but Adjutant Kiel caught him by the arm. Finally, he was prevailed on to end the ceremony, but he went out and down that aisle shouting and yelling he'd get to the bottom of this.

A few hours later the Gestapo came swarming into Borsig's and forbade anyone to leave until further notice. Among the several score arrested in due course were two brothers of the train porter branded a swine by Ley a few days before. The train porter himself was taken into custody, accused of spreading false rumors that Ley carried his own coffee and butter and ate varieties of meat while traveling on the railway. If proved guilty, this porter can sit behind penitentiary bars as long as ten years.

2

The Nazis are very quick to punish anyone in the land gossiping or willfully spreading harmful stories about the higher-ups in the government and party.

They say this is the most poisonous weapon there is, and one of the most effective, like the old party line on the telephone. So they watch carefully and clip any wagging tongues. It helps keep the pot from boiling over, especially at times of real tribulation. At times, for example, when the real big guns in the Nazi party revert to the primitive and for a moment act natural. Such as was the case in Munich, home of the Nazi party and native hunting grounds of Hitler's right-hand men like burly Adolf Wagner, the Bavarian Gauleiter, and Christian Weber, the power behind the throne of the Nazi party and owner of the great Munich race track with its stable of the best-blooded race horses in Europe.

Wagner, the Gauleiter and Nazi wild man, has a scar on his right cheek and a voice on the radio identical to Hitler's. We foreign correspondents and the Germans themselves were of the opinion that Wagner could substitute for Hitler on the radio without anyone being the wiser, so close was the vocal resemblance, except that, in forgetful moments, Wagner belches and that is a habit totally out of keeping with Fuehrer dignity.

Christian Weber is also of the Wagner type, although lumpier and more deeply scarred from forgotten brawls than the Gauleiter. They have much in common, such as a reputation for a readiness to double-cross everybody except Hitler, whom both fear.

Wagner, as Gauleiter of Bavaria, holds official rank comparable in our scheme of government to the governorship of a state; Weber is the hidden boss of the Nazi party and the personal steel-tipped whip of the Nazi Fuehrer.

What might be out of place in the exalted office of the Reich chancellery in Berlin would not be out of place in the party office of Christian Weber. He can do the necessary political dirty work constantly required in a beer-hall machine like the Nazi party, without staining the Fuehrer's own hands. He is good at it, and at raking in the golden reward.

Weber started life on the race tracks and never defines his parentage; he became a notorious race-track tout, a shady bookie, and, when necessary, served the stables or acted as track bouncer. His prowess in "adjusting" deals and getting things done as if by magic attracted Hitler's attention to him in the twenties, when the future Nazi dictator was badly in need of hard-fisted men who weren't too squeamish about doing some knifing in the dark or similar shady jobs for him.

Weber met all these qualifications, and Hitler made him the political boss of the Nazi party. He is that today, but instead of touting at the race track in Munich he owns every inch of ground and every stable there.

He runs the annual Braune Band (Brown Ribbon) Derby featured before the war by horses from the finest European stables. He coins money in piles from these racing events, edging out the better horses in favor of his own whenever big dough is in the offing on a race.

On such occasions you do not know which horse is running for Weber in addition to the scheduled one, but if you should find out, bet all your money on Weber's dark horse and you will win a fortune on that day. It is foolproof, in accordance with Weber's foolproof methods.

In the 1941 Braune Band race a jockey on the wrong horse crossed the finishing line a split second ahead of what in reality was Weber's horse and of course the judges immediately awarded the prize to the winner. Next day that horse was declared ineligible on the grounds that its owner was of Jewish blood and under the regulations no longer could enter or own race horses anywhere in the Reich. Weber's horse thereupon took the purse of 80,000 marks.

I have no proof or direct knowledge of the rake-off Hitler gets on these Weber deals (all Nazi-party real-estate deals and a score of other money-coining projects are handled very slickly by Weber), but Hitler has limitless funds for spending purposes, not all of which can possibly come from the sales of *Mein Kampf*.

Scores of Nazi big shots take it for granted that what Weber does is done for Hitler under cover, and they act accordingly. If Weber can live in palatial estates, so can they. If Weber can run the biggest race track in Germany, why can't they get extra money by the same method, be that race track or monopoly on construction projects in their own sectors. If Weber can win huge purses on the race track, why can't they get in on the gold mine? All they need do is play along with Weber, and all of them do, with exceptions.

Wagner is a big enough man with Hitler to afford him-

self the luxury of an independent attitude as far as Weber
is concerned. Weber knows it and consequently likes to
play ball with Wagner, slipping back into old habits only
occasionally. When necessary, he invites Wagner out to
dinner and takes him to the smoky and medieval Nuremberger Bratwurst, famed before ration-card days for its de-
lectably grilled chicken. You still get it today, for, like Horcher's in Berlin, the special food supply comes in official
delivery wagons by the back door and the clients out front
consist exclusively of the Nazi hierarchy. Therefore the
flame on the open grill of the Nuremberger Bratwurst burns
merrily, and the chickens on the spit spread the same ap-
petizing odor, but a mere mortal can't get in unless invited
by a big shot.

Weber feels at home there, and when he invited Wagner
one night he was particularly anxious to please. He had the
best table where everyone could see him and come over
to kowtow and click heels with a Nazi salute. He started
Wagner off with caviar on ice and champagne, mixed
now and then with a shot of vodka. Wagner ripped the
chicken apart with bare hands and Weber followed suit,
since the Nazis made this a fad of recent years in the Nuremberger Bratwurst. They like to act natural, pretending
to be the same simple souls as of old days, and they claim
that the business of state and party can best be finished off
between or during juicy mouthfuls of food.

By the time Wagner had reached the belching stage,
Christian had polished off with him whatever political bar-
gaining was required. They slid into racing talk as naturally

as jockeys on a holiday, and soon Weber waxed eloquent over the latest wonders in his stable. The mixture of champagne and vodka made his face glow, bringing out the scars in livid streaks. Wagner was still licking bones and fingers, letting Weber do most of the talking.

"*So sag ich dir, mein lieber Adolf,*" said Weber with smug self-satisfaction, "*es wirkt wunderbar.* An old jockey I used to know told me to try it. I did, and today you can pick out the horses I own on my track by their glossy hide. I tell you, it is wonderful. Every morning and every evening, as that old jockey told me, I have the trainers feed them a good mash beaten up in dozens of eggs and rich milk. They like it, and look at how they shine. I have given orders to all my stables to use that recipe. You should try it in yours."

But Wagner didn't take the tip. He struck a sudden strange attitude, staring balefully at his host. His clenched right fist struck the table a resounding blow, causing the heavy plates and glasses to bounce and clatter. A score of Nazis at other tables looked up with a start.

Wagner was waving a fist in Weber's face, whose mouth was open with unguarded surprise. "*Schwein!*" Wagner roared. "*Schwein!* Now I know where those eggs and that milk for sick soldiers are going to. You sidetracked those farm deliveries and I got the blame for it. I couldn't meet the quota and you fed your horses on it.

"All Germany is sparing on eggs and milk and you squander it on horses. I get the blame for running short on the Bavarian quota and you polish the hides of your horses with milk and eggs. *Es ist ja eine ganz grosse Schweinerei!*"

Then, before Weber could duck, Wagner seized the tablecloth in both hands and whipped it over his host's head, plates, glasses, bones, champagne, and all.

He hit the covered face with his fist and Weber rolled off the chair to the floor, tangled up in tablecloth and tableware. Wagner roared and swore like a drunken trooper on a rampage and stomped out of the place, hurling back charges that nobody could frame him with tricks like that. He turned around in the doorway once more and warned one and all that Wagner is boss in Bavaria, none other, and intriguers against him had better watch out.

I imagine Wagner knew what he was saying, for it is no secret that mean little bits of intrigue wreck Nazi careers much quicker than big plots or bad mistakes. Weber was not above undermining the powerful Gauleiter, and numerous hidden tricks like the sabotage of Wagner's egg-and-milk deliveries could accumulate nasty suspicions against him in Berlin.

3

Consider the sad case of Ernst Udet, who almost single-handed made the Luftwaffe a fast and deadly instrument of stukas, parachuters, and blitzkrieg daredevils. He was a victim of carelessness, of too trusting a nature.

Udet, unlike Wagner, did not see a warning symptom in things around the office or field that went wrong. He trusted the Nazis in the swivel chairs of his department of the Goering Air Ministry and blithely shot dice or chewed the rag with some of us Americans as in the old days before an order went around prohibiting such association "with the enemy."

One morning last September he found himself in the midst of a shake-up. General Chaersik, an administrative general of old Nazi leanings who was in charge of contracts and deliveries at the Air Ministry under Udet, was removed from his post along with a dozen other higher-ups.

It seems that contracts okayed and signed by Udet were never fulfilled, or at least some were not, although the money was paid out. Most of us foreign correspondents who knew Udet and his German friends, too, were sure that Udet was merely the victim of his underlings and that he probably knew nothing about the graft and corruption in his own department.

But he was the responsible man who signed those contracts and had to take it on the chin. There was no getting around that.

Now some years ago the Nazis at Hitler's suggestion set aside a large estate not unlike a big farm over in East Prussia for temporary "recuperation" in cases of Nazi key men under a cloud. They are kept there under house arrest until their case is cleared up, washed up, or hushed up. It depends on circumstances, provided grave charges like high treason or anti-Hitler activity are not involved. Udet was an open-and-shut case for the State Farm and throughout September and October he sat it out up there. The farm is huge; there are riding horses and swimming accommodations in addition to good food and fine living quarters, except that the occupants are pledged by word of honor not to go off the property.

Just before I left Berlin in late November of 1941 I heard that Udet's case was to be hushed up, and within a few days I also heard that Udet had been reassigned to his post but under another man. It was an outright demotion, and to a man like Udet was not only galling but it was a stain on his honor. He was colonel general in military rank and a large share of the Luftwaffe's brain power. It is hard to see how he could be expected to work under order of an inferior. Udet just wasn't built that way.

Shortly after his silent return to the Goering Air Ministry we heard whispers in Berlin that Udet was dead. I knew it wasn't so, because I saw him eating quietly by himself at the table always reserved for him in Horcher's, the most exclusive and most expensive restaurant in Europe.

I was having a farewell lunch with a Nazi official that day, but Udet never as much as looked up at anyone passing his table. Obviously, he didn't care to greet company or resume the jovial mood of other days. He was a man in disgrace, a soldier with a deep wound in his heart. He knew he couldn't go on and that there was only one way out. His face showed that, and the news of his death a short time later brought me no surprise.

It was like Udet to die of his own choosing by the same method with which he had risked his life a hundred times—trying out a new plane or bomb but trying it out in such a way that he couldn't come out alive.

He had pride and courage, manly ingredients completely

lacking in some of the most obnoxious of the Nazis, as, for instance, Julius Streicher. This man of addled brain and sick body nevertheless was boss of all Franconia until late in 1940, in addition to which he had an evil hold on Hitler and therewith the Nazi party. Streicher used to swagger through the land or through the capital of his *Gau* (province) Nuremberg like a master of old through his slave plantation, constantly slapping the heavy horsewhip in his hand against his polished boots.

Bald as a billiard ball and with shoe-button eyes, Streicher shrieked at every opportunity against the Jews and was publisher of the reeking anti-Semitic sheet *Der Stuermer*. He couldn't talk or act rationally and by 1940 was clearly a case for the insane asylum.

But I recall that at the Olympic Games in 1936 he moved like a shadow at Hitler's side and prevented the Fuehrer from receiving for a moment Jesse Owens, the black flash. He did it by having all adjutants firmly but quietly made aware that he, Streicher, would personally horsewhip every verdammte one of them if Owens got past that reception door beneath the Olympic Stadium. Hitler waited five minutes, and when Owens failed to appear, as expected, left without getting wise to Streicher's hand.

In the summer of 1940 Streicher's name finally stank to high heaven. I spent a day in Nuremberg after the French debacle of July and saw men and women openly ripping down his picture. They told me frankly that he was a swine and had gone far enough, which was quite a strange kind of language to hear in contemporary Germany.

Hitler youths were sent to all public schools and buildings to remove the Streicher picture, and for a time it looked as though the offices of *Der Stuermer* would get mobbed. A few days before, I was told, the wife of another of his adjutants had been buried by her grief-stricken husband and relatives. The husband killed himself on the morning of the day when I was in Nuremberg. Three other women had died the same way, and even more revolting charges were recounted to me.

The Nurembergers had enough of it, Nazi head man or not. They said so out loud, in the face of the Gestapo, which doesn't often happen.

Hitler quietly removed him from his post as Gauleiter of Franconia and for the next six months had him kept under lock and key in an insane asylum. There were no charges against him, and no punishment. He now lives under guard at his farm a few miles out of Nuremberg, ridden by hallucinations and subject to epileptic fits. Hitler never visits him, but *Der Stuermer* still appears throughout Germany with Streicher's name on the masthead. It is one of those things you run into in Naziland.

Streicher is not the only former familiar part of the Nazi party and of Hitler's entourage to fade into the background like discarded waste.

There is Field Marshal Werner von Blomberg, who fell by the wayside when he married a young girl and therewith committed an infraction of military rules for high officers. There is Hans Brinkmann, former brains in the Reichsbank and financial adviser to Hitler, who cracked under the strain and is now in a strait jacket in an insane asylum.

There was, until 1940, the familiar hard-boiled figure of Julius Shreck, chauffeur to Hitler since the rowdy twenties. The Nazis—and some said Hitler—had built a sort of legend around Shreck and said nothing could ever happen to Hitler while Shreck was at the wheel.

He did save Hitler's life more than once, swerving the car in a flash to miss the deadly rocks which came tumbling down in 1938 on the road between Berchtesgaden and Munich. The year before he stepped calmly on the accelerator when bullets whipped and bit against the bulletproof windshield.

He was tough, all right, and made a point of swaggering about in public when not driving the car. He was a bear with women, mauling them about in cave-man fashion, but bragged around that this got results without waste of time. He was apt to mention women's names at the beer table, expanding on his latest conquests to intimate details if the champagne flowed freely and there were enough men to listen.

He did that once too often, after an affair with an army officer's wife. The young officer, of proud military family and disdainful of low-caste Nazis anyhow, walked into the Brown House in Munich (Nazi-party headquarters) and before a dozen astounded Nazi eyes socked Shreck on the nose before the chauffeur knew what had hit him. Then the officer called him a coward and challenged Shreck to a duel with pistols.

Shreck was in the soup. He had to accept but during the night tried to have the officer arrested by the military, and, failing that, tried to have him waylaid on the way out to the meadow in the woods outside Munich at dawn.

But that didn't work, and an hour later Hitler was without his hard-boiled chauffeur. I understand the army went to bat for the young officer and compelled the Nazis to leave the case in military hands. Then, through the Nazi-party press, it was melodramatically announced that Julius Shreck had suddenly died of complications from a blood clot in the right leg. He even got a wreath from Hitler, with the usual red ribbon and golden initials of the Fuehrer.

Woman trouble also eliminated a traditional figure from Hitler's elbow. That is the bloated body of Wilhelm Brueckner, original personal adjutant to Hitler and captain in the World War. Brueckner was never more than a step behind his Fuehrer, practically dressing and undressing him and certainly making all appointments of importance. You couldn't get near Hitler without passing muster with Brueckner, who sized the candidates up through bleary eyes and cheeks puffed from alcohol.

More than six feet tall, he towered like a protecting wall behind Hitler, shoving his own body forward with steam-roller effect wherever the crush for Hitler autographs got heavy.

In 1938 we foreign correspondents, or those in the know, began to hear rumors that Hitler was getting impatient with Brueckner because of his heavy drinking. What annoyed Hitler more was the fact that Brueckner lived surreptitiously with a married woman with two children, leaving his own wife sitting in Bavaria as object of all the hot gossip in the land.

Hitler sooner or later was bound to make use of this opportunity to remove his old shadow, as he likes to do from time to time, and it wasn't surprising to hear one day that Brueckner was called on the carpet by Hitler and given four months to clear up his marital affairs.

Brueckner arranged a divorce from his wife in Bavaria and married the woman with two children the day after she, too, got a speedy divorce, with the help of Nazi machinery. A week later Hitler sent Brueckner into retirement, curtly informing him to remain out of sight until further notice. That was the last seen in public of Brueckner, body servant of the Fuehrer for many trying years. He sits in a Bavarian house on Wiesensee today and broods over his lot. There isn't much you can do after getting fired by Hitler.

4

I never could look at these Nazis around Hitler without feeling that they must have an iron constitution and be somewhat awry in the head. Otherwise, they wouldn't want to be around him or be able to stand the pace and strain. I suppose in the last analysis all of the higher Nazi key men are abnormal, sustained by drink, or swell-headed with self-importance. I don't know of a single Nazi in Hitler's setup who hasn't got some peculiar quirk of mind or body, just enough to make you wonder what makes them tick.

With this curiosity in my mind after nearly seven years around them, I went to particular pains in February of 1941 to get along for an evening with Victor Lutze, successor to the liquidated Ernst Roehm of the 1934 blood purge as chief of Hitler's brown-shirted S.A. The word around Berlin had been that Lutze is a nincompoop, picked by Hitler as a safeguard against further trouble from ambitious men like Roehm.

Be that as it may, Lutze came as requested to a dinner at Boemer's political club in Leipziger Platz, chest sticking out and eager to prove himself a good fellow to these foreign correspondents. I sat alongside of him through dinner and drew him out on political questions.

"Is it true, Herr Lutze, that you have circulated instructions to the S.A. that war with America is inevitable and that they must get ready for it?" said I boldly.

Lutze, who'd been telling me all through the soup and fish courses how he keeps his fingers off foreign politics, rubbed his nose for a few moments before answering. "Yes, that is what I've done," he declared. "Yes, we are telling the S.A. to get ready for a war with America. It is inevitable, that war."

This was in February of 1941. His frank confirmation of rumors I'd heard took my breath away and fitted nicely into other things that came to my ears. But I was puzzled by his frankness. Was he trying to throw me off the track by this direct admission? I stuck to my guns and said: "Why?"

Lutze was ready for that one. He answered:

"We are at war now, and it is just a matter of time before the shooting between us begins.

"We Nazis intend to be ready for it and to accustom our people to this eventuality. It will help a lot to remove the shock of having yet another powerful enemy lining up against us. The public won't mind as long as it is made fully aware of the development beforehand.

"That is why we are working hard now to spread the news around, first through the S.A., then through the army, and then through the public at large."

I asked: "How long do you think the war will last then? There is an idea floating around it will be finished in 1941. Even some speeches have suggested as much."

"The war cannot finish before 1943, at the earliest," Lutze said. "You Americans will see to that. But we Nazis will win the war, long or short as it may be."

That was at the beginning of 1941, and figuring back now, it is easy to guess how thoroughly and systematically Hitler plotted and prepared for the war against America. It all comes out in the wash.

After dinner Lutze and the bunch of us took over the bar, where champagne began to flow freely. The weather over Berlin was pretty bad and there was small chance of an air alarm, so we could take our time. For the next two hours we talked of everything under the sun, pumping his Nazi mind on all topics of interest, while the cigarette smoke and long draughts of champagne heated up the atmosphere. Lutze, like most Nazis, slugged down a full glass at a time and laughed at slower imbibers like myself.

"Here, drink like a man," he said boastingly after the sixth bottle. "Look at me. Every morning at six I'm up for a horseback ride. I ride two hours and tire out three horses before I go to breakfast. Then, if weather and time permit during the day, I get into my plane and ride around in the clouds for a couple of hours. Freshens you up. I'm always on the go till after midnight and drink my fill to boot. Down with it. *Prosit!*"

I checked up on his routine a few days later and found that he told the truth. They're all like that, these men around Hitler. Restless and ever busy proving to themselves and others what a super-race they are. At times it gets a trifle tiresome.

Lutze also began telling us about the wild horses he tames or rides bareback in Westphalia, roping them in with lassos in the manner of our cowboys. That, too, proved correct, and I discovered that some four to five hundred horses are running wild in the hills there.

"Did I ever show you my favorite trick?" Lutze said suddenly, after draining enough champagne to float a ship. He took his champagne glass and filled it to the brim, saying:

"It scares a lot of women out of their wits, and Hitler gets a good laugh out of it. He has me pull this one at state banquets or when things get boring and he wants to get rid of the old wives who hang around too long. It breaks the ice when there are too many stuffed shirts and their women sitting at the table and some of them faint. Look!"

Laughing and shouting, he reached up to his left eye and

neatly removed the eyeball, dropping it into his champagne
with a deft twist of the hand. Then he stirred the drink
and gulped down the whole works, champagne with glass
eye to boot. He opened his mouth to show that he had
swallowed the glass eye, but a moment later he made as
though to belch hard and out came the glass eye.

He wiped it indifferently amid his own shouted laughter
and replaced it in the left eye socket. There was, I must
say, scarcely anything to betray that false eye, unless the
light happened to reflect too strongly in the glass.

"There you are, perfectly simple," he said with a sweeping gesture. "You should hear them shriek!"

"And what does Hitler do?"

"He laughs to himself and never lets on that he has seen
me do it before. He is a better actor than some of our stage
and film stars. It's a good way to get rid of some of those
ancients."

This man Lutze reminded me a good deal of Walter
Funk, the chubby, round-faced little man picked by Hitler
to succeed Schacht of the high collar as president of the
Reichsbank and Finance Minister.

Funk, formerly right-hand man for Joe Goebbels, likes
to act natural, too, and rid himself of official starchiness. At
a banquet given by the foreign press corps in 1939, before
the war, Funk threw caution to the winds and before all
eyes navigated toward the orchestra. He waved the orchestra leader aside and, seizing his baton, went to town, ripping
off the speed and the notes as he thought the job should be
done. He fell on his back once, but we picked him up,

brushed off his dinner clothes, and the show went on. Hjalmar Schacht would never have done that.

A few weeks later, on a sultry autumn night, the foreign press (a dozen of the important ones) were guests at the beautiful villa, amid a parklike scene and lake, of Gustaf Gruendgens, stage and film star number one in the Reich and also director of the State Theater in Berlin under Goering's patronage.

The feast began before midnight at tables set out on the lawn like an open-air restaurant, with torches stuck in the ground casting off an eerie reddish light. It was typically Hollywood, and a gypsy band slightly hidden under the trees played appropriate music.

Pert little stars from film and stage were there to enliven the interest and the scene, all of which contributed to a gay night. Funk was there, too, sleepily enjoying one bottle of champagne after another. At 3 A.M. the girls discovered that the water was lukewarm and a swim in the lake would pep everyone up. Off came clothes, and soon a dozen were swimming in the moonlight, the white of their bodies showing through the clear water.

Funk strolled leisurely down to the lakeside, a bottle of champagne in his hand. Without once giving it a second thought, the Reich Minister for Finance and president of Hitler's Reichsbank removed every stitch of clothing and revealed a body not unlike a beer barrel on stilts.

Standing there as nature cast him while the girls and men in the water and outside of it shrieked with delight, he finished his champagne with much gurgling and then dropped himself into the lake with the splash of an elephant. For over an hour there was splashing and shrieking as girls and boys and Hitler's minister disported happily in the water, waiting for the moon to go down.

Anyway, he is one of a type, this Funk. Another one is August Bohle, the young whippersnapper of British birth who is in charge of Germans abroad. He is the Nazi who organized the consular machinery so that it functioned as a sort of Gestapo network, reporting closely on all activities and political attitudes of Germans in foreign lands, for a time directing all functions of the German diplomatic machinery.

He put a Nazi-party functionary into every German embassy and consulate abroad, chiefly to stooge on the officers. He organized a network of communication and exchange of information nowadays tantamount to espionage. It was an attempt to keep every German abroad under the thumb of the Nazis, and to make use of them.

This Bohle didn't like us correspondents much. Some of us knew too much about the good-looking secretaries he surrounded himself with either in his offices on the Tiergarten or while on trips. I had severely rapped the knuckles of the stooge he always sent to the Ristorante Taverne to get an earful and had forbidden him to sit at the table reserved for correspondents and their friends.

Finally, in arrangement with the Propaganda Ministry, a few of us went to Hamburg to cover a big shipping festival dedicated at the same time to some thousands of Germans who were returning from abroad.

Hitler was to be there aboard his armored yacht, the *Aviso Grille*, and it looked like a worth-while bit of copy. But in Hamburg we found out that Bohle was in charge of arrangements and receptions, which didn't look so good. He welcomed us at dinner with a little sardonic smile and said he hoped we'd enjoy our stay there.

The accommodations, he stressed, were limited and for that reason we'd sleep in cabins aboard German ships for the night. A pretty little miss took down everything he said, which was just as good an excuse as any to have her there at his side and in a room next to his at the hotel.

Bill Shirer and I drew the same cabin. Something told us to watch out. The cabin was on the liner *Monte Rosa*, lying at a pier unloading cargo. The cabin was okay but it stank to high heaven, for the cargo being unloaded consisted of hides from the Argentine. Every time they let down a batch of those steaming hides, the load dropped straight past our cabin porthole and Bill and I got the full benefit of their perfume.

We gave it up and found another place to spend the night, at our own expense. It was Bohle's way of getting even. Just a Nazi with a twisted sense of humor, and I suppose he got a kick out of lying in bed and thinking about it. As I said previously, all these Nazis have something queer in their heads, otherwise they wouldn't be the way they are, or where they are.

CHAPTER 3

Goering's Troubles with Hitler

A PONDEROUS POLITICAL MACHINE like that of the Nazi party, sprung from the beer halls of Munich and nursed along on street brawls by hard-fisted men who'd sooner fight than eat, is a magnified version of the old Tammany Hall at its worst.

Inside this machine you are bound to have a touch of the primitive, functioning at all times on the basic law of the jungle that only the fittest survive. The little wolves and hyenas of a decade ago become the high and mighty through a process of ruthless elimination; a big one falls here and there and is forsaken immediately by those who used to curry his favor.

I have seen this law of the jungle at work within the ranks of the Nazi party and inside the political volcano in the Wilhelmstrasse ever since I went to Berlin for International

News Service shortly after Hitler had come to power. I saw the blood purge of 1934 and got arrested in Munich by the Gestapo for telephoning, or trying to telephone, a descriptive story to our office in Berlin. I heard the rattle of rifle fire in the Berlin suburb of Lichtenberg a few days later as heads rolled in the sand by the score, and watched with dismay as the man hunt for those on the black list spread terror into every nook and corner of the capital.

All passed over, like the raid of a satiated wolf pack on the shepherd's flock. It has never been repeated in just that way, but the shake-ups and cleanups within the Nazi ranks and those of the Wilhelmstrasse have come and gone as regularly as the four seasons.

I sat around Berlin with my ear to the ground for nearly eight years and time and again watched the moving finger write finis to a high or low career. True, I didn't again hear the rifles crackling over in Lichtenberg as in 1934, but in effect and principle it was the same thing. The scores and even the thousands of men holding down medium or high jobs in the Nazi party and government alike nowadays shave every day and wear spick-and-span uniforms or civilian clothes with neckties, yet they are the same who a few short years ago shaved once in several days and looked askance at people who wore clean shirts with neckties. On the surface they wear the mantle of official dignity; beneath the skin they are carrying on in exclusive clubs and hotels the same fight for survival they fought out on the street, and the jungle mill of elimination, intrigue, and rivalry grinds away just as busily as ever.

That goes for the Nazis in Hitler's Third Reich from top to bottom today, and no holds barred.

If you were one of the foreign correspondents sitting on that boiling lid in Berlin, the whiff of scandal or brewing political storms in high and low quarters around Hitler came drifting on the wind from all corners. It might be one time that some of the more hard-bitten generals of the old line were bucking the Hitler tide and having a showdown. Or it might be that some high-placed Nazi in Hitler's entourage had fallen into disfavor and was on the way out. It came to your ears, by chance or by whisper, and soon enough it was just a matter of waiting for the storm to break. Whatever the case, up to now Hitler has always won out.

I heard without much surprise, therefore, the recurrent rumors around the town in 1940 that Goering and Ribbentrop were quarreling again. There had always been bad blood between them, soured by political rivalry and jealousy. Goering considered Ribbentrop a political upstart and outsider and made no bones about saying so; Ribbentrop considered Goering a fat slob filled with vain ambition and crazy enough to get it in his head that he would be an ideal Fuehrer II. That and much more kept the sparks flying between those two.

So one night at the beginning of November 1940 I sat in pajamas on the sofa of my apartment on the Luetzow Ufer adjoining the War Ministry in Berlin and listened to my visitor's account of the latest row in the chancellery between Goering and Ribbentrop. He had much to tell,

safe from prying eyes and listening ears or dictaphones.
Long ago I had made sure that the unseen hand of the
Gestapo should not reach into my apartment, and those
who came there by night felt wholly at ease. The telephone
was tapped, of course, but we in Berlin had learned to say
nothing over the wire that we didn't want strange ears to
hear.

"Herr Ribbentrop went to Hitler and complained that
Goering was up to his old tricks of meddling in foreign
policy," the man from the inside of the Wilhelmstrasse told
me, between gulps of real coffee I had brewed for him.
"Of course Hitler knows all about it, but the situation between those two has again reached the stage where it's
time to stop juggling and make a decision one way or another." The man put down the coffee cup and smiled.
"What finally got Ribbentrop mad," he added with a touch
of satisfied malice, "were those gaudy trips of Goering's
to Budapest, Belgrade, and Rome with his Emmy. He had
gotten some sort of good-will assignment from Hitler to
make his excuse valid to the governments concerned but
the real purpose on the one hand was a shopping tour
and on Hermann's side a chance to be glorified and put his
finger deep into the political pie. Goering has always been
good at this sort of thing and Ribbentrop knew it. In Belgrade, you know, Goering sprang some sort of friendship
and economic deal between Yugoslavia and Germany and
in the other places he was trying to do the same thing. He
ordered a dozen boiled eggs for breakfast and threw half
of them at the flunkies because the eggs carried a Danish

stamp or something on the shell. He got a beautifully engraved dagger of Mohammedan design from the Yugoslavian Government and bawled out the Foreign Minister for not using German steel. In Belgrade they decided that he was crazy but admired his blunt ways of doing things the way they like to see them done.

"So they signed a deal and told stories at the dinner table about Hermann and his Emmy.

"So now," my informant went on, "Goering got the idea that he could make a whale of a deal by going to Sweden. He has a touch of the Swede in him, you know, and considers Sweden a sort of private reserve for himself. That is where Ribbentrop blew up and went to Hitler. He can't take it any more, without losing face on the outside. The rumors are pretty thick anyhow that Ribbentrop is losing out, and another trip of Goering's to a foreign capital for a deal would just about make Ribbentrop look like two cents. So Ribbentrop had a case and last night went to bat with Hitler."

It wasn't the good French cognac we were drinking by now that made us look at each other and smile. Mutually we had in mind the nasty moments of subcharged atmosphere which must have ruled the offices and corridors and private rooms in Hitler's chancellery the night before. Trouble like that always gets around in that building, carried chiefly by the moods and temperamental outbursts of an agitated Hitler. He will juggle and stall for weeks and months, fighting shy of any definite decision like the man with a bad tooth trying to avoid an appointment with the

dentist. It excites and disrupts him to face the showdown.
He relies to a great extent on the fear and lack of courage of
those who come to him seeking a positive decision, edging
them off at times with a snarl of temper or by simply shoving aside the whole affair as not yet ready for solution.
Only when cornered with a condemned man's courage by
a gray-faced Ribbentrop or glaring Goering does he come
to the point, and if there is no other way out, his verdict
falls. Then it usually echoes around the town like a thunder-
clap.

"Well, it looks to me as if Ribbentrop put Adolf on the
spot then," I said to my visitor and poured out two more
glasses of the cognac. This bottle was one of the few I had
left after bringing it all the way from Paris some months
before. The French had urged it on us and pointed out that
they'd sooner sell it to us Americans than to the swarms of
Germans swamping all shops immediately after the occupation of Paris. I knew the French stores were empty now,
cleaned out to the last shelf of everything. I was glad I had
kept the Germans from at least a few mites of the French
stocks in merchandise and liquor. "What did Hitler do
and how did it all come out?" I finally asked my informative
visitor.

"Oh, he saw the point and gave in to Ribbentrop. He
called in Goering this morning and told him to remember
that Herr Ribbentrop is Foreign Minister of the Third
Reich and fully qualified and authorized to handle all questions of foreign policy. He is not to be interfered with by
anyone else. Goering was to run his own part of the show

and not butt into Ribbentrop's field. That ended the conversation on that subject, for you know how Hitler is at such times. He takes refuge in being the Almighty and wards off any argument at such times by making it all sound like an order. Then he shook hands with Goering and invited him to lunch. It mollified Hermann, and, furthermore, Hitler clinched the whole thing by making Goering the Reichsmarshal with a uniform all his own. He gets a special baton studded with diamonds and plated with gold, worth at least around thirty thousand marks, and a specially designed cap decorated with gold leaf. So there is peace in the family again, even if down beneath the surface there is bad blood as always between Goering and Ribbentrop."

2

I noticed long ago that a Nazi can never put one over on the other fellow without gloating about it. Sooner or later he puts salt in the wound, if only to keep the ball rolling.

I was to be the accidental witness to this sort of thing a few days later when the Soviet Embassy staged its annual commemoration of the November 7 Revolution. I had gotten my engraved invitation for a tea and reception starting at 4 P.M. It would be worth going to, and might even produce a little story for the cables, for it got around town that everybody in the political, diplomatic, and military world was going to show up. No wonder, for the Soviet Embassy receptions in those days were noted for the luscious and lavish helpings of caviar, vodka, and real coffee.

I got into a taxi and drove down Unter den Linden in the heart of old imperial Berlin to the drab-looking square old box of a faded palace where in the days before World War I nothing less than a Russian prince ruled as Ambassador and where Czar Nicholas and his wife stayed during their state visit to the Kaiser. Police and the usual sidewalk spectators lined the entrance and looked sharply at everyone who came. An ordinary blue suit like mine with its white shirt and red tie just for the sake of a little atmosphere got quicker attention from the uniformed German police and the non-uniformed Russian G.P.U. than all the uniforms and diplomatic top hats. You had to keep that engraved invitation prominently in sight to get by.

Inside, the Russian Embassy had changed little from Czarist days, except that an oil painting of Stalin hung in the main hall through which you pass in order to get into the reception chamber. The heavy gold frame holding that painting was the same one which held the life-sized painting of Czar Nicholas II, and the Imperial Crown with its Russian double-headed eagle still caught the eye above the head of Stalin. The heavy red carpets, the old-fashioned glass chandeliers, and the imperial table and silverware were as good as ever. A lone marble bust of Lenin against a wall of the main reception room was all there was to remind you that Soviet Russia ruled here, and not the court of St. Petersburg.

I went perfunctorily through the usual reception line, announced and presented according to etiquette by one of the bright young men from the German Foreign Office.

The Russian Ambassador at that time was a nonentity named Skwarzekev, shaking in his boots every time the G.P.U. looked at him and showing fear in his eyes if any foreigner really came up to do some talking.

Beside him stood a woman dressed in plain black from head to foot, not necessarily ugly, but very much a part of that embassy. She played the role of wife in public and of G.P.U. chief behind the scene. In addition there was the bright and ascetic little Pavlov, said by some to be one of Stalin's illegitimate sons. Whatever the case, this blond young man talked perfect English and always came up to ask numerous questions while urging you to help yourself to the good things on the table. He was the lad who did the real reporting to Stalin out of Berlin on the goings on. So it wasn't surprising to see him recalled to Moscow to take charge of the Central European Political Department back there as soon as Dekanozov from the Soviet inner ring replaced the other man as Ambassador. That was early in 1941, proving that Stalin was smelling the wind and wanted somebody on the spot in Berlin who could tell him what was really being cooked up by Hitler.

I looked around the reception chamber and found almost everybody of note on hand. They were feeding their faces like hungry children at a tea party, stuffing caviar and meat or lobster sandwiches into their mouths as fast as two hands could get them there. Glass after glass of vodka and cup after cup of coffee went down the throats of the Fieldmarshal and the wife of the diplomatic clerk alike. No quarter was given or asked, and the stolid-faced Russian help struggled mightily to keep the mob at bay. I have always felt that human nature displays its worst side in these official receptions all over the world, and looking around the reception chamber in the Soviet Embassy that day, I found no reason to change my mind.

Goering came in clanking in the blue uniform of the air force, a stripe of white two inches wide on the seams of his trousers. He had on the usual carload of medals but made short shrift of formalities. He plowed his way forward through the crowd straight to the table where I was helping myself to some caviar and vodka, firmly elbowing aside the excited and highly decorated ladies who came with a rush for Hermann. But it was his off day for some reason or other and he was fixedly interested in that bulbous brown caviar from the Caspian. He grabbed a plate and sank a spoon into the caviar pot. He might as well have been swinging a spade, and the portion that came out upon that plate would have cost many a German a month's wages.

I looked at him and said nothing. It was this directness of Goering and his don't-give-a-damn attitude which accrued for him a sort of popularity. Every ambassador, every military attaché, and all the important Nazi world stood around that room and had their eyes fixed on him, but he was eating caviar and too busy to notice them. Out of the corner of my eye I saw Ribbentrop coming in from the other room, apparently making a beeline for Goering. Far be it from me to eavesdrop, but business is business, and if those two were going to let go within hearing of strange ears, then conscience would never bother me. They knew the rule better than I that in Naziland you look around and especially over your shoulder before you do any talking. I wasn't invisible, although naturally I looked the opposite way so as not to draw their attention to me.

Ribbentrop of the fast-graying hair and the slight forward stoop stood quietly beside Goering for a moment, as if waiting to see how much caviar a man could eat without stopping for breath. He lit a cigar and nudged the new Reichsmarshal. Goering glanced around and his eyes started dancing a little more nervously. He uttered a perfunctory greeting and went on with his meal.

"We haven't met since we clarified our personal relationships and defined our mutual duties and authority," the affected voice of Ribbentrop said in an undertone. "You know, Goering, I have always said that we will get along fine if you mind your own business and let me be the Foreign Minister."

Ribbentrop was gone and left the Embassy before Goering could catch his breath. I wasn't interested any longer in eating, for the caviar would have stuck in my throat. I grabbed a vodka off the nearest tray and faded into that crowd as fast as I could, and as far away from Goering as possible. For I have seen him get mad, and besides, I had no desire to be known to him as one of those who had heard what Ribbentrop said. He has a way of losing his temper right out in public, and woe to the man or woman who crosses his path at that moment.

Goering held his temper in check that day but it can be

taken for granted that he made a mental note to get even. Experience in big-time politics has shown him that everybody has his ups and downs. He knows that Ribbentrop, probably for the duration of the war, is sitting pretty and can hardly be dislodged from his seat alongside the mighty. But someday things might change, and then would come the day of reckoning. That's the way it goes in Naziland.

It wasn't unusual or very hard to hear tales in Berlin or from the outside that a row was on again between some of the Nazi big shots, landing this or that one in the doghouse. Incidents like the above feed such rumors, gaining in circulation over the grapevine as varied versions get started from bits of truth always leaking out. There is usually some basis to the wildest rumor, which in the end may serve to lead you to the real thing.

Consequently, I listened with open ears to the gossip in Berlin over the succeeding months clear through the summer of 1941, getting always the same undercurrent of trouble between Ribbentrop and Goering, or Himmler and Goering, and finally Hitler and Goering. It used to be constantly between Goebbels and Goering, but as far as I know never very seriously between Hitler and Goering. Therefore it was worth tracking down.

For the sake of clarity, it must then be pointed out here that Goering has just about as many jobs in the Hitler regime as he has medals. He is probably best known as the Reichsmarshal and Commander in Chief of the Luftwaffe. But he is an equally busy man as boss of the so-called four-year plan and of all internal measures deemed necessary to win the war. He is the man who dictates to the German what and how much he should eat or drink; he runs big industry and sees to it that rich and poor alike march in step. He is a manifold dictator within his own right.

Goering is also what might be termed a conservative Nazi, leaning heavily in sympathy and viewpoint toward the military, and is not very enthusiastic about giving the Nazi party much of a free hand. He holds some sort of rank in it but has never felt at ease in his brown shirt. In the heyday of Nazi-party feasts, circuses, and parades, Goering donned the brown uniform when he had to, but he ducked for home at the first opportunity. Nowadays you seldom see him sitting around with the Nazis. He can and does find ever so many excuses. For the same reason, it can easily be imagined why the career men in the Nazi party have no special love for Hermann Goering. That, too, is one of the things about Naziland you mustn't forget.

With so many irons in the fire, each big enough to require a man's undivided attention, it is but logical that sooner or later he must ride the bumps. The political jungle and the clash of interests are bound to interfere, to say nothing of the moods and tempers he has to contend with. Goering takes it all in his stride and goes home to play with his electric railway or hunt wild pig on his Schorfheide estate if he gets fed up. He can always seek refuge, too, in the war and devote all his time and energy for a while to the personal direction and conduct of Luftwaffe operations.

But there are moments when he must speak his mind, even to Hitler, and try to put his foot down or have an understanding on vital matters in hand. Last spring and during the succeeding months all these problems seemed to come at once, actually taking off a bit of weight from his portly figure and giving the world the fixed impression that he was on the outs with Hitler. On the outside they even said that he was under arrest, which annoyed him no end, for it meant that people believed a lower-ranking man like Himmler was telling him what to do. Goering grumbled and resented it, ending by having himself filmed for the newsreel around the Russian front and with Hitler.

But it wasn't as simple as all that. Sitting back in that web of intrigue and gossip of official and unofficial Berlin, I picked up the threads one by one and with a little additional information from behind the scenes soon had in hand the causes that were making Goering lose weight.

In the first place, Heinrich Himmler, of the Gestapo, was feeling his oats. In collusion with others like Sepp Dietrich (commander of Hitler's crack bodyguard of some 25,000 men in the field), Himmler was pressing Hitler for an air-force unit attached solely to S.S. troops and as independent in operations of the Luftwaffe as Hitler's bodyguard of the regular army. That is, they fight as part of the regular army but in a sector all their own by plan and on command of Hitler himself. These highly equipped troops are always the first to dash into a captured capital, probably with the idea of symbolizing the arrival there of Hitler. Himmler wanted a similar arrangement for his

S.S. troops, on the contention that they go into occupied lands and do special work such as subduing resistance and cleaning up the enemy wherever they find him. He argued, therefore, that a special air-force unit directly under his command should be made available.

Goering scotched that plan with much shouting and roaring, declaring that he was boss of the Luftwaffe as it stood or not at all. He would brook no interference in that respect and no rivalry bound to spring from such an offspring of the Luftwaffe. He won out, but naturally not without raising dust between himself and Himmler, all to the silent delight of Ribbentrop.

Then, after Hess had flown the coop, new troubles broke on the horizon with the advent of the little Nazi Bormann as successor to the Deputy Fuehrer. Bormann was one of the radical fanatics from the beer halls for whom Goering had no great love. Hess in many ways had been a conservative like himself and a stanch pillar to lean on in times of strain and stress.

Within a few weeks after being in office Bormann started trouble by launching a new pressure campaign against the Catholics and an all-out crusade against the Jews. Soon convents all over Germany were being closed and the rabid flame of fanaticism lurking in many Nazi breasts throughout the Reich was being fanned to dangerous proportions. The Gestapo dragged thousands of Jews away from home and threw them to die into ghettos in Poland.

Goering and other conservative men of influence of the Reich were swamped and besieged with protests and pleas, all frantically pointing out that the renewed persecution of the Catholics was getting them up in arms just at a time when the war and hardships of sacrifice in Russia required every ounce of unity and support from the people.

Again Goering took the bull by the horns and went to bat with Hitler. He was fortified about that time by co-incidence in the person of his foremost Luftwaffe ace Werner Moelders, victor in scores of air battles and holder of the highest Hitler decorations. Moelders had gone home to the city of Münster in Westphalia on leave. He found the historic old city partially in ruins, battered and torn apart in many places by R.A.F. bombs. But what hurt more than all that was that his sister had been run out with other nuns from the near-by convent by the Nazi fanatics, and the good Catholics of the town were in a high state of indignation.

Moelders lost no time in reaching Goering. He told him plainly and without mincing words that as a soldier of the army he could not refuse to continue to fight but he could turn in all decorations and honors bestowed on him. That this he intended to do forthwith unless the Catholic perse-cution was brought to a halt.

Goering seized on that written document from Moelders and also took with him to Hitler a whole stack of appeals from influential persons in all corners of the Reich. The outcry and protests had in fact become so audible by that time that Goering merely had to clinch the deal with suf-ficient evidence. Whether he liked it or not, Hitler had to order suspension of Bormann's campaign against the Catholics, but all of us from inside Germany know that this is merely a truce. Sooner or later the Nazis again are going to lock horns with the Catholic Church and settle the issue in their own way. The Bormann war on the Jews could not be stopped and raged with unbroken cruelty clear through to the end of 1941. The Nazis were boasting and bragging that no Jew would be left inside Germany before very long.

It can be imagined that all the above again didn't improve Goering's standing. It handicapped him, also, for the greater struggle which developed and originated suddenly with the departure of Hess. For a long time, and especially since the beginning of the war, a section of opinion had crystallized against the further continuation and existence of the Nazi party itself. This was particularly true, by and large, in the higher military circles, where it was pointed out time and again that the army does the fighting and therewith absorbs all the available man power, leaving no room or place for semi-military organizations such as the S.S. or S.A.

The parading and marching and carrying of side arms by storm troopers always had been a sore spot with the army, and in fact was part of the cause which led to the 1934 cleanup. Much of that blood purge was intended to show once and for all who was to have the upper hand. Actually, higher German officers under the regulations cannot be members of the Nazi party, although the late Fieldmarshal Walther von Reichenau belonged to it for many years. But no high-ranking man in the party by dint of his position therein gets the least consideration from the army. When drafted he comes in as the buck private or in whatever rank he left the army the last time he served. You can imagine what a howl there was when some of the Nazis who got caught and yanked in from comfortable offices and fine limousines had to do the goose step as ordinary soldiers of the ranks.

There was another side to it. Men of higher government and industrial standing, and some courageous ones in the educational fields, kept harping on the fact that there should not be two governments in the Reich; in other words, they considered and always will consider the Nazi party a shadow government to the proper machinery of state in the Wilhelmstrasse. They said it should be done away with once and for all.

When Hess moved off to Scotland the shock to the Nazi party was terrific; its standing was at low ebb and everybody said that the Third Reich of Adolf Hitler definitely had been transformed from a party into a military state. There was cheering and celebrating and much toasting in the circles who hate the Nazi party, with a lot of handshaking among themselves in farewell to a political setup which had gotten many people well fed up.

Inside the chancellery there were heated sessions and strong words about the Nazi party. Hitler paced the floor and flared like a torch every time the subject was mentioned. Goering, and with him many of the higher generals, was losing no opportunity to press home to the Fuehrer that now was the time to co-ordinate once and for all the ruling machinery in a single centralized form. As it was, there were Nazi governors in occupied lands and Gauleiters in all the provinces at home, reporting variously to Nazi-party chiefs in Berlin or to another governmental department elsewhere.

The Nazi party ran all labor and social undertakings in the Reich, yet everything remained under split authority and in a sort of nebulous state in relation to the state proper.

What the military men meant, of course, was that Nazi-party bosses were running the show and everything else was subjugated to the interests of the Nazi party. The military forces had maintained an independent standing but only because of the war and the constant battle for independence. Why, not so many years ago Himmler actually was playing with the idea of getting Hitler to appoint him Minister of War. They had put the skids under the plan, but it showed what could happen.

Thus the arguments ran back and forth and the Russian War put no stop to it. Goering and the military around him looked at it as another improved opportunity to press home the point, and the touchy subject was injected into the conversation time and again at Fuehrer headquarters. Hitler refused to listen and on the contrary appointed Nazi after Nazi to important posts in embassies abroad and in occupied lands.

Goering in those days of summer at Fuehrer headquarters also was carrying the battle to him on the church and on similar related problems. It got so that Hitler looked askance at the ringleader who seemed to differ with him in the most trying moments. He broke into a temperamental outburst one day and gave Goering a tongue-lashing. They were no longer addressing each other by the familiar "Du." You can count on your fingers those who can talk to the Fuehrer with that much intimacy.

"Remember this, Goering, I am first of all a Nazi and I shall remain a Nazi and a fanatic all my life," Hitler is said to have told Goering at Fuehrer headquarters. "I organized and built this party from the bottom up and I intend to keep it strong and ready for everything. It has its faults and weaknesses, as it always had, and it changes as time goes on. The Nazi party in no sense of the word is what it was in temper and purpose some years ago; it isn't the same as it was a year ago, and in fact it will not be the same a year from now. But the Nazi party is my party, and when I have finished creating the New Germany of my time it will be a Nazi Germany. Nothing on earth can change that."

We heard in Berlin those last weeks I was there that the thing is not yet settled. There has definitely been since this summer marked cooling off in relations between Hitler and Goering. It put Goering in the doghouse but not behind the bars. He moved about as freely as ever, putting steam behind the punching power of the Third Reich, but up to the end of 1941 he had not rehabilitated himself in the eyes of the Fuehrer to the point of the old heartiness and the use of the familiar term "Du." But in Naziland, it must be remembered, everything is subject to change from day to day and night to night. You may be on top of the heap today and down in the dumps tomorrow. It's all a matter of political potluck and of knowing how to skate on thin ice when occasion calls for it.

For a man like Hitler has no real friends, and he goes at all times on the principle of the survival of the fittest. He can take no chances and brook no interference, unless he wants to go down in an unguarded moment. The same goes for Goering in a different way, and for Ribbentrop and all the rest, all of whom know that they are living on a volcano apt to erupt in their faces any day.

CHAPTER 4

Goebbels and His Game with Hitler

A GLOOMY ATMOSPHERE hung over Berlin the night of
August 29, 1939. Everything smelled of war and nobody
wanted it. The air was full of deadly rumors, and the German faces in streets and cafés were long and sour. The goings and comings of the ambassadors in the Wilhelmstrasse
spoke eloquently of the terrible importance of the issue in
the balance, and their cars racing up and down frequently
moved past long columns of troops flowing to railway and
road junctions leading east. It was known that the hectic
negotiations between London, Paris, and Berlin so far had
reached more or less a deadlock, with Hitler demanding
that the British and French exert pressure on the Poles to
send a specially empowered delegate to Berlin to talk terms
whereunder Poland could buy for herself another lease on
peace with Germany.

A lot of us American correspondents and many of our European colleagues smelled another Munich and looked disgusted. I had never seen the British and French correspondents so excited and up in arms, and they all swore that if Hitler got away with it again, they'd all go home in a body. I went over to the British Embassy early in the evening to nose around for the lay of the land in that quarter and found a whole stack of bags and trunks in the main entrance. I poked my head into the office of Sir George Ogilvie-Forbes, the First Counsellor, and found him hard at work ripping up official documents.

"Come in, old boy!" he called cheerily, his Scotch face a little shinier than usual. He and I had been friends for years and I knew he would give me the right steer. "Well, looks like our people in Whitehall mean business this time. Sir Neville has been asked to come over to the chancellery at 7:15 P.M. to pick up Hitler's answer to our message of yesterday. Smells like an ultimatum to me. I wouldn't be surprised if this were the last time you and I meet for a time in Berlin."

Old George was wrong. I bumped into him again two days later in the Adlon Hotel, where he was having lunch with Virginia Cowles. I had run into her time and again when things were happening in Naziland or elsewhere and knew her for a good newspaperwoman, in addition to which she was easy to look at. That always helped the conversation with Sir George. A little later I was accosted in the lobby by the Gestapo and warned to keep away from the English. They were henceforth to be regarded as in-terned and not to be contacted. That was how I knew that England had finally quit stalling and gone to war.

But on the night of August 29 the issue still hung in the balance and most of us had a dull fear in our breasts that Hitler would win out once more. A few hundred Berliners stood somewhat dejectedly on the Wilhelmsplatz staring at the chancellery and wondering what was going on inside. They didn't want war and a good many of them still clung to their faith in the Fuehrer. They were dead sure he was striving with might and main inside that building to find a way around war, as he had done so many times before. Surely he would not risk a conflict with England and France for the sake of Danzig and the Polish Corridor?

Now and then a few would raise their voices and call for him to appear on the balcony, a customary procedure initiated and encouraged by the Nazis. They felt, I suppose, that the gravest burden of responsibility in history rested at that moment on the Fuehrer's shoulders and they wanted to encourage him. He didn't appear, although by nine o'clock the crowd had swelled somewhat. They were sure then that Hitler was deep in his overwhelming task, working probably without a moment's rest. Ah, yes, the Fuehrer in times of stress always sacrificed himself unstintingly for the Fatherland and worked sometimes days without sleep. That was the murmur and comment which ran through the crowd on the Wilhelmsplatz during those fateful hours, properly inspired by the usual Nazi stooges circulating around by order from Goebbels. It keeps everybody in a sympathetic mood.

Up on the fourth floor of Dorotheenstrasse, across from the Adlon, I had the whole staff of the International News Service working full blast. It was one of these familiar moments in Naziland when anyone in the newspaper business had to go short on food and sleep. I sent down for beer and sandwiches and kept the mill going. We were six hours ahead of New York and service messages coming in from Jack Oestreicher, our foreign editor in New York with a reputation for speed and brilliance in writing, indicated that the afternoon papers were getting out extras every hour and lapping up all developments. Seymour Berkson, the fast-thinking night manager, was also shooting orders for the morningers. We had to keep on our toes, for seconds counted and minutes were vitally important. These were moments when you could mar or ruin completely a reputation built up over years of hard work. You had to keep a cool head.

Then, with the fate of the world hanging by a thread, I got a phone call from a little dancer I kept in touch with. I was too busy worrying about Hitler and German troop moves toward Poland to bother with her and almost hung up. But she was very insistent that I come at once to the café in the Behrenstrasse and talk about something. That was two blocks away from the office. I thought it over and a hunch deep down inside urged me to see her. I told the boys in the office to keep a sharp ear and eye open and that I'd be back shortly.

She met me halfway down Behrenstrasse instead of in the café, a smart thing to do in case somebody with a suspicious turn of mind had listened in on our phone conversation. We both glanced casually around and over our shoulders by habit to make sure we were not being followed and arm in arm walked along to an inconspicuous little cabaret doing pretty good business in nudes and wisecracks next door to the big Metropole Theater. This place specialized in an interior of private booths looking out on the floor show. It was popular as a lovers' hide-out, unknown to tourists, and no man in his right senses took his own wife there. Only the wife of somebody else. They turned out the lights every time an act came on and nobody minded. Except that there was no curtain or screen to give you complete privacy.

We came in just as three hula dancers were on the floor, all of them German girls shaking the flesh in the best Hawaiian manner and shrieking a song to boot as they twirled their straw dresses around. My little dancer had reserved a booth beforehand and we sat down in the semi-darkness. I ordered a bottle of champagne, high in price but low in quality, still wondering what she was up to. I told her again I was exceptionally busy that night and would not have time to sit around for long. I told her war might come by tomorrow, depending on what Hitler was doing at that very moment.

My little dancer smiled and said it couldn't be as bad as all that. Hitler had probably fixed up everything his own way and wasn't worrying very much about war. Only people like me, she said, were running around and worrying themselves sick about the war and what Hitler was going to do. I told her never mind about that but to come across with what was on her mind. I was beginning to lose patience.

The lights went on after the hula act, although you could hardly have read a book in the bluish dimness. My dancer friend was smoking a cigarette, right cheek propped in the palm of her hand so that her mouth was hidden from anyone watching from across the floor. "Look without seeming to into the corner booth on the level with your eyes," she whispered, and added, "Be careful, and don't draw attention."

I lifted a glass of champagne and drank very slowly, raising the glass so that I could look straight across to the corner booth without being obvious. Two men sat alone there, nearly hidden by the semi-darkness. They had on light raincoats, with the collars drawn up to their ears. They both wore large, horn-rimmed glasses. The booths on either side were also taken up by men in dark clothes, men with nondescript faces. They were carefully watching the crowd and especially anyone who walked near to the corner booth.

I set the empty glass down.

"It's him and Goebbels," the girl whispered very cautiously. "They came half an hour ago, after the booths were made free for a reserved party. I called you as soon as my friend here passed the word."

I had seen enough to know I was looking at Hitler and Goebbels sitting surreptitiously in the cabaret here after a hard day's work of gambling for high stakes in Poland against the bids of England and France.

"You see, there cannot be much danger of war," the girl dancer whispered, nearly echoing my first thoughts. "They must be out to celebrate the end of the crisis."

It was not the first time Hitler and Goebbels had come here before the war—the place closed a year later—but I never would have looked for them in the cabaret on that night of all nights. The laugh was on the crowd standing with beating heart on the Wilhelmsplatz, and on a few million German people waiting for momentous decisions by the Fuehrer of the Third Reich. The fact is he handed his memorandum over to Henderson at seven-fifteen that evening and his armies had orders to roll into Poland before dawn of September 1, regardless of the outcome of negotiations, for Hitler was convinced that at the worst the British and possibly the French would carry on a shadow war for a few weeks and then make a deal. So he played his cards with cool self-assurance. That night he celebrated war, not peace.

He probably liked that floor show, for he sat there in the dark booth with Goebbels for another half-hour before vanishing as discreetly as he had come. The slick brain of swarthy little Joe, always on the watch to provide lighter moments for his master on short notice, clearly had plotted that evening's program. He probably had dinner with Hitler in the chancellery after the British Ambassador was handed the latest scrap of paper and suggested to Hitler the idea of a night show as the best antidote to the strenuous work in hand. In bygone days, the six-foot Putzi Hanfstaengl might have been called upon to play a soothing piece on the piano, but Putzi was run out years ago. Joe Goebbels of the foxy mind and passionate nature has more slippery ways of catering to the Fuehrer's emotions and moods, fitting them neatly to each occasion. He is, therefore, the closest of the Nazis to Hitler in private life despite all the scandal and political gossip recurrently involving Goebbels.

Hitler, all those in the know say, likes the elfish little clubfoot and in times of stress keeps him closely under his protective wing. The long knives of Goering, Ribbentrop, and Himmler drawn at times against him have never touched Goebbels, for he hangs safely onto the coattails of his Fuehrer. When in Berlin the big boy comes to his house —in the city Goebbels has a new palace worth a million marks next door to the American Embassy building on Pariser Platz—at least twice a week for dinner. Then Magda the wife washes the five little girls very nicely and puts on their cutest little dresses, for the Fuehrer always makes it a point to come before their bedtime to play around like a good uncle. He always brings them presents, and huge bunches of flowers to Magda. He doesn't even mind driving to their villa in Bogensee, some sixty miles outside Berlin. That also cost something like a million Reichsmarks to build, but it gives the children a home in the country.

Two or three times, after particularly unsavory and clandestine affairs the little propaganda shark had with women of stage and screen, Magda called it quits and sued

quietly for divorce. Twice she went over to Switzerland
to sit out the separation. Each time Hitler would step in
and make peace in the family, ordering Goebbels to lay off
and exhibit to the Fatherland his happy home life. Each
time, after harkening to this call and coming back, Magda
again showed the country at large how to win Hitler medals
for raising the birth rate. At such times Joe would be off
again on the forbidden path, and usually the high sign came
when a pretty new star rose from the ranks over in the Ufa
movie studios with the suddenness of a meteor. The explanation never lay far away.

He'd buy them a car and provide a luxurious apartment
once they proved their mettle and their charms. Then he'd
come around in the dark of night and romp their troubles
away. For instance, if a film director bucked and saw no
star material in the girl, it was always a good idea for the
studios to remember that Goebbels is dictator of all the film
industry and signs the checks. He also picks the directors
and the stars to be presented to Hitler from time to time,
which is almost a necessary ritual in the Third Reich if you
want to rate at all.

There isn't an angle Joe hasn't his fingers on, either film
or theater. On his birthdays if you are in the film or theatri-
cal game, you chip in for a nice expensive present; on any
other day you snap to it when he gives orders and you take
your hat off when his latest flame comes into the shop.
Whether you like her or not. Except that the matter must
never be whispered about near Magda. Never, even, when
he drops the current affair for a new one. His 1941 passion

was, and so far as I know still is, at the beginning of 1942, the film star Ilse Werner, petite and blonde. The public gossip goes merrily on.

I know the war interfered somewhat and cramped his style in drawing Hitler in on discreet escapades. It was Goebbels who used to stage parties at home or in the Propaganda Ministry and invite foreign or German girls from the shows, frequently Americans among them, and then have Hitler walk in for a good look. A few days later the girls who stuck in the Fuehrer's eye got invited to come around to the chancellery for a party or even down south for a private showing at a high price.

A few American girls got in on the pickings and some others claimed they did. A rare few of the European girls with finesse and hell-bent ambition got further than the reception room with the Fuehrer; a lot of them used to run around the Continent claiming they slept with him. Leni Riefenstahl, the German film star, for example, until they shut her up. She is now in Berlin making a movie.

Shortly after 1933 Hitler made it a point to be nice to important foreign visitors. Everything was done for their comfort, and even those with special longings among the menfolk were accommodated. The delicate task of arranging for such clandestine things was naturally left in the hands of Goebbels, who knew just what to do. He silently took over the guardianship of the notorious house of "Kitty," a luxury villa located near the Kurfuerstendamm until its removal to Giesenbrechter Strasse off the main café district in 1935 and arranged for an exclusive clientele. Im-

portant foreign visitors who came to Berlin to talk with
Hitler or make deals with the Nazis could cavort in safety
and seclusion in the richly furnished rooms of "Kitty,"
herself a fallen aristocrat of shopworn but perceptible
beauty. The diplomats, with some exceptions, were in on
the house in Berlin but never brought friends they couldn't
personally vouch for.

It was, on the whole, harder to crash the gate at "Kitty's"
than a studio in Hollywood. The girls, before the war, were
the classy kind from film or stage who had the time and
inclination for a little activity on the side. Goebbels never
came there himself, but a lot of ambassadors and embassy
men did along with a score of key men in the Hitler regime.
All they needed was the Goebbels password. The ex-Crown
Prince bumped into a well-known German general there
one night—the general is now a field marshal—but, on the
whole, Kitty was pretty good in guarding against such mistakes.

In 1935 Kitty had some bad moments, although not so
bad as Goebbels himself. In fact, the headache out of Kitty's
shop went all the way up to Hitler and to the High Command of the German Army. A dashing Pole with a flashing
smile and a monocle larger than a silver dollar got introduced at "Kitty's" as in the Polish diplomatic service and
became a very welcome client.

Baron Jurek Sosnowski, as he called himself, was particularly keen on three titled girls who used to come there once
a week or so to pick up a bit of change. These girls, very
representative of the high-class goods you'd meet at

"Kitty's," were the Baroness Benita von Berg, the Baroness Renate von Natzmer, and Irene von Jena. All held responsible positions as secretaries to generals of the High Command, for their families had long records of brilliant military history.

They could be trusted, particularly in a place like "Kitty's," where they were sure to satisfy and impress the important visitor who might even have some information of value to Goebbels and Hitler to impart. The Nazis always like to know some intimate details on the private lives of their guests. Baron Sosnowski seemed to appreciate their charms more than anyone else and even had the three girls visit him separately and discreetly from time to time in his apartment on the Luetzow Ufer. This is next door to the War Ministry and is where I lived since getting chased out by the military from my mandarinlike apartment in the Bendlerstrasse on the beautiful Tiergarten.

Sosnowski was a slick operator and got away with his espionage for Soviet Russia until nearly the end of 1934. Then the German military counterespionage caught up with him and one night at "Kitty's" he and the Baroness von Berg were quietly but firmly taken by the collar and led away to prison. The Baroness von Natzmer and Irene von Jena were taken out of bed in their apartments and escorted to the same prison. Kitty dropped from sight for the next six months, by which time the three girls had been put on trial before the People's Court and two of them, Von Berg and Von Natzmer, died under the headman's ax. Irene von Jena got a life sentence and Sosnowski twenty years in the penitentiary, but one year later he was exchanged for a German spy sitting behind the bars of a Polish prison. When the storm had died down, Kitty quietly reappeared in a new location off the Kurfuerstendamm and resumed business on a somewhat less lavish scale, but nevertheless along the same lines. But henceforth, until this very day, every girl going there must make a direct report to the Gestapo and to Goebbels on every man she meets.

As I said, the war has interfered somewhat with Goebbels' activities for his master. But he is right there with his bag of tricks when opportunity knocks. In Paris, before the signing of the armistice in Compiègne, Hitler quietly marked time by taking over a beautiful château in St. Cloud, where Goebbels and the rest of the Nazi court assembled around him. Carefully shepherded by men with revolvers in their pockets and guided by two German agents who knew Paris like a book, Goebbels took Hitler out on a round of the far-famed Paris night life, peeking in for short visits at places like the Monocle Club, the Rue Pigalle and its tawdry spots. Then they toured the way of all flesh in the Rue Blondel and the Rue Provençale, in addition to the Sphinx, all of which places remained open except for a few hours during the actual occupation and today are doing a flourishing business on prices rigidly fixed by the systematic German methods. Goebbels flew back to Berlin and next morning Hitler sallied forth in grand style to take the terms of surrender from the French in the woods of Compiègne, where he looked long and hard at the monument of Foch and the tablet commemorating the capitulation of the German armies on November of 1918. I watched him staring at the stone tablet with folded arms for nearly a minute and later denounce it as a stain on German honor and a black mark on European history. Before leaving the spot, after meeting the French in the same railway coach where the Germans had signed in 1918, he ordered that tablet blown up and everything destroyed except the statue of Foch. The armistice railway car was taken to Berlin and now stands in the war museum on Unter den Linden for the Germans to gape at. That was Hitler's way of settling scores with the Treaty of Versailles.

It isn't always, of course, that Goebbels clicks with Hitler on ideas or plans designed in the long end to curry undying favor with his Fuehrer. Off the record in Nazi annals of September 1934 stands the fantastic stunt little Joe cooked up for a mighty sensation but which Hitler threw aside in an outburst of temper, bawling out Goebbels for a fare you well. It was one of those occasional mistakes in judgment clubfooted Joe will make from time to time and then cover up before enemies like Himmler and Rosenberg make political capital out of it. He has wriggled out of every mess so far. People say he is far too clever ever to get cornered.

I had gone down to Nuremberg in 1934 for my first look at a Nazi Party Congress on an invitation I had wangled out of Rosenberg through Boemer. This gave me the privilege of remaining foot-loose, leaving I.N.S. coverage in the hands of Hubert Knickerbocker. I was assigned quarters in the Grand Hotel with Boemer, and for the sake of floating around unrestricted behind the scenes of this

annual Nazi circus I kept out of sight of my colleagues
from the foreign press over in the Wuerttemberger Hof.
That is how I was tipped off by Goebbels' Nazi enemies
to the crazy stunt he tried to pull but which never saw
the light of day. In fact, he was in the doghouse for a week
until Hitler took him back on his train to Berlin and made
up.

On the second day of that brown whirlpool of marching
and singing and heiling by two million men in the medieval
streets of Nuremberg, I heard that something terrific was
brewing, something far from the ordinary in Nazi procedure. The air was buzzing with it, and Nazis in brown
shirts of high rank stood around in batches in the halls and
lobby of the Grand Hotel and gossiped about it. Most of
them, judging from their faces, appeared indignant. I heard
them talk about going to Hitler in a body to have a stop put
to this mad plan of Goebbels.

I nosed around all day looking for a chance to get in on
the low-down. By 8 P.M. I had the promise from two of
Goebbels' nastiest enemies in the Nazi party to get the story
of what was going on, with the implication that I could send
it through and therewith give little Joe a terrific kick in the
pants. In those days, it must be remembered, there was no
censorship whatever and the field of news was wide open
despite the fact that the Nazis had begun to expel correspondents from Germany if they were particularly un-
favorable and of a crusading spirit.

After dinner I sat in the bar of the Grand Hotel and
watched closely for the appearance of the two men who

had promised me the story. Everybody from Himmler to Goering and half-a-dozen ambassadors showed up, for in those days the Nazis still had their feet on the ground. Shortly after 9 P.M. a young Nazi adjutant I knew came into the bar looking for me and asked me to come along. He took me out of the hotel by the back way, and outside in a car the two men I had been expecting were waiting. They drove through the crowded streets past the big moat into the ancient part of the city and to the back entrance of a Gothic edifice serving, apparently, as a city museum. There were a lot of guards around, black-uniformed men of the S.S., but the rank of my companions was high enough to get into the building without question.

Inside, in a room reached through heavy wooden doors with iron bolts, we were received by a man with white hair, evidently the keeper of the place. A heavy and nail-studded wooden box stood on the table of the cloisterlike room. At a nod from my companions he inserted a key and unlocked it with several clicks, lifting the lid to show its contents.

I stared in curiosity, not sure of the meaning of all this. On velvet cloth in the box reposed a scepter, a crown, and an orb. They seemed to be made of iron, with a few jewels gleaming on each. The orb had a cross on top, like the cross on a church spire. There was nothing very startling about the objects.

One of the two Nazis asked me if I knew what I was looking at. I said it must be the ruling insignia of some Germanic emperor, kept here for exhibit.

"You are looking at one of the greatest treasures and symbols in Germanic history," the Nazi beside me replied. "There you see the crown, the scepter, and the orb of Charlemagne, brought here from Aachen under guard along with a number of other remaining insignia of that great empire in early European history. These treasures in the past couple of hundred years were removed from Aachen only twice, each time to save them from great danger.

"That crazy fool Goebbels has now secretly brought them here. He hatched up a spectacular program to march in procession up to Hitler after his speech in Luitpold Hall on Sunday and present him the crown, the scepter, and the orb of Charlemagne. You see, it would amount to the transformation of the Third Reich from our Nazi conception to a new Germanic empire, provided Hitler accepted the symbols.

"We hear that Goebbels did not seriously expect Hitler to accept and turn himself from the Fuehrer into the Emperor, but Goebbels was all set to make it the most dramatic event of the year. He had a lot of material printed and ready for distribution to the press on the background of Charlemagne and his comparison to Hitler. He had trumpeters and everything ready for his dramatic scene. Nobody but Goebbels could have thought of that.

"We ended his idiotic scheme tonight by going to Hitler and placing the whole thing before him. He just about jumped off his chair and had Goebbels summoned over to the hotel. He is there now and getting an earful."

The two Nazis obviously were pleased as Punch in their

knowledge of having at last succeeded in rapping the knuckles of their hated rival. They talked about it all the way back to the Grand but in parting cautioned me against letting anyone find out the source of my information. I sent the story. The next day consternation reigned in Goebbels' quarter, for the London *Evening Standard* came out in banner headlines with the whole thing. If I am not mistaken, Goebbels accused Knickerbocker, but it all blew over after awhile.

He was always blaming us foreign correspondents for the bad press he got in the outside world. Not until Boemer came along to take charge of all matters pertaining to the foreign press did Goebbels change his tune. In the old days, up to 1935, he could hardly get any foreign correspondent in Berlin to accept an invitation from the Propaganda Ministry. We boys hadn't forgotten the time when he invited us to go to a Hitler speech on the heights of Ehrenbreitstein, the old German fortified point overlooking the Rhine behind Coblenz, where General Allen of the American Expeditionary Forces had his headquarters after World War I. Goebbels placed a special railway coach with plenty of food and drinks at our disposal as far as Cologne, from where we drove next morning to Coblenz. There we naturally found brown-shirted Nazi cordons lining the narrow road up to the heights, with thousands of people crammed in behind the cordons waiting for a close-up glimpse of Hitler.

We didn't know that Goebbels had run a hefty campaign in the local newspapers against the dirty foreign press and its conspiring foreign correspondents in Berlin. On the windshield of each car bearing us up to Ehrenbreitstein had been pasted a large red sticker with the designation "Foreign Press." We had to drive very slowly, and the mob had a field day hissing and howling us down, with a little spitting thrown in for good measure. We realized soon enough that snaky Joe had thrown us to the lions and was probably chortling happily to himself over the neat revenge he was getting. We kept that lesson well in mind.

We got even a couple of years later when Joe became deeply involved in his clandestine affair with the beautiful Lida Barrova, a Czech girl who had become the leading German film star. She was married to Gustaf Froehlich, the tops of all German male film stars. Joe played fast and loose with this girl, and had the whole town talking about it. We boys sitting around and licking our chops were also getting additional low-down on the q.t. from Goering's stooges, who had orders from the fat one to grease the skids for little Joe.

That was how we knew within a few hours after it happened that Joe got socked on the chin and knocked down in the Ufa film studios by Lida's husband. It was on a Saturday morning and Gustaf, instead of going off on a scheduled trip to Vienna, had gone to the studio to finish off a few retakes. Goebbels came walking blithely out of Lida's dressing room, all set to take her for a drive and private luncheon out on Peacock Island near Wannsee Lake, an exclusive spot frequently used by the Propaganda Minister for lavish parties. But Gustaf's fist suddenly spoiled the day by landing on Goebbels' chin. Gustaf had known all about his wife's affair and was suing for a divorce anyway. I suppose it gave him a lot of satisfaction, though, to see swarthy Joe sprawling in pained surprise on the studio floor, fingering a swelling jaw. It goes without saying that Froehlich was arrested in short order.

Goering's whispering campaign saw to it that all the cafés of Berlin were talking about it, all of which coincided with the opening night of the première of Lida Barrova's new film. Howls, hisses, a whistling concert, and derisive shouting marked every appearance of the girl on the screen. Lights were turned on in the film house after the first ten minutes and the manager made a speech imploring the audience to remain orderly.

The storm burst forth anew as soon as the film resumed, spiced this time with rhymes and verse sung by groups in the crowd very pointedly alluding to the relations of Lida and Joe. Voices yelled out asking why Goebbels had not come to the première and taken a bow despite his black eye and lopsided jaw. When the lights went on again, the Gestapo filed into the aisles and threatened to arrest the audience, but they got nowhere. The show was stopped and everybody went home laughing at Goebbels and saying he ought to be shot. They stood in line to see Froehlich's pictures and cheered themselves hoarse every time Gustaf appeared on the screen. To this day he is the Reich's most popular star, and there is nothing Goebbels can do about it.

The scandal became so widespread, what with us boys whooping it up as much as we dared, that Hitler had to step in and read the riot act to little Joe. The upshot was that Lida Barrova was quietly exiled to Prague, with a permanent annual pension from Goebbels of something like thirty thousand marks. Gustaf was set free after a few days and that was one of the times Magda Goebbels went to Switzerland with the intention of getting a divorce. But here again Hitler stepped in and smoothed everything over. Somehow little Joe got around him again and a few months later the whole thing was forgotten. That is why people say Goebbels will never be cornered and will last as long as Hitler lasts, but not a minute longer.

CHAPTER 5

The Story of Rudolf Hess

On a bleak and dull morning in Berlin, on December 15, 1940, when the heavily embroidered square-cut flag of Hitler hung in cheerless folds from its pole up above the Reich chancellery, the Fuehrer of Naziland summoned his inner cabinet which most closely resembles anything like a German *Kriegsrat* or War Council. It was to be a day of momentous decision, changing the course of the world.

We, the foreign correspondents of surviving lands of the free press and those already under the yoke of Hitler's new Europe, went about our business in the Wilhelmstrasse the same as usual. I stood outside the side entrance to the Propaganda Ministry and looked across the dirty ruts of snow to the iron-grilled residential entrance to the Fuehrer's chancellery. Both the right and the left gates into the yard were open, guarded by two of the green-uniformed police and steel-helmeted S.S. men. Two army sentries stood like ramrods with feet apart and rifles on shoulder on each side of the door beyond the lawn, never opened or used nowadays, but offered to the awe-struck eyes of visiting Berliners as the visible shrine where their lord and master goes in and out.

A Swedish correspondent standing by my side nudged my elbow. Far down the Wilhelmstrasse, from the direction of the gargantuan Air Ministry, a piercing blue light was showing and the huge and florid-faced traffic cop in the middle of the intersection of Voss and Wilhelmstrasse was hastily clearing the street of cars and pedestrians alike. The powerful car with the blue light and a shrieking whistle of three tones was bearing down toward us at something like sixty miles an hour.

People rushed to the edge of the curb and pointed excitedly. We stood there on the sidewalk and waited, sensing that something was up again, yet knowing that all that went on inside the Fuehrer's chancellery usually remained secret, or, if not, it might take weeks and months to piece together on the basis of the stray bits of information through highly placed contacts what had transpired. Even so, it could never be published unless the powers that be in the Wilhelmstrasse saw fit to place some sort of prepared propagandized version before the world.

"I saw Brauchitsch come in fifteen minutes ago," the Swedish correspondent said to me. "It looks as if this is going to be more than just a daily meeting of the big shots.

There is all that talk again about the invasion of England next spring."

The baby blue Mercedes limousine, resplendent with nickeled accessories and its impressive-looking six wheels, came bursting up nearly to where we stood and with violence sufficient to scorch its buna tires wheeled into the chancellery yard to halt at the arched and unimpressive-looking side entrance.

From the front seat alongside the driver arose the ponderous figure of Reichsmarshal Hermann Goering, the great collar of his double-breasted overcoat up around his ears to the rim of a splendid gold-leaf cap. He stood there for a moment looking out at the street, a bejeweled marshal's baton in his right hand. The few dozen spectators standing with hands raised at Nazi salute on the cold sidewalk took the cue and raised the familiar cry:

"*Unser Hermann! Heil!*"

A bullet-headed little man in the faded brown uniform of the Nazi party shouted the loudest and kept looking around to see that everybody took proper part. His glance rested momentarily on both of us, but he looked away again. Our very clothes and attitude had betrayed us to him as the hated foreigners.

Hermann Goering's nervous eyes, flicking about like two little balls of black and white on a water fountain, looked comfortably over the pillows of his tremendous cheeks. He was pleased. If the Fuehrer's summons had broken into his morning game of playing with his electric miniature railway and spoiled his mood, it was forgotten now. His people had cheered him, their hero, and next to the Fuehrer their leader.

Hitler himself had designated him as next Fuehrer over the head of Hess before the Reichstag at the start of the war. Wasn't it right and proper that they become accustomed to him as their next Hitler and rush around in eager haste to greet him whenever his signal sounded?

Standing there five feet ten in his boots and almost a yard wide, Hermann Goering smiled and to the mob in the street raised his flashing baton in response. Then he stomped away into the interior. The police and army and S.S. sentries unfroze from their rigid positions and around us there was excited babel of comment.

In the next fifteen minutes, when snow began to fall again with a wet touch on cheek and neck, half-a-dozen less pretentious limousines arrived one by one and drove into the chancellery yard. Grand Admiral Raeder, Field-marshal Keitel, and Von Ribbentrop, the Foreign Minister, swept past us. The last to come was a plain dark limousine with a red standard embroidered with a gold swastika on the right-hand fender. Inside next to the driver sat a man with heavily beetled brows, dark as the jungle, and with a preoccupied face. He looked at no one and no one raised a voice in cheers.

"*Der Stellvertreter*," the eager-tongued little man in the Nazi uniform told the wide-eyed sidewalk starers. "*Ja*, it is Hess, our Deputy Fuehrer. I have talked to him once. He is a quiet man and doesn't say much. But he shakes the hand well."

Thus did the innermost circle of Hitler's ring assemble for the fateful meeting of an epoch. It all came out through the succeeding months in dribbles and whispers, passed on to the few ears of those who had the inside track and knew where to tap in the dark. Even today heads would roll in the sand in Naziland if names were to be mentioned here or elsewhere in connection with the story I am about to tell.

Hitler did not receive them in the huge paneled office with the french windows and the fireplace at the end of the room opposite his desk. He met them in the large cabinet room, oblong and dignified, a long, highly polished table in the middle. Around this table stand the baronial chairs of his ministers, each covered in red leather and engraved with a black swastika eagle on the background of white.

A folder of expensive leather stamped with the swastika eagle and designating the particular minister marks the place for each man to sit. The Fuehrer's chair is in the middle, slightly larger in size, and has an A. H. in addition to the eagle. Hess and Goering flank him (before the flight of Hess), and in ordinary cabinet meetings some twenty-one Nazi ministers sit around that table.

In this sacred innermost meeting of the War Council probably eight men sat around the Fuehrer in that sound-proof room. Joe Goebbels of propaganda magic was one of them.

Hitler played his usual game of keeping to his office and holding appointments with minor mortals until it was one minute to twelve. Then bully-beef Schaub, personal shadow

and valet of many skeletons in the closet, very quietly lifted
the house telephone and spoke to another adjutant over in
the cabinet room. He nodded and laid down the instrument.
He snapped to attention with a crack of heels and his hand
stretched forward like a Roman greeting his Caesar.

"Mein Fuehrer, die Herren warten," he said in a guttural
voice made hoarse by the heavy wash of alcohol in the hours
of leisure. He took the folio of papers lying on Hitler's
desk, next to the leather-bound copy of *Sulla* autographed
by Mussolini with loving words to Adolf, and marched
away to open the doors before Hitler into the cabinet room.

The subdued conversation there stopped, bringing dead
silence. There was no smoking, although some of those
present like Ribbentrop are inveterate addicts to cigars or
cigarettes. You simply don't smoke in front of the Fuehrer.
It is an inviolate rule, to be observed with the same care
and personal wisdom of not indulging in alcohol before
you appear in his presence.

"Der Fuehrer!" the adjutant Schaub said mechanically,
as mechanically as those heels of the highest in the land
snapped to salute. Hitler came in with that loping walk he
assumes in his chancellery, the right hand describing less
than a half circle as it lifted in the nonchalant Nazi salute
familiar to all in the land. Peering straight into the eyes of
each man, he shook hands, beginning with Goering and
ending with Goebbels. Schaub and the other adjutant disappeared, while the remainder of those in that room
grouped themselves in confidential expectancy around their
leader.

All the niceties of dignity and formality had been observed with the usual care. Hitler prides himself on being the most legal ruler the Reich ever had, substantiated in office repeatedly by a popular vote nearly 100 per cent.

Some nasty minds in the Reich claim to know that Joe Goebbels got more than one hundred per cent on his tabulating machines and had to do some revising from the Nazi-party figures turned in over the tickers all over the Reich at the last election, but I am no certified accountant and could not prove the case to you either way.

Hitler takes himself seriously and will flare up in a temperamental rage at the least impingement by act or attitude on the dignity and holiness of State and Fuehrer. I incurred his momentary displeasure some years ago when I offered him my pencil instead of a fountain pen to sign his name to a photo held out to him. He threw the pencil down without comment and reached for someone else's proffered fountain pen. That's Hitler.

The meeting back there then got under way in the best of form. Nobody arose and challenged Hitler or fired the opening gun. There is only one voice of authority, one man of initiative, one boss of the show. Whether in cabinet session or in this small circle of the all-highest, there is the Fuehrer alone who counts, and he proposes and disposes as he wills. All else is secondary; all else is a matter of fitting mind and body and appearance to the form and the will of the quick-tempered man with the mustache.

I can imagine that what Hitler said caused many an intake of breath and a tug at the heart. There is seldom an appeal to the basic law and principle enunciated by the Fuehrer on such occasions, and the thing to do is to make him feel he has revealed a new inspiration conceived of the Divine mission conferred on him by a Power not of this earth; after that, provided you are willing to take a chance and go to bat on an idea of your own, there may be an opportunity to persuade the Fuehrer that perhaps this and that normal factor or factual situation in the world might be taken into consideration.

Ribbentrop knows how to do this by the smooth road of sales talk smacking still of the days when he drew commission on whisky and champagne sales in Whitehall; Goebbels, the swarthy and oily one, is past master at the art of playing on his emotional cords, and bluff Goering every once in awhile takes the bull by the horns and says what he thinks to the Fuehrer.

But those are exceptional occasions and are reserved to the privileged few. For example, you could never catch Brauchitsch or Keitel or least of all the slow-speaking, ponderous-thinking Rudolf Hess doing so.

Of course I was not present at that historic meeting. I know that it took place, I know who was there, and I know accurately, in broad outline, what was said. I also know, from close study of his methods and of his style over a period of eight years, and from the interviews I have had with him, how Hitler talks. I think, therefore, that the following direct quotation is a close approximation of what Hitler said:

"Gentlemen, I have called you here to lay plans and take

steps in pursuance of which we shall bring this Reich of ours nearer to its great goal.

"We have fought this war for more than a year now with great success and at the moment we are the masters in the west of Europe. We have crushed France and face an England already sorely troubled and worried over the future. In fact, there is a possibility that within the next six months England can be brought to a point ripe for the final blow by force of arms or by means of a dictated compromise.

"I have reason to believe that this situation is far more advanced than we have hitherto believed possible, and I draw your attention to the fact that the conquest or capitulation of England by force or by compromise in actuality would mean the end of the military war over here in Europe. Come what may, then, America would likely swing away and for a decade or so withdraw completely into its own hemisphere.* The sore spots in Europe and in the Far East, and the economic warfare, might continue to harass us in many forms, but on the whole I repeat that the war as such would be ended over here."

Hitler looked intently at the men around him. His fingers played nervously with the folder before him.

"Gentlemen," he said with the intensity of suppressed passion, "we are all agreed that the German people are patiently bearing through this war. They will bear many

---

*Hitler purposely refrained from revealing to his inner council at this time his intention of plotting a Jap war and his own against America in case the invasion of Russia failed to achieve its goal. Hitler, as in many instances, deliberately deceived his council by withholding this intention.

years of it, if called on to do so, and uncomplainingly endure the hardships that every war calls for.

"But I am a realist, and as a realist I face every situation. As long as this war goes on, as I said, the German people will bear it and will bear with me. Let the end of the war come with a sudden rush, and our people will welcome it with open arms. They will give vent to their restrained emotions and plunge like crazy people deep into the conviction that the last big war with all its misery and sacrifices has passed away.

"It would be almost impossible to get them to face another big war in our time."

The handful of men around Hitler murmured and nodded.

"*Richtig, mein Fuehrer, richtig,*" Goering said more audibly than some of the others. They all knew, from Gestapo reports throughout the country and other devious means by which the Nazis constantly feel the pulse of the country at large, that Hitler had spoken the plain truth.

Hitler slapped his hand on the table. "*Jawohl!*" he declared with emphasis. "The German people will fight the world if called upon during this war, but the German people cannot be taken out of this war and later be put into another one. It cannot be done, and what we must do to fulfill our program and reach our goals must be done now."

He rose slowly from his chair and stood before them like a judge who pronounces sentence. He seemed not to be seeing them any more or talking to those few men at the table, but rather he saw before him half a million men lined up in rows of brown and black, staring at him as the one god in their world, and he was talking to them from the heights of Olympus.

"I mean," he said in the rising voice of an orator, "that this war must not be ended unless an essential part of our program has been fulfilled.

"National Socialist Germany came into being sworn to destroy Jewry and Bolshevism. We are the mortal foe of Bolshevist Russia and Bolshevist Russia is the mortal foe of National Socialist Germany.

"We have at the moment friendly relations brought about and based on extraordinary circumstances. Stalin knew when he signed our agreement in 1939 that it would be only a temporary truce, a political and ideological armistice. He knows as well as I do that Europe is too small to hold both of us. He knows that the world revolution can never be a world revolution until and unless National Socialist Germany is out of the way. I know, and all of you know and so does every one of our people, that peace can never come to Europe and security can never come to Germany unless Bolshevist Russia falls to the ground.

"I said in Nuremberg in 1936 that if I could only have the Ukraine, I could bring prosperity and paradise to Germany. I have told you time and again that our real Lebensraum lies not in faraway colonies strange in climate and geography to our Germany, but in the vast spaces east of us. I have told you time and again that Europe must be made independent of the outside and free of the constant threats of hunger blockade, as the only way ever to assure peace for the future.

"I now tell you again, and remind you that Soviet Russia not only remains a real military menace to our existence but holds the key to all we have planned for.

"Gentlemen, the time has come to switch east and have the final reckoning with our greatest enemy. England can wait; it is a matter of form as to what procedure can be used to settle our quarrels there.

"Perhaps, when we launch our attack on Bolshevist Russia, the British Empire will swing around along with the rest of Europe and a large part of the world and help us smash the common enemy.

"I count on this being a popular war, both here and abroad, and the bridge to our final goals in the future."

I have pieced together what I heard in Berlin over the past year from sources and contacts who know. Such intimate information comes through channels that can be established only after many years of hard work and intimate knowledge of the men around Hitler and the things that make him click. He is, in fact, a remote individual to the man at large in Germany but an open book to those who know his mind and methods. He sits in the middle of a web of high-powered intrigue, plotting, gossip, and a maelstrom of clashing jealousies and interests and there is little in his private or official life that does not sooner or later trickle down to ears like mine trained to listen in the proper place.

Thus I came to know the story of that day in December inside Hitler's chancellery in Berlin.

2

The men who had heard Hitler walked out in a sort of trance. They were carrying a great secret, sworn to silence and pledged to the task of preparing the military forces as well as the Reich itself for the job of mastering Soviet Russia.

Goering drove away in his baby-blue car to his princely estate in the snow-covered woods out in Karinhall, some fifty miles from Berlin, and played like a good father with his baby daughter. He wallowed on the floor and let the child crawl over him, shrieking and laughing, until the actress mother, Emmy Sonneman of one-time film and stage fame, came to take her away for an afternoon nap. It gave Goering a chance to sit at his great desk in the hunting room with the huge windows and figure out the staggering job facing his Luftwaffe for the coming spring.

A few miles distant, over the woods and hills of the same Schorfheide area, Joe Goebbels was home for the day like a faithful husband visiting wife and children in his Bogensee villa, a low, rambling building with a touch of the Spanish.

His still pretty but fading blonde Magda, mother of five daughters by him and a son by a. first husband, had put on her prettiest dress in expectation of the Fuehrer. He was coming out there for dinner, as he frequently does, and the children were on their best behavior to play with him before going to bed. It was all so familiar, and they all knew just what to do.

Goebbels stood in front of the blazing fire on the hearth and stared at the woods out beyond the french windows. He had much on his mind, what with the great new task of soon letting loose the floodgates of Nazi passion and pent-up bitterness against Bolshevists and Communists and keeping in mind the dates and charms of film and stage stars back there in the city of Berlin.

Ribbentrop returned to his office and lit a cigar, coldly assured within himself that the Fuehrer thought highly of him. The military went over to Bendlerstrasse for a consultation with key men of the General Staff, but the moment had not yet come to tell them the things in mind. Strategic plans in any case were filed away against Russia in the proper pigeonholes; for the military it was merely a matter of switching and realigning the forces at their disposal and getting them into proper place for the moment designated by the Fuehrer.

But across the way from the chancellery and the Foreign Office a silent man sat at his desk staring straight before him. Hess, brooding by nature and fanatical follower of Hitler in his quiet way, was celebrating an emotional triumph within himself. In August of 1939 he had broken down and cried and sobbed like a baby with shock and mortification when Hitler and Stalin signed the deal; he retired to a sanitarium like a spurned lover to recuperate in mind and spirit when England seriously declared war on Germany. All had come at once, sinking him into the blackest depths of despair since the days when a gassed lung from the trenches made his life hang on a thread.

He sat at his desk now, trying to grasp what had happened. The Fuehrer had indicated that the war with England might soon be over.

To Hess it was like the return of an undying love to his home and hearth. He was a friend of England; he was of that peculiar Nazi belief—favored and encouraged for a long time by Hitler himself—that Germany and England were the chosen people of this earth, fated to rule and fit for a natural friendship.

He was also a fanatical Nazi, bitter against all things Communist and sworn hater of the gospels preached by Moscow. The Fuehrer had said that the time was here to smash Russia, and to Hess that meant that a new life was about to start. It was just a matter of going about and doing it the right way.

He sat there and dreamed of the great moment when England and Germany would be at peace.

The weeks went by and Christmas and New Year came and went. Around Berlin the gossip mill was going full blast, speculating on what spring would bring and where the blitz would strike. Versions were a dime a dozen, fed by the Nazi propaganda machine in all its myriad forms. Behind the scenes the pace was equally furious but less smooth than had been anticipated after that meeting of December 15.

There was dissension and open difference of opinion between Goering and Ribbentrop; for example, on the proper way of proceeding to the kill. Ribbentrop was for smashing hard at England at the same time as at Russia; Goering argued that a double front going full blast at the same time would rest too heavily upon the shoulders of the air force if not on the military as a whole.

Hitler was playing his favorite game of juggling all and saying nothing.

Hess had a favorite theory that once you told England in direct manner that peace was available at an honorable price, and, furthermore, that into the bargain would come the smashing of Bolshevist Russia, the trouble in the west would be over.

He harped on the numerous friends of Hitler and himself and Germany over in England; he recalled to the minds of all that in Germany itself a handshake with England could be made popular overnight. He took Hitler at his word that England was near the breaking point and pleaded that the time had come for a negotiated peace in the west.

All the fervor and passion of his Nazi heart came flooding to the surface and nothing on earth could shake his conviction that a golden opportunity lay within grasp. It must not be mishandled; it must not be overlooked. He paced the floor of his home and his office, thinking and planning, desperately seeking for a way to convince the Fuehrer of his viewpoint.

In all those weeks at the beginning of 1940 there came to our ears repeatedly rumors from outside of Germany that Hitler was seeking a new peace. At one time it would be the King of Sweden who had been asked to intervene in London; at another time it would be the Pope or Sven Hedin or even President Roosevelt. Ever and again the ponderous voice and spokesman of the Wilhelmstrasse denied any and all intentions of seeking peace.

"Victory must precede all talk of peace from our side," Ribbentrop's mouthpiece and spokesman of the Foreign Office, Minister Paul Schmidt, pontifically told the foreign press corps in his daily conferences time and again.

"Only the sword can decide now. We offered our enemies peace and compromise time and again and they slapped down our offers. Now we shall fight through to the end, and all talk of peace and peace offensive is enemy propaganda of which we wash our hands. We must ask you not to commit the blunder of sending such harmful stories from here, lest we be compelled to impose upon you the hardships of censorship."

Therein lay the strength and effect of Hitler's repeated peace offensives. They were launched in devious ways abroad and sharply denied at home. It kept the whole cloaked in nebulous rumor and uncertainty, making people talk and wonder without losing interest. It also served the twofold purpose of gathering from the four corners of the earth the world's reaction to such a plan and, on the other hand, camouflage what really went on below the surface to Hitler's great advantage in preparing and carrying out the surprise moves he so dearly loves.

By April, Hess had definitely lost his case, and the attack on Russia had been fixed for April 22, although the Yugoslavian coup against Hitler eventually postponed the war on Russia until June 22.

More than ever Hess had it fixed in his mind that peace

with England could come almost simultaneously with war on Russia, and in fact England might even be swung over to moral support of Germany against the Bolshevists.

He was convinced that the forces eager to end the war, believing in Anglo-German co-operation as the keystone to peace in Europe, would overthrow Churchill's war government and thus prepare the way for a common stand against Soviet Russia.

It all seemed so very logical to him, the expert on England and the friend of all Englishmen. He hated Ribbentrop for thwarting and opposing him; hated him with a cold fury that upset his stomach and irritated the suffering lung and the ragged nerves. His scowl grew deeper day by day; he scarcely heard what people in conversation told him or saw what went on in his own circles.

A wheel was spinning around and around inside his head; his heart was filled with black hatred for arrogant Ribbentrop and with an unquenchable conviction that if only someone like himself could get to talk man to man to influential Englishmen, a great triumph would be achieved. If the Fuehrer would only consent to arrange a meeting between himself and some high-placed man from London, the war in the west would be over. What a triumph, what a boon to civilization, what glory for the Fatherland and the Fuehrer!

3

The events in Greece and the minor British resistance merely convinced Hess more than ever that England would welcome a deal. His health bothered him, and he spent two weeks in a sanitarium before going back to his desk.

On the calendar before him was a note that he was to visit his great friend Willy Messerschmitt in Augsburg, in the south of Germany, during the coming week and make a speech to the airplane experimental workers there. He was also slated to make a speech at a rally of Germans from abroad in Augsburg on the succeeding Saturday.

Hess thought of his hobby and pleasure in flying fast planes and he knew that his friend Messerschmitt always was willing to close an eye to the Fuehrer's edict against such private indulgences. Flying your own plane around always brought such relief from the pressure on the brain and from the troubles and tribulations on the earth below.

Hess had other troubles, too, right there in his own plain office in the Wilhelmstrasse.

Long ago he had sensed, and lately become more sharply aware of the intriguing little Nazi, Bormann, his deputy, always around where he could rub elbows in slavish fashion with Hitler or kiss the ground he walked on, except that his portly figure scarcely permitted this physical act unless he lay flat on the ground.

Hess knew the man would even do that to curry the light of favor from above. He didn't care, idealist that he was, or worry much about the whispers heard from time to time that he would soon be muscled out. All that had started, he preferred to assume, from the appointment at the start of the war by Hitler of Goering as man Number Two in the Third Reich, when rightly by title and succession he should be the successor of the First Fuehrer.

Hess thought again of the pleasant town of Augsburg and the warm smile of his rather bushy-haired friend the great Messerschmitt, turning out fast new planes with the speed and precision of a sausage machine. Up there in the air all by himself, Hess felt, he would be at ease in a Messerschmitt, away from the quarreling men of Berlin. He decided that, come what may, he'd keep the date in Augsburg.

I remember so well the night of Monday, May 12, 1941. I was sitting at the Stammtisch (regular reserved table for old guests) in the famed Ristorante Taverne in Berlin, owned and run by devil-may-care Willy Lehmann, who launched to fame in the old days as pioneer film director of stars such as Pola Negri and Lya de Putti.

Half of today's best directors in Hollywood know Willy and worked with him back in the forgotten studios of Berlin. His restaurant still caters largely to film people, the diplomats, and the foreign correspondents. The big shots in Naziland come there, and the Gestapo is always around to listen. But they get no change out of the Taverne. On air-raid nights you can sit there with Willy and hope for the best, cracking a few bottles of his best champagne before curling up to sleep until the all-clear sounds. It makes existence more bearable.

The phone rang for me about 9 P.M. I had just washed the dirt and dust of the southeast, from Yugoslavia down to Corinth and back, out of my hair and eyes after following the German Army in its Balkan campaign. Willy told me the call seemed urgent.

It was an important informant, a man who never called me on the phone unless it was really something. Hess had vanished, flown the coop in a plane, he said. The voice on the phone was pretty excited but kept on an even keel. An official communiqué would soon come, giving some details and branding Hess as insane.

I could take a chance, the voice on the wire added, and get the story out over Berne, although it wasn't dead certain yet that the announcement would be forthcoming that night. All this called for an immediate decision on what to do in the face of trying circumstances, without forgetting that once a bombshell like that hits the hot wires of International News Service, it is gone and cannot be blotted out. A wrong steer in this case, and never again could I look Barry Faris, the boss, in the face. His clients in America would see to that. But to get beaten on a story like that would be almost as bad.

Well, that's where intuition and years of hard work on contacts in a town like Berlin come in handy. That kind of dilemma faced me many a time, got me almost thrown out on my ear or behind Nazi bars three or four times, but I never pulled a real boner. In a flash I knew inside of me that the man on the wire was safe, and I jumped on that phone. Only minutes later the International News Service was breaking that story to a startled world.

This was on a Monday evening in Berlin, but Hess had skipped on Saturday. He had gone to Augsburg on schedule to talk to the Messerschmitt workers there on Friday and to make his public speech to the Germans from abroad on the following day. He stayed with Messerschmitt on Friday and in the afternoon inspected and flew around in the newest little air devil his friend was just getting okayed for the Luftwaffe. It was a masterpiece, under three tons in weight, and fast as a shooting star. The 109F, or something like that, they called it. A plane to gladden the heart of the most blasé cloud-hopper.

Hess flew around for a couple of hours and came down visibly refreshed. He was delighted with the machine's performance and asked for another jaunt in it after tomorrow's speech. Messerschmitt told him to come in any time of the day and help himself, reminding him with some trepidation of the Fuehrer's ban on this sort of thing during the war.

"Oh, that was because Goering took a couple of turns over burning London last year," Hess said laughingly. "A few more like that and Hitler would have had to create a new medal to give him. Just don't worry about it; nobody will be any the wiser, and whatever happens, I'll take the blame for it."

That settled it, and the next day Hess was off again for a joy ride up in the clouds. He never came back and in the evening hours parachuted to earth in Scotland. Two of his adjutants were arrested and nearly shot; Messerschmitt and some other close friends of Hess's, like Professor Karl Haushofer of geopolitics, felt the hard hand of the Gestapo. They got off later, but it was a close shave.

In Berlin the stock of the Nazi party dropped with a bang, reaching the point where a brown-uniformed storm trooper could hardly appear on the street without getting a razz. I saw it come to blows in a bus when a Nazi protested over the wisecracking joke someone told, and the argument ended when the Nazi was thrown off bodily. That was something novel to see, and hasn't been seen since. For the Nazi party, it was generally agreed, was a goner, and from now on the army had a clear road. At least, that is what they all thought.

Inside his million-dollar chancellery Hitler was roaring mad. His ears were red and he was seeing red, but after hell-raising up and down the halls and rooms all night, he cooled down and summoned a conference to put the best face on what had happened. He issued an edict banning Hess and declaring him insane; then he appeared in public on the advice of wily Joe Goebbels and received an ovation.

Then an order went out to all government officials and public employees prohibiting further discussion of the Hess case. A damp silence settled over the land, enlivened only by the whispering gossip and the cutting wisecrack. Neither press nor radio ever again broached the matter, not even the debate on it in the House of Commons. Hess was gone, an official outcast and branded a maniac by Hitler himself. Yet everybody knew it wasn't as simple as all that, and Hitler knew it best of all.

He sat in his office with the bust of Frederick the Great and the painting of Bismarck above the fireplace and figured things out. Obviously Hess, with that fixed conviction in his suffering mind that the war could be ended with England by a direct approach and appeal to reason, had hit upon his daring plan only after he was aloft—perhaps on that

first-day joy ride above Augsburg—flying around and
around in wide circles. A few short hours, a few clear
words into the right ears, and the world would be at his
feet. Yes, it was easy to see what had happened, exasperat-
ingly easy to see.

The Fuehrer stamped his boot into the carpet of expensive make. They were already saying Hess had skipped
to get away from Naziland; they were saying Hess had fled
the Gestapo; they were saying Hess had been sent over by
Hitler to beg for peace, perhaps as a trap for a deeply laid
plot.

All that and more came to the Fuehrer's ears. It didn't
make much impression; he waited and worried for a hint or
a symptom that Hess had revealed the great Russian secret.
There was the rub. The Balkan mess had compelled him to
postpone his plans against Russia and the bulk of his blitz
troops were still in Greece. He wasn't ready. Hess, loyal
though he knew him to be to himself and the Fatherland,
nevertheless may have committed the unpardonable sin of
telling the English of Hitler's plan to attack Russia. He
would do it with the best of intentions, this crazy Hess,
but what an idiotic mistake.

The Fuehrer scratched his chin and gave orders to ex-
pedite immediately the realignment of all troops in accordance with prepared plans. In a few days the roads leading from the Balkans and toward the east teemed with German troops hastening to assigned positions.

In Berlin, Hitler kept his fingers crossed and banked on
two things: that the English would reject Hess and any-

thing he had to tell them and that nobody either in England or Russia would seriously believe what Hess had to say.

Cleverly he kept the suspicion alive that Hess had gone with his own knowledge, with Goebbels spreading it tirelessly around outside that Hess was a crackpot. The rare magic worked, although the Russians began moving troops, and soon again Hitler was riding high.

And before attacking Russia he appointed little Nazi Bormann successor to Hess.

CHAPTER 6

The Rise and Fall of Karl Boemer and of His Policy toward America

THERE IS a short but dignified avenue in Berlin leading from the busy Potsdamer Platz to the edge of the Tiergarten, flanked by important buildings such as the exclusive Esplanade Hotel and the gaudy gay spot Moka Efti farther down.

It is the Bellevue Strasse, where until some years ago the American Consulate under the doughty and indomitable Raymond Geist had its headquarters. Right across from this building, where the American eagle is still engraved on the wall, there is an unimpressive edifice with a simple iron gate through which a car can drive under the portal into the inner courtyard.

A plain back-and-white board sign hangs over the entrance: THE PEOPLE'S COURT.

That is a name dreaded just as much all over the Reich

as the Gestapo. Both deal largely in matters closely affecting your own person and both more frequently than not deal out sudden death. There is not much chance of appeal from either of these two Nazi punitive machines.

The People's Court is a sort of specially combined civilian and military court-martial, whose five judges are appointed by Hitler personally and who are responsible only to the Fuehrer. He alone has the power to suspend or alter a verdict reached by this court. The judges consist of an officer of each of the three military branches, a functionary of the Nazi party, and a presiding judge of the profession. All goes according to the accepted form of court procedure, with a prosecutor and defense attorney in addition to the usual witnesses, but 80 per cent of the cases end up in a death sentence or long prison sentences at hard labor.

The building now used by the People's Court formerly was a library for sciences and literature endowed by the Kaiser. The marble staircase leading upstairs is still there, and the courtroom and judges' chambers retain their paneled oak. Photos of Hitler with one of his severe looks hang everywhere on the wall. Defendants of the various services or of government positions take their oath by holding in the four fingers of their left hand the Nazi flag standing alongside the table. A rare few spectators receive permission to get in on a session, depending on the nature of the case on trial. There is no gate-crashing, and the majority of hearings before the People's Court are *in camera*. For cases coming before this deadly court are primarily based on charges of treason, espionage, subversive activity, or plotting against the welfare and safety of the state or its representatives. The trial may last a few hours; it may occupy the court in exceptional cases from morning to night of one day, but seldom longer. The prepared evidence in the case and the circumstances usually have been clarified by the Gestapo and the Military Intelligence to such an extent that the procedure in the courtroom itself more often than not is a matter of formality. It isn't very often that the uniformed judges behind that table have to keep dinner waiting at home or omit the evening's beer and schnapps at their Stammtisch in their favorite *Kneipe*.

But that is what happened on the night of October 17, 1941. The case in hand, a dangerous secret known to and talked about in all the diplomatic whispering galleries of Berlin, did not reach a verdict until Saturday evening of the next day. Then it rang down the curtain not simply on the meteoric career of Nazi big-shot Number Four but it reverberated through the hearts of men on the inside like an earthquake and sounded finis, among other things, to what up to now could have been described as an attitude of restraint on the part of the Nazis toward America; tempered also by the tenacious hope in the breast of the man on trial that somehow or other Germany and the United States could be kept from coming into open war against each other.

The man of the thinning blond hair in the prisoner's box before the People's Court on October 17 was the hitherto gay and audacious Ministerial-Director Professor Doktor Karl Boemer, friend of all things American and with a par-

ticularly warm spot in his heart for American correspondents in Berlin. His imposing title when boiled down
into plain language gave him a rank equal to that of a German ambassador abroad. That, at forty-two years of age
and considering the fact that he joined the Nazi party only
in 1932, was something to boast about. It was common
knowledge that "Bel Ami," as he was popularly known
from his easy success with the fair sex, would inevitably
advance within the next year or so to the coveted title of
Staats-Sekretair, one step away from the rank of minister.
By and large, he was fourth in importance in the Reich by
dint of power and influence.

Karl Boemer had flashed his way to the top of the Nazi
Government by sheer brilliance mixed with a cocky dare-
deviltry that gave him the reputation in the Wilhelmstrasse
of being about the only man who'd tell Goebbels, for
example, to his face that he was all wrong and making a big
mistake. His intimate knowledge of America and Americans enabled him to talk and to act with authority in that
respect, and it is generally recognized by friend and foe in
Berlin that Karl Boemer as chief of the Foreign Department
in the Propaganda Ministry did his job most efficiently. He
was the only man in the Nazi Government who outdid
Houdini by working smoothly for two rival taskmasters at
the same time: Joe Goebbels of the Propaganda Ministry
was his chief on one side of the street and Hitler's Minister
of the Press, Otto Dietrich, from the Reich chancellery the
other.

Goebbels and Dietrich, each jealously guarding his prerogatives and personal foes of long standing, were about as easy to handle and pacify in one basket as a tomcat and a rattlesnake. But Boemer did it, and did it so well that both big Nazis swallowed the knocks and sometimes acid criticism he dished out when the situation called for it. They showered him with expensive presents and told him he ought to be shot.

This, then, was the man who stood before the People's Court in October fighting for his life. He was brandmarked with having broken nearly six months before a great Hitler secret: in an unguarded moment of overworked nerves and strong drink mixed with the passionate love for a woman, he had blurted out to sharp-eared guests of a foreign legation in Berlin the fact that within a few weeks Hitler was going to attack Soviet Russia and march his armies clear to Moscow and the Volga. You can imagine the commotion and the gasps among Germans and foreigners alike in the legation that evening, with telephone calls to foreign capitals throughout the night. And the busiest of all these international telephone lines that night in May was the one between the Soviet Embassy and the very private office of Joseph Stalin in Moscow.

The secret was out, and so was Karl Boemer. Without realizing it until too late, he had become the victim of clashing political interests, of international intrigue, of rivalries in the Wilhelmstrasse, and finally of the policy of moderation and restraint toward America for which he had tenaciously fought in past years.

As far back as 1936 he had sold Hitler on the policy that

America must never again be provoked into any war or participation in a war against Germany. He had convinced Hitler—and that meant pacifying and reconciling Goebbels to his viewpoint and swinging Ribbentrop into it—that America is a land of fads and phases, easy to flare up in emotional things and quick to forget and forgive. In time he swung Hitler and therewith the Nazi policy toward America around to one of swallowing everything and anything hurled at them from across the Atlantic.

Up to the war, and in fact until after President Roosevelt's election to a third term, Boemer held his own. The Nazi press occasionally was permitted to blow off steam as a safety valve in the wake of some particular incident in America such as the Communist raid in New York on the liner *Bremen* and the tearing down of the Nazi flag, but on the whole the press and official policy were careful not to aggravate openly the Reich's relations with the United States.

Boemer had legions of friends and also silent support in many high and low places of the Reich for his policy of restraint toward America. He ran into many political storms and hot sessions behind the scenes of Naziland as the war lengthened and grew tougher and the sentiment in America against the Nazis became hardened and bitter. He set his jaw and redoubled his efforts, hoping against hope that the worst would pass and that events in the end would vindicate his policy.

He could not know that as far back as May of 1941, in the innermost secret of his heart the Fuehrer already was hard at work plotting a desperate alternative for America, an alternative which would permit no such handicaps as the Boemer policy and that therefore he would have to be ruthlessly eliminated. Hitler's plan of swinging the Japs into line against America for an ultimative showdown after the invasion of Russia tolerated no median course and in fact called for the immediate and definite education of the German people into a hostile state of mind toward anything and everything American. It called for an all-out propaganda campaign of vilification, of mud-slinging, of condemnation, and of placing in the eyes of the German people all blame for continuation of the war on the man in the White House whom Hitler dreaded and feared. It called also for the softening of the shock in the people's minds, through instigation of their antagonism, which the active participation in the war by America was sure to produce. Boemer obviously, if not intentionally, stood in the way of the Fuehrer's plans in relation to America. He had to be eliminated, one way or another. To Hitler the dictator there were many ways of doing this, but he had to consider the effect of removing a pillar of the Wilhelmstrasse on the minds and morale of the hundreds of political career men who make his regime click.

It wouldn't do just to kick him out, as the natural reaction of everybody else would be that his own turn might come next. For Karl Boemer, on the whole, had become a sort of political barometer and landmark in Hitler's capital.

Then, in an unfortunate moment, Boemer himself provided Hitler with the golden opportunity to wipe him out.

It came as a culmination to a brilliant but hectic career, ear-marked by an impulsive and erratic nature and stamped with the restlessness of the born adventurer. I first got to know Boemer in the late twenties at the University of Missouri, where he came to lecture before the School of Journalism I was attending at the time while working my way through as college correspondent for the St. Louis *Post Dispatch*. In 1931 I ran into him again at the World Press Congress held that year in Mexico City. I was correspondent then for International News Service and Boemer somehow had wangled himself an appointment as delegate for the German newspapers of pre-Hitler days. Back in Berlin he had several books on the press to his credit, but he was nevertheless short of cash and somewhat vague as to future plans.

I ran into him again at the beginning of 1934 while casting about for ways and means to establish inside contacts with the Nazis. My New York headquarters had transferred me from London to Berlin as correspondent for the office there, and I was a complete stranger in a maelstrom of news and events needing quick and efficient coverage. Guided by chance into the headquarters of Alfred Rosenberg, the Nazi philosopher and now ruling dictator over Russia, I found myself face to face again with Karl Boemer. He was as surprised as I was.

In those days Hitler, still shaken by the 1934 blood purge, continued to lean heavily on the silent and reserved Rosenberg. He had the latter in mind for his next Foreign Minister and to that end Boemer threw himself into the task without sparing. He carried the cause for Rosenberg far and wide and by the time Hitler for reasons of his own turned away from Rosenberg to pick on Ribbentrop for Foreign Minister, Boemer had made such an impression on Hitler that he was switched to the Foreign Office to shake the dust of tradition and routine from that venerable machine.

Rosenberg made only one condition: that Boemer remain at the same time his own press chief. Joe Goebbels was having a hard time hitting the right propaganda tune in the outside world because he had never been across the German borders, so one fine morning he went to Hitler and convinced him that the Foreign Office could never replace the functions of the Propaganda Ministry and that consequently a live wire like Boemer should be assigned to him. Meek little Otto Dietrich, newly appointed Press Chief of the Reich by Hitler and desperately looking around for someone who knew what to do, for once took the bull by the horns and asked Hitler for the services of Boemer. After the usual arguments and counterarguments, Hitler fell back on his favorite method of compromising by transferring Boemer into the Propaganda Ministry assigned to the job of impartially aiding both Goebbels and Dietrich.

It was a radical thing to do, fraught with political dangers, and it placed Boemer constantly between two fires. But he faced the situation without flinching and made friends with both Nazi moguls by flatly refusing to play favorites. His

main job was to put steam behind the Nazi foreign propaganda outside of Germany and that meant extensive re-
organization of the existing machinery. An essential part of
the immediate job was to find men suited and qualified to
handle their job; a second major task was that of establish-
ing closer contact with the foreign correspondents in Berlin
and in particular with the American correspondents. That
was something the Nazis had not succeeded in doing up to
this time, chiefly because Goebbels and others of the Nazi
party like Julius Streicher and Labor Leader Ley in those
days used to point fingers at us foreign correspondents and
call us liars and poisoners of people's minds.

Boemer stopped all that, launching therewith a new
policy for aiding foreign correspondents in every possible
form. He opened channels of information and approach to
Nazi key men hitherto closed to the ordinary foreign correspondents; he organized a fast-clicking Department of
Information open day and night to questions and phone
calls, and finally looked about for ways and means to lighten
the personal difficulties and troubles of foreign correspondents in Berlin.

Over in the Foreign Office, Ribbentrop had picked as
successor to him a very young and portly man named
Paul Schmidt, fresh from the provinces around Kiel as
storm trooper and propagandist of the S.S. Boemer liked
him from the beginning and went out of his way to boost
him up the ladder of governmental rank. He brought him
around to the Taverne of nights and introduced him as a
coming young man. In this exclusive Berlin restaurant,

Boemer fostered a deepening partnership with Schmidt and when the occasion called for it drank him under the table or vice versa.

By the time war began, Schmidt had risen in the Foreign Office to a rank equal almost to Boemer's, partly because of the intense jealousy and rivalry existing between people like Ribbentrop, Goebbels, and Dietrich. Ribbentrop was not going to have Goebbels or Dietrich running the press policy and propaganda output of the Foreign Office; he was not going to have himself and his ego overshadowed in the slightest by anything Goebbels or Dietrich could do. It aggravated and piqued his *amour propre* to have a Goebbels or Dietrich man of high rank always outshining and outdoing his own representative and mouthpiece, chiefly because the latter lacked equal authority. Therefore, he threw all orthodox procedure to the winds and promoted Paul Schmidt over the heads of young and old alike. It caused much gnashing of teeth, and in the breasts of men who had labored for years to achieve an official rank of even medium nature there rankled a resentment against the portly young man they regarded as an upstart. He paid back by cracking the whip and surrounding himself in the Foreign Office with very young henchmen of his own choosing.

2

Boemer saw the knife too late. I warned him repeatedly not to lay himself wide open. The shock came early in 1940, a few months after Boemer had hit on the idea of organizing and providing a sort of clubhouse where foreign correspondents could always be assured of meals at a low price. He felt that as the war went on, times would get harder, and for the foreigner in the Reich might come unpleasant moments. At the Taverne one night he proposed to Schmidt that they get together and ask Ribbentrop to surrender to them one of the vacant legations or embassies of the warring powers, such as the house formerly used by the Polish Ambassador. They could draw on propaganda funds to redecorate the place to suit their plans and purposes.

Schmidt enthusiastically agreed and said no more about it. A few months later, at the weekly get-together of an inner ring of foreign correspondents of the first rank, where Nazis of importance and with valuable information to pass on to us were invited and to which, until the last six months of 1941, they were eager to come, Paul Schmidt sprang a surprise. Boemer was not present at the gathering that night and Schmidt, after pledging us to silence, invited us all for a midnight ride. Driving through the black-out, we halted in front of a gloomy house off the Kurfuerstendamm on Fasanen Strasse and were invited to enter. A burst of light and a lavish clubhouse with expensive easy chairs in red leather, carpets an inch thick, a dining room, and an upstairs floor with a bar and billiard room, greeted our astounded eyes. We looked at each other in amazement.

"Gentlemen of the foreign press, this is your house," said Schmidt with a smirking smile. "Herr Ribbentrop places it at your disposal. He will welcome you into it at a formal opening I am planning for next week."

I stood there with the rest of my colleagues, a sense of foreboding in my heart. Here was something very nasty. We all went home after the champagne and the sandwiches shaking our heads and discussing the unpleasant surprise in store for Boemer.

A few days later, when Schmidt staged his opening party and had Ribbentrop there to give us the usual handout of international co-operation and good will to all on the part of the Reich, Boemer stood there amid the very modern lighting smoking cigarette after cigarette. He even added a few words in the name of Goebbels and Dietrich to those of Ribbentrop. Then he went home to nurse the wound in his heart.

From that day on open rivalry flared between Schmidt and Boemer. The old friendship and mutual drinking bouts ended. Boemer stormed from his own big office in the Propaganda Ministry into that of Goebbels the very next day and demanded to know if Goebbels would stand for that kind of a dirty Ribbentrop trick. Half an hour later he came out with half a million marks at his disposal to build the finest club in town. He went to Leipziger Platz and practically confiscated the stately old edifice originally housing the exclusive and aristocratic Imperial Automobile Club, throwing all but fifty thousand marks into its rebuilding. The fifty thousand marks he spent in stocking up on French chefs and whole truckloads of fine champagnes and liquors. He built a bar twice as large and twice as attractive as the one in Paul Schmidt's club; he included a working room for foreign correspondents with telephones, desks, typewriters, and instantaneous radio service. The dining room carried a large bill of fare and Boemer, ever the ladies' man, had one room done entirely in green silk enriched by two grand pianos. In short, he showed his mettle by putting it all over Schmidt. You could almost see the sparks flying between those two now.

We foreign correspondents of the non-Axis countries, standing on the side lines and trying to do our hard job well, scratched our chins and told one another of our mutual misgivings. We didn't want to get our fingers caught in something that was none of our business, yet here we were hardly able to avoid the thin ice altogether. Invitations came frequently and with recurring coincidence from both clubs at the same time; if you went to one place the stooges of the rival club immediately relayed that information and in effect you had a mark against you there. I made the best of the situation by eating lunch a couple of times each week in Boemer's club and spending one evening each week at the bar upstairs, while Saturday nights I reserved for the equally boring but inescapable drinking bout with cabaret girls and film stars who performed gratis at Schmidt's club and gurgled to you about the glamour of foreign corre-spondents or the nastiness of people in Hollywood.

But Schmidt had other tricks up his sleeve. He withdrew from public circulation and surrounded himself with a mantle of dignity and exclusiveness. Boemer, on the con-trary, increased his pace, driven by restless nerves and a crushing daily program of work and high tension. He sought relief in champagne and cognac, hotfooting it around the night clubs with a new favorite every week or two. For a time his new home with his blonde little wife and adopted child out in Grunewald near Berlin helped him keep on an even keel, and he deftly avoided the hidden traps laid for him time and again over in the Foreign Office. The lavish gifts from Hitler, Goebbels, Dietrich, and scores of high Nazis and diplomats continued to pour in, giving him no inkling in the spring of 1941 that the Fuehrer he served was planning a showdown with America after the attack on Russia and even then was waiting the moment to do an about-face on his policy toward America. Schmidt didn't know it either, but he watched every move Boemer made.

One night in late February, down in Garmisch-Partenkirchen of Olympic fame, a couple of other American newspapermen and myself in company with Boemer went over to the Alpenhof Hotel for an evening's relaxation. We had come down there from Berlin after a hard winter for some alpine air and rest. The town was full of rich men's wives and daughters sent there to escape the bombs at home; all the left-over glamour girls with somebody else's money in their pockets were on hand to liven up the situation. A friend of Boemer's came over to our table to introduce a woman, neatly dressed but with a long nose giving her a faintly hatchet-faced look, and worst of all, she had fish eyes. We looked at her without interest, listening to her companion recite to Boemer her wonderful qualities as a pianist. Boemer's interest quickened visibly; he always was a passionate addict of the piano and could play everything from the classic to the popular for hours without stopping. He asked the couple to sit down, and it wasn't long before I knew from the light in his eye that he was definitely interested. The girl's attitude showed clearly that she had come here determined to get on in the music world by hook or by crook.

That started things, and a couple of weeks later, as might have been expected, the girl showed up in Berlin. Bel Ami was definitely in love, and he was a man who wore his heart on his sleeve. Day after day and night after night he could be seen in his club with this strange new flame, wildly pounding out duets on the two pianos in the room of green silk or soothing his strained nerves in the barroom. I told him to his face, and so did Guido Enderis of the New York *Times*, that between the liquor and the woman he was bound to crack up. He agreed, and said that all good things must come to an end. He said he could always join the army in the field, having an officer's rank, and thus secure himself military promotion and the decoration for bravery for which he yearned. He was hipped on that; in fact, Boemer went into the trenches of Flanders as a sixteen-year-old volunteer and won the Iron Cross of the First Class. In some ways he was a crazy guy.

When Hitler attacked Yugoslavia and Greece in April of 1941, Boemer arranged for the usual trip of some foreign correspondents with the German Army and he himself went along. As always on such moves to the front, Louis Lochner of the Associated Press and I were assigned to his car, giving us sometimes an added advantage over those in the cars behind us. But on that hard trip through the southeast, with its dusty and hungry days for us, Lochner and I strove with might and main to bring Boemer back to his feet and tear him loose from the grip of the woman back in Berlin. By the time we returned from Athens, we thought we had succeeded, particularly as Fish-Eyes was absent for some weeks on a piano tour.

But we were mistaken, badly mistaken. Bel Ami had definitely lost his heart to her, and he mooned around like a dying calf. Even the hotbed of whispering and speculation going on all around Berlin over Hitler's next move failed to stir the old fire in him. On the evening of May 15 his old chief Rosenberg asked him to come over to his office right away for an important conference. Boemer went and for a while became his old self when Rosenberg in the intimate company of his oldest and truest co-workers revealed that he had just come from Hitler with an appointment of dictator over all Russia in his pocket. Yes, it was true. The day for the attack on Russia was fixed for the not-too-distant future. The disgraceful previous necessity forced by circumstances of keeping silent on Bolshevist Russia and putting a good face on everything at long last would be broken. The Nazis there in Rosenberg's office shook hands with tears in their eyes. All of them would gain tremendously by the new turn of the tide.

3

Karl Boemer went home to his patient wife and put on a dress uniform for the reception that night at the Bulgarian

Legation. He went there in a high state of excitement, one of the handful of men inside the Reich that night possessed of the greatest Hitler secret in years. For days the air had vibrated with rumor and speculation on what was to come next. Some said the invasion of England; others believed that Stalin and Hitler were going to join forces after a deal splitting up the Middle East and the rest of the continent. A dozen other versions floated around, but Boemer could afford to smile and look dumb.

The usual crowd of Axis diplomats and their wives were on hand, brimming with gossip and mischief. Men with keen dark eyes from the Balkans watched Boemer drink his fill, and later they engaged him in conversation in a secluded corner. They talked of the manly art of drinking, stressing the Russian custom of pouring down a glass of vodka with every breath. They told of the matchless capacity for vodka of Stalin and Molotov in Moscow, asserting that no man could equal those two. Boemer said he could do it, and lifted glass after glass.

The room spun around him after awhile, and he became talkative. A friend of his who tried to persuade him to come home was rudely shoved aside. In the legation, Paul Schmidt of the Foreign Office and some of his aides had watched Boemer from afar, sure that he would make a spectacle of himself and thus add another black mark to his record. What they didn't know for the moment was that the sharp-eyed questioners around him were goading him on, flattering him with fine words.

"*Ach*, Herr Boemer, you big men know so much," one

of them whispered to him. "But they say here you don't know any more than the rest of us about the Russian situation."

It was the kind of bait held out to him at exactly the right moment. They had angled for this the whole evening, maneuvering and fencing to arouse his *amour propre* and provoke him into spilling any information he might be hiding under his hat. The fumes of vodka did the rest.

"I know all about everything," Boemer shouted suddenly. "Two months from today our dear old Rosenberg will be the boss of Russia and Stalin will be a dead man. We will smash the Russians quicker than we smashed the French. We'll show the Bolshevists who is running Europe. Hitler is running Europe; Hitler, not Stalin. These Bolshevist pigs will find that out now."

The shocked officials from the Wilhelmstrasse, Schmidt included, tried to stop him from his wild outburst. He stumbled through the reception rooms and raged and raved that he was going to be a Staats-Sekretair. His army chauffeur finally got him outside and away.

That is why the chancelleries of Europe on that fatal night teemed with excitement; no doubt Stalin worked the night through, and if from previous information drifting in from the Hess case and other sources he still had doubts on Hitler's intentions, he now knew what to do. The Red Army rolled toward the western borders, scores and scores of fully equipped divisions ready for war.

In the Wilhelmstrasse next day Goebbels tried to save Boemer from his blunder. He hastily dictated a letter to

Hitler, explaining the background and pointing out that Boemer was overworked and had made his bad mistake without any premeditated intention. It could be overlooked, and what he had said could be denied as another of those rumors circulating around by the dozen. A long report on the affair from the Foreign Office and Goebbels' letter were handed to Hitler simultaneously. Hitler took one look and hit the ceiling. An hour later special Gestapo men picked up Boemer in his office in Wilhelmstrasse and took him over to Himmler's headquarters in Albrecht Strasse as Hitler's personal prisoner. Those in the know around Hitler later told me they fully expected that Boemer would be shot almost immediately, but there again Hitler's strange quirk of following legal procedure came to the surface. He turned the case over to the Gestapo and that is how it came about that Boemer, the Number Four in Naziland, sat behind the bars from the middle of May to October 17, 1941, before his trial came up before the People's Court. In the meantime his vacant chair in the Propaganda Ministry was filled by a nonentity; from the day he vanished you could feel the atmosphere thicken against America and Americans in Berlin.

Day by day the outburst against America and Roosevelt in the press and on the radio became intensified, agitating and poisoning the German people's minds against us. It didn't take much imagination to know that Hitler was pressing a new button. In the Foreign Office, Paul Schmidt achieved full ambassadorial rank and within the space of weeks practically muscled out the Propaganda Ministry in all things that count in dealings with foreign-press policy and foreign correspondents. He was tops now, unrivaled and unchallenged. He, the green young man of a few years ago from out of the sticks, had won out and it remained but to make sure that Caesar was dead.

So he went to the People's Court with his aides on that first morning of the Boemer trial cocksure and confident he would nail Boemer to the mast.

All the mighty string-pulling of the past six months had failed to move Hitler to lift a finger in behalf of Boemer; it was but logical for Schmidt to assume that the die was cast and that the life sentence, if not a death pronouncement, was sure to come. He stood blandly before the court and declared that mercy must not be shown in such a case. He never looked at the man in the prisoner's box, coldly delivering his testimony.

Two famous girl dancers, several girls from the night clubs were put on the stand as witnesses and questioned as to their relations with the prisoner. They all liked Bel Ami, and admitted that they had fun in his company. By the time lunch recess came, Schmidt and his aides were sure of their case. The shock for them was all the greater, therefore, when lightning struck at the resumption of the session at 3 P.M. They could hardly believe their ears when the doors opened and up to the witness stand hobbled none other than Minister for Propaganda Doktor Paul Joseph Goebbels, dark eyes flashing and the grooved mouth firmly set. It seemed incredible, almost unbelievable, but here before the dreaded People's Court stood as witness now a minister and right-hand man of the Fuehrer. The momentary silence was like that of the tomb.

White-faced and visibly shaken, Schmidt sat in nervous silence on the spectators' bench and listened to the incisive oration flowing from the lips of silver-tongued Joe Goebbels. He traced in detail before this court of life and death the career of the blond man in the prisoner's box, dwelling at length on what he described as the great services rendered the Fatherland. He told them that the man in the box had sacrificed his health through sheer overwork; he reminded them to keep in mind that a great German patriot stood for judgment before them, not because of a willful crime committed, but because of an error of carelessness precipitated in a moment of sheer physical and mental exhaustion. He testified for nearly an hour and a half, leaving no phrase unturned. He held them spellbound and somewhat awed, ending with a sweeping announcement that the Fuehrer himself had sanctioned this appearance of his minister before the People's Court. Then he stamped out as quickly as he had come, never once glancing at the portly man from the Foreign Office and his aides on the spectators' bench.

Two minutes later the door opened again and in marched Otto Dietrich, straight from Fuehrer headquarters in Russia. He, too, had gotten Hitler's permission to come here, and in fact had used his private plane to make the dash. For nearly an hour he recited in favor of the man who in effect had guided and shaped the press policy of the Reich for foreign lands in the past several years.

It had been cleverly arranged, this massing of the big batteries for the last. It made it conceivably easier for Boemer himself to get up at last and speak in his own defense. He had no excuses to offer on the secret spilled, but he did have a double-barreled argument in his own favor.

"I did not break the secret of Russia to foreign ears," he declared with firm voice.

"I merely repeated that which had already reached enemy ears. I remind the gentlemen of the court that the self-imposed mission of Rudolf Hess in his flight to England centered largely on his conviction that by telling England that Hitler at last would smash Russia, he could effect peace with England and even bring England to our side. The secret of Russia went to England with Hess, and I say again to this court that I unintentionally repeated and probably confirmed to a greater extent what must already have been known to the other side."

That was about all Boemer had to say. The next day the court resumed, giving long play to the pros and cons of the defense and prosecuting attorneys. At four-thirty in the afternoon the court adjourned for a verdict and two hours later came in to pronounce sentence.

"We find the defendant guilty of an irresponsible act injurious to the state," the judge in the black robe and cap said. "But in view of the special circumstances and conditions demonstrated in this case, this court sentences the prisoner to the merciful lenience of two years in prison. The six months already served during the investigation are to be made retroactive."

Boemer the big shot walked out of the court and into the green police van waiting below with a firm step and lifted head. For the first time in its existence the People's Court had really been lenient; he was to hear from Goebbels the next day that within the next six months he might fall under a Fuehrer amnesty. Once out from behind the bars, he could vanish for a time into the wilds of Russia, holding down a post assigned to him far away by Rosenberg.

Thus inside this Germany of Hitler's I witnessed again the ruthless play of jungle politics. Hitler conveniently got rid of a man with a policy gone sour; a new phenomenon in the person of Paul Schmidt at the Foreign Office replaced him. The road was free for the war against America, and we, the foreign correspondents in Berlin, knew that day that the verdict which had fallen before the People's Court had also fallen on us.

CHAPTER 7

Hitler's Viceroys in the New Order

O<small>N A SUNNY DAY</small> in September of 1938 Adolf Hitler stood amid half a dozen of us foreign correspondents up in the tapestry room of the medieval castle overlooking gable-roofed Nuremberg and became loquacious. He was in an expansive mood, as he can be when the sun is warm and two million men are marching around town hailing him as a triumphant Caesar home from the wars abroad. His eyes shone and he was almost gay, already confident within himself that things were going his way. Perhaps, by strange instinct mixed with the keen attributes of the bloodhound, Hitler already at that time smelled Munich and the triumph he was to gain over the British.

He liked to hold forth in surroundings of ancient Germanic glory, and each year in September, until the war interfered, he came to Nuremberg for ten days of riotous

Nazi-party marching and singing, featured by tidal waves of oratory to massed formations of storm troops. At such times of the *Nuremberg Partei Tag* he lived in the Hotel Deutscher Hof, rebuilt in luxury style with special Fuehrer apartments on the second floor and a balcony overlooking the street. But he frequently visited and received guests in the castle on the hill, where each year a special staff of servants and a supply of excellent culinary equipment ruled any ghosts out of place and drove aside the taint of museums and dead ages. There, in the heavily beamed oak-wood room which long ago served as reception chamber for the fierce and mighty Barbarossa, Hitler felt at home and each year played luncheon host to diplomats and correspondents, receiving each group on a fixed day in accordance with the program of the Nazi Party Congress.

Below us, in the cobblestoned streets winding crazily through rows of feudal walls and towers, brass bands played lustily and Nazi columns marching four abreast throatily sang: "*Heute gehoert uns Deutschland; morgen die ganze Welt!*" It is a travesty on the actual text of the song, which reads: "Today Germany hears us; tomorrow the whole world." Yet in my eight years in Germany I heard brown storm troopers singing only the following version: "Today Germany is ours; tomorrow the whole world!" The Nazis, disregarding official frowns, let the cat out of the bag and substituted *gehoert* for *hoert*.

I glanced at Hitler to see if his ears had caught that little byplay on his claims and policies, but he paid it no attention. He was engrossed at the moment in pitying the shortcomings of Europe, in damning Stalin and Bolshevism, and in eulogizing the wisdom and vision of himself and his ideology.

He folded his arms across his chest, striking an attitude not unlike Napoleon standing on the battlefield. *"Ja, meine Herren,"* he said with weighty self-importance, "I have told my men time and again, and I shall say so in a speech to-morrow for all the world to hear, that we *wild Nazis* are after all the best Europeans. We have thrown off the shackles which held us; we have trampled on the dusty customs and standards of a decayed Victorian age; we have had the courage to reawaken Germany; and we have the courage to reawaken and, if necessary, to lead this sick Europe. The graybeards in many of its chancelleries cannot do it; the masses are helpless, and the army leaders in the various lands are interested only in themselves. New blood is needed, young blood, and men of courage. They must be Europeans, not from outside their own continent. They can put Europe back on its feet. I can help them, once they are in the saddle. I can work with them, and together we can create a new Europe, a Europe rid of internecine strife and suicidal tariffs. Together we shall work as Europeans, for the common good of Europe, and that will be the time when the world will discover that we wild Nazis, as I said, are after all the best Europeans."

Thus spoke Hitler one year before he marched across the borders of Poland and into World War II. It is easy to see that his blueprint for the New Order in Europe already had taken shape, even if it hadn't materialized. He did not define the ways and means of getting the new blood, the men of courage he spoke of so glowingly. He did not tell us that day, for example, that in his mind these men already had been chosen, picked by him for the task of mastering and ruling the conquered parts of Europe with an iron hand. He did not say that booted Nazis who had served him well were selected one by one to sit in the capitals of Europe and create that new Europe he spoke of. Wild Nazis, he said, are the best Europeans. He meant that rabid Nazis *only* could rule the Europe he intended to master and enslave. He was, on that September day in 1938, already very sure of himself and of Europe.

Later I had reason to recall his words in the castle of Nuremberg when the tide of war swept governments away and Nazi rulers appointed by Hitler swung the swastika scepter. Poland went down, then Norway, Holland, Belgium, and even France. Hitler sent new blood into these lands: the courageous men and the *best* Europeans he had visualized for us. They wore Nazi uniforms, these henchmen of Hitler, who carried out his instructions to the letter and today rule Europe for him with an iron hand. They are the ones who work with him and they are his conception of the *best* Europeans.

Every time the German Army swept through the next victim on the Continent, the Nazi Fuehrer summoned to his office a deserving servant and with the gesture of a generous king endowed him with powers unlimited over the region he assigned him to. One by one he dispatched these personal viceroys to the conquered capitals of Europe, each one responsible only to himself and charged with transforming the conquered territory into part and parcel of the Nazi New Order in Europe. The ways and means of doing this were left to the gentle discretion of each viceroy, whose hands he reinforced by placing at their disposal all the violent efficiency of the S.S., a body of highly trained military guards specially equipped to pacify and dominate any land taken over by force. The consequent shootings and mistakes of administrative rule did not matter to him; of them he expected no more or less than a thorough job of keeping the region under the Nazi thumb. When the only gentleman and non-Nazi in the lot, Baron Konstantin von Neurath, failed to show sufficiently the ruthless iron fist as master of the Czechs, Hitler peremptorily removed him and sent to Prague the cold-blooded assistant to Himmler, Acting Gestapo Chief Reiman Heydrich. That, to the Czechs, was the unkindest blow of all.

I know Heydrich fairly well, or at least well enough to keep away from him as much as possible. He is forty, a former naval lieutenant by profession, and the best human bloodhound Himmler has found so far for his extensive work of hunting down the thousands of people filling the prisons and concentration camps of the Reich. He has a mind and mentality something like an adding machine, never forgetting or lapsing into the sentimental. From his viewpoint every man and woman under the sun must be regarded with suspicion and looked at as a case for investigation. Nobody ever gets a break or considerations of mercy. Heydrich isn't that way.

This tall young man, in the uniform of Group Leader of Hitler's Elite Guards and now boss of the so-called Protectorate (former Bohemia and Moravia), has a straight, long nose and eyes set close together. His face is always smooth shaven and he talks in the clipped sentences of a man accustomed to dealing with people who can only listen and take orders. When Heydrich looks at anyone, his eyes narrow with suspicion for every word they may say and he watches them like a cat playing with a mouse.

A German high in the government service told me: "I know that several people disappeared in the past few years because they had knowledge and proof of the fact that Heydrich on one side of the family comes from Dutch Jews." This was told in a whisper although we were in his home, a safe place, and he laid a finger on my arm to impress me with the need for silence. A hint to Heydrich's ears that this devastating skeleton in his closet is walking around the Wilhelmstrasse would bring swift retribution in the dark. But Heydrich is not the only one against whom the charges of unpure Aryanism are in the Berlin air. The same goes for people like Ley, Goebbels, and Milch of the Luftwaffe. Only in the case of Heydrich, however, do they talk of existing proof of their allegations.

One night this ruler of the Czechs was invited to meet and talk with a group of us foreign correspondents meeting every Thursday evening under the patronage of Goering's *National Zeitung*, a daily publication in Essen. This weekly meeting was known as the Stammtisch, run with an eye to exclusiveness by a Berlin correspondent of that paper,

Erich Schneyder, whose job it was to bring to these meetings and in contact with foreign newspapermen the key men in Naziland. The idea was to get across to the important correspondents in Berlin some of the fundamental Nazi viewpoints, and before the war quite frequently to "break" through this medium a story of major importance. This method had its advantages, for men like Ribbentrop could always retract or deny what they had told us next day if the story backfired the wrong way.

But a lot of the big shots among the Nazis came around to the Stammtisch with tongue in cheek, distrustful of all foreigners and fearful lest something in dispatches across the borders be attributed to them and frowned upon in highest Nazi quarters. Therefore they usually made it a condition that they were not to be quoted, and the evening in such cases developed into one of political discourse mixed with Rhine wine and beer.

Heydrich was one of those who didn't care to be quoted. In fact, he laid stress on it, on the grounds that many of us had axes to grind and always put Himmler and the Gestapo in a bad light. Then he launched forth on a long dissertation aimed at whitewashing the Nazi-controlled machinery of justice and the Gestapo methods of policing. Without batting an eye he claimed that only something like 60,000 people of all kinds are sitting in Hitler's concentration camps within Germany, not counting the Jews, although he was perfectly aware that the figure commonly accepted by people who ought to know stands at around 1,000,000.

"I suppose you never shoot anybody without first thoroughly investigating the case from all angles," a rather cynical Swiss correspondent remarked dryly. "We hear so much about mass shootings and the direct-method procedure of the Gestapo and the S.S. that we sometimes wonder."

Heydrich stared with close-drawn eyes at the bold man from Switzerland, evidently weighing his words. For a moment it looked bad. Then Heydrich got hold of himself. "This is all utter nonsense and enemy propaganda designed to damn us in the eyes of the world," he said in an icy way. "People we shoot should have been shot long ago. There is no great trick in finding the guilty in big subversive plots in an occupied country, once you have the key to the situation and know the ringleaders. All you have to do after that is to follow their tracks and pick up the facts one by one. It is like unrolling a ball of yarn. The rest takes care of itself."

He said this sometime before Hitler sent him to Prague to carry out the 1941 blood bath there as successor to Neurath. Heydrich later certainly acted out in detail what he had told us that evening at the Stammtisch. He shot everybody and anybody who had anything to do with the ringleaders or wandered into the network of Heydrich's Gestapo. The fact that hungry stomachs in Czech factories and shops compelled to work day and night for Hitler's war machine motivated part of the sabotage did not bother Heydrich; he blamed it all on Moscow and London paid agents and blazed away with his guns.

At the Stammtisch he told us that he and his Gestapo were powerless to arrest individuals, unless the usual machinery and process of justice functioned properly beforehand. Baldly he claimed that all talk about shadow arrests in the Reich is vicious slander designed to terrorize and undermine the German people's peace of mind. He got a little edgy, with a spot of color in his pale face, when our silence conveyed our thoughts. Like all Nazis, Heydrich hates to find himself in a position where people act skeptical and show signs of disbelieving any patterned Nazi statements. It irritates him.

He locked horns with a Swedish correspondent who quizzed him on the rumored godlessness of the S.S. and the teachings within their ranks against Christianity. The Swede stuck to his guns in the face of Heydrich's growing fury, but every foreign correspondent there chipped in in open support for the colleague from Stockholm and that churned up an atmosphere bordering on the dangerous. Heydrich's lips were set tight as a drum, and he talked through his teeth.

"The S.S. is a splendid body of men trained to safeguard the Fuehrer and the Fatherland," he said with a baleful glance at the circle around him. "We do not consider it necessary to march into church every Sunday or to listen to sermons which mean nothing. The S.S. is trained to believe in God, but we do not intend to be handicapped by superstitious rules and regulations laid down by the Church of Rome or by any other ecclesiastical organization. Christianity is a term, and if we choose to worship

God our own way, then none should point fingers and say
we are heathens. The first and only principle of service in
the S.S. is fanatical loyalty to the Fuehrer and the Fatherland. If a bishop or a priest oversteps the bounds of his office
and agitates in his community against his government instead of sticking to purely religious functions, then I see no
reason why I should not justifiably interfere. I also see no
reason why a large body of men like the S.S. should even be
exposed to the possibility of running into a non-Nazi atmosphere such as is generally apparent in the Catholic Church.
But that doesn't mean that we are godless."

Heydrich shortly thereafter cut the evening short, refusing to go into details on the tribal religious rites and prac-
tices which the S.S. indulges in along with radical brown-
shirt troopers steeped in the distorted philosophies of Alfred
Rosenberg. He left with a curt Hitler salute, scarcely making an attempt to hide his displeasure and inner fury. We
knew it was the last time he would come to the Stammtisch,
and some days later we heard that he had complained bitterly and with a menacing hint to Schneyder about the
insolence and shocking attitude of foreign correspondents
in Berlin. Himmler, his immediate superior and man of the
everlasting tiger smile, filed that report away with the rest
of the dossiers against us, to be brought out and made use
of at an opportune time.

The Stammtisch since that day has fallen more and more
under a shadow, as has everything which goes against the
grain of Himmler and Heydrich. We in Berlin shook our
heads when the appointment of this cold-blooded and

vengeful Heydrich as master of the Czechs was announced
with a flourish by Hitler, for a single evening of him on his
best behavior was enough to convince every one of us
that he is a bad one to deal with if you are on the wrong
side of the fence. He knows no mercy or tolerance, prid-
ing himself on the efficiency and sadism of the devil himself. He showed that in Prague, and to Hitler and Himmler
he demonstrated himself as one of the ablest of Nazi viceroys hitherto to take over any part of conquered Europe.
He must be, to Hitler, an ideal Nazi servant and New Order
co-operator and consequently one of the *best* Europeans.

It may be that Heydrich's shining example in Prague set
the pace and cut anew the pattern of Nazi domination for
the other and older Nazi viceroys in Europe. Some of them
are apt to lie down on the job once in a while, and eventually
get summoned back to Berlin for a bit of revitalizing by
Hitler. That happened during 1941 to the savage young
Nazi Gauleiter cracking the whip over Norway, Joseph
Terboven, who used to be boss in Cologne until Hitler sent
him to Oslo as his viceroy there. Terboven's official title is
Reich's Commissar for Norway. He was one of the rough
and brawny youngsters from the coal mines in the Ruhr
who waved the swastika and planted it firmly over Essen
and at Krupp's cannon factory long before Hitler assumed
power. Among other rewards in the earlier days, he ran
for a time and cashed in on the Goering-sponsored newspaper, Essen *National Zeitung*. Then he went to Cologne
as Gauleiter and finally to Norway as the specially picked
tough guy relied on by Hitler to hammer the equally tough

Norwegians into shape and make them march obediently to Hitler's New Order in Europe. He, Terboven, is certainly the boy to swing the club up there in the hardy regions next door to the polar wastes.

We foreign correspondents heard time and again in Berlin that Terboven wastes no time on ceremony or sympathy up in Oslo. He loses patience easily and lets the fur fly at the least provocation. The Norwegians are hardheaded, but they found their match in this heavy-muscled and round-headed man from the coal mines. They found that when balked, or loaded with liquor, Terboven could stare with protruding eyeballs that never winked and convey an answer that needed no words. He could be plainly bored and act the same way.

Terboven is the kind who relieves his feelings by going off on a terrific spree. He is apt to be a little oversensitive, too, and seek solace in drink. Particularly after those uncomfortable moments one has with Hitler in Berlin during these revitalizing conferences at the chancellery. Terboven's fanatical loyalty and doglike idolizing of everything and anything pertaining to the Fuehrer cannot be doubted, but he has his moments of self-pity and rumination. For example, after sessions with Hitler, when he cannot explain why the Quisling fifth column in Norway isn't making progress. That hurts his Nazi heart and he has a way of consoling himself by going to the Kaiserhof bar, where he surrounds himself with cronies of his own choosing to drink away his sorrow until the late hours of the night. He even forgets himself on such occasions, roaring forth bawdy songs and upsetting the bar furniture. He has cost the hotel many a broken window, and the distracted manager is always running around trying to collect on Terboven bills. Although, in the end, the Nazi party wipes off all outstanding claims. That is not a complicated process, for long ago the Hitler party purchased the hotel as the simplest way of dealing with the problem of meeting unpaid bills from beer-hall spenders who switched to champagne and caviar in celebration of their rise to power. That became a habit.

Terboven was in a particularly pugnacious mood one evening after a final two-hour session with Hitler in the early part of 1941. He was to fly back to Oslo next morning, taking along the usual set of instructions and orderlies. He sprawled and held forth at the large round table in the left-hand corner of the Kaiserhof bar, gulping down English whisky at twenty-eight marks per bottle (around eleven dollars) and later champagne. The five S.S. men with him were the new orderlies and gunmen he was taking along to pep up the Nazi policing of Norway and nip in the bud a growing undercurrent of dissension and almost open revolt on the part of the Norwegians. They drank to the success of their task and toasted the prowess of the S.S. Other customers in the bar had left early, either to avoid difficulties of transportation in the black-out or perhaps to escape the proximity of a Nazi higher up on the rampage. It is a byword in Berlin never to be caught as eyewitness and summoned to testify against anyone ranking above the common Nazi trooper.

Terboven reached for the telephone now and then to call telephone numbers he gloatingly described by word and body motion to the drunken men around him. He made dates for the night with all the girls who answered, without bothering to be subtle. Albert, the barman, quietly closed the door leading into the main lobby and went back to sit on his stool behind the bar. He was used to these carousings and could be relied upon to keep his mouth shut. He was almost a legendary figure to Nazi big shots, all of whom knew him from the old days when Albert swung a mighty fist against Communists invading his bar to tackle the Nazis in their lair.

But Albert was getting old, prematurely old, a victim of four years in the trenches of World War I and dying by inches from a gassed lung and aching wound in his right leg. Hitler never came to the bar but frequently he'd send for Albert to talk about the trenches and the wounds. It was Albert who arranged and supervised many a Nazi cocktail party or had charge of the drinks to be served at their private dinners. He was, on the whole, a part of the Nazi party, and he knew them like a book.

But Albert had his likes and dislikes. He wasn't very keen about the S.S. or troopers from its ranks who came in there to act big and drink beer. He detested Terboven, who always made trouble and never paid or tipped. He was being particularly obnoxious tonight, and Albert kept one eye on the clock. At 11 P.M. he would have the right and obligation to close the bar in accordance with strict police regulations.

Terboven called for more champagne and for cigarettes. Albert wearily supplied both, at the same time drawing attention to the fact that in ten minutes he'd have to close up and ask them to leave. They laughed and shouted uproariously, demanding to know who would put them out. Albert reminded them in his soft-spoken way of the police hour and pointed to the Nazi-party sign on the bar mirror urging its members to set an example by respecting the official closing hour. Somebody, Terboven or one of the S.S., hurled a full bottle of champagne and scored a bull's-eye on the mirror. Glass and sign came crashing down, in addition to a number of bottles on the counter below.

Albert looked over at the damage behind his bar. He turned to Terboven, whose eyeballs were protruding and staring balefully at the barman by now, and said: *"Es geht zu weit. Ja, meine Herren,* this goes too far. I am obligated to call the manager. I cannot take any responsibility for this or for your refusal to leave at closing time."

Terboven, not a very tall man and heavy-set, suddenly came from behind that table like a flash. He displayed surprising agility, and before Albert could even move a step back, he went down on the polished floor at a blow from Terboven's hamlike fist. The five S.S. drunks rose like one and pummeled the man on the floor, while Terboven added hefty kicks with his boot. They took the champagne ice pails and emptied them on Albert, commanding him to get up and bring more champagne. Then they went back to their table, cursing him and telling each other in vociferous language that this was only a sample of what would happen to the Norwegians if any of them as much as let out a peep. They banged on the table and howled for champagne.

Drops of blood marked Albert's painful stagger across the room. He leaned on the bar for support and with an effort telephoned on the house instrument to the manager. He never finished, for Terboven and the five others were on him like men gone berserk. They dragged him from behind the bar and struck resounding blows. They trampled all over him, shouting and yelling, Terboven loudest of all. Then they rolled him down the small flight of stairs leading out into the hall, shoved him out through the door, and slammed it shut. Then they took over the bar.

The manager came in time to stare aghast at the bleeding and suffering barman, who was crawling through the hall. He helped him to his feet but had to summon the night porter to lend a hand in carting Albert upstairs. The doctor was summoned, and afterward the manager went downstairs to make sure everything would be hushed up. He was white as a sheet and trembling. He paced up and down the hall for hours, until at last Terboven and his crowd staggered out of the bar and up to their rooms. They'd obviously forgotten about the barman and went to bed singing and howling. Next day, still showing signs of the night's dissipation, they drove away to the airfield with much formal saluting and clicking of heels for the ride to Oslo.

Albert was a Bavarian of peasant stock and not easy to kill. He showed up behind the bar a few days later, against the doctor's advice and obviously a sick man. He was silent and boiling with fury. Nobody dared say anything, the hotel manager least of all. Albert told the whole story to one of his very closest friends, who insisted that Albert see Hitler about it. But Albert never did, or didn't have time to, for five days after he came back to the bar he was dead. The kicks and blows had added the final touch of pain and misery to the war veteran's wounds and in the middle of the night snapped out his life. He was mourned by the Nazis in grand style, all of whom sent wreaths to the funeral and drank a farewell toast at his bar. They said he died of war wounds, as old veterans do, and hoped his spirit would go marching on with the many who died for the Fatherland. Nobody mentioned Terboven, or if some one of us in on the know had slyly asked the hotel manager about Terboven and Albert, he would have got a scared look and blank face. For in Naziland it is poison to know too much, or to know anything about the headmen around Hitler and their past, all of whom have skeletons in the closet and who at one time or another have sold their soul. Otherwise, you don't serve Hitler well.

For instance, there is Arthur Seyss-Inquart, the be-spectacled Hitler viceroy of Holland, whose wooden leg causes a limp on parade and at reviews, but it does give a wonderful crack of heels to the salute. His blond hair occasionally slips down over his brow when he removes too suddenly the S.S. cap with its death-head insignia, giv-ing him at a distance the aspect of the student and in-tellectual. He may be, although long ago he sold his soul to Hitler for material gain and earthly power. Seyss-Inquart is an unpopular man, a renegade from Sudetenland who fled from Czech rule to Austria and eventually became there the maggot in the apple. He traded on the friendship and confidence of others, worming himself with especial care into the bosom of the trusting Kurt von Schuschnigg, last Chancellor of Austria. There were many inside Austria in the hectic days before the Anschluss who were distrustful of Seyss-Inquart, openly giving vent to opinions that he was a Hitler agent. But Seyss-Inquart worked hard to disprove all rumor mongers, shoving himself always into the thick of the political battles on Schuschnigg's side and damning the Nazis as traitors and madmen. He conferred with the leading Jews in Vienna and urged them to pass the word among their people that he, Seyss-Inquart, was not their enemy or even remotely a Hitler ally.

One day, when the political volcano was boiling dangerously near the end of 1937, Schuschnigg decided to take energetic action by forming a Staatsrat endowed with special powers, with himself presiding. That was tantamount to the formation of a powerful junta and it was bound to draw criticism, but Hitler's shadow was lengthening over Austria and hard-striking counteraction was needed if Austria was not going to fall into Nazi laps through revolution and conflict within itself. The primary things expected by Schuschnigg of those men selected for the Staatsrat were courage and unstinting loyalty, otherwise the catastrophe was bound to come. He selected his most trusted followers, Seyss-Inquart among them. He summoned the first meet-

ing in the cabinet room of his chancellery on the Ballhaus-
platz, where Dollfuss was killed by Nazi gunmen, and
solemnly swore in each man on an ancient Bible kept there
for such vital occasions. They sat around the table then
under the chandelier of cut glass and listened carefully as
Schuschnigg outlined the grave task ahead. He spoke not
only in a general way but turned to each of them for emphasis on the particular responsibility he must assume un-
flinchingly on his shoulders.

All were agreed and clear on their duties by the time the
first sitting was over. But just as they rose to disperse to
their offices, Seyss-Inquart came to his feet and requested
a moment's attention. A little silence fell around the table,
although Schuschnigg may not have noticed it. He nodded
to Seyss-Inquart to go ahead.

A Schuschnigg minister, now living in enforced retirement in Tyrol, told me the story. Seyss-Inquart glanced
slowly around that table and sought the eyes of each man.
Obviously he wanted to be listened to in dead earnest, and
he reached over to lay his clenched hand on the sacred
Bible.

"There is some talk going around that I am in sympathy
with the Nazis or even in touch with Hitler," he said
slowly, and looked straight at Schuschnigg. "Herr Chancellor, and men of the Staatsrat, I wish here, before all,
with my right hand on the Bible, to swear to you that I
shall never cease in the struggle against Hitler and his
Nazis, or against those working with him and for him. I
give my word of honor and my oath that I shall loy-

ally work with and stand by our Chancellor and Austria. I am not one to stand in your midst like a Judas and betray you. I am not here as a Hitler agent or Nazi sympathizer. I stand here as one of you and shall never be anything or do anything other than to work for independence and security of Austria."

It was a masterly gesture and carried the day. They shook his hands and forgot their previous doubts. For weeks after they had no occasion to doubt his sincerity. Then, in little ways, he gave grounds for suspicion again. But Schuschnigg retained his faith in him and probably got the shock of his life when Hitler, at the historic meeting of February in Berchtesgaden, laid down a demand that Seyss-Inquart be appointed to a key position in the cabinet, something which had been deftly avoided up to then in order to avert open friction in the ranks. What Hitler wanted was control of the Austrian police and inner situation, which he got by compelling Schuschnigg to appoint Seyss-Inquart Minister of the Interior. The cat was out of the bag and Seyss-Inquart's first official act was to amnesty all Nazi prisoners. A month later, on March 12, Schuschnigg was Hitler's prisoner, and as the German Army marched triumphantly into Vienna amid the clang and clamor of Nazi celebrating Seyss-Inquart proudly donned his S.S. uniform as Gruppenfuehrer and welcomed Hitler to the capital he had conquered for him without firing a shot. He had conquered it by treachery, by what we nowadays call fifth-column work, and the reward was an embrace from Hitler plus the power to rule the land for the moment. This was really a great milestone in Seyss-Inquart's life, and it helped immensely to prepare and harden him for the august job of Reich's Commissar of the Netherlands. He was sure he could beat the marble-headed Dutch into line for his Fuehrer.

It is not his fault that enthusiasm and the spirit of cooperation in the New Order of Europe are dismally lacking in Holland, despite two years of guidance and coaching from Seyss-Inquart. He went there, as I remember him telling us in Berlin sometime ago, determined to win the good will of the Dutch and show them the great future ahead of Holland under the Fuehrer of Naziland. He tried to treat them like friends and accept them as brothers, never once intending to interfere with their own national customs or standards of life. Anyway, that's what he said, although the Dutch tell us the opposite. They say he did try that system of making friends, but friendship for the price of your soul. You were invited to his house as an influential Dutchman and expected to leave in a blaze of good fellowship but sworn to work hand in glove with the Nazis. Seyss-Inquart, in other words, tried to swing Holland to Hitler's side by fifth-column methods and devices, the only method he is adept at. When that failed, he showed his teeth and soon enough the S.S. and Gestapo were hard at work slamming Dutch heads and making them feel the steel-tipped whip of Hitler's New Order. Today there are ration cards with just enough bad food to keep from starving; there are death sentences for the slightest offense and staggering money penalties on whole communities on the least provocation.

The Dutch newspapers, once so flourishing and powerful, have been reduced to official Nazi-supervised sheets, allowed to live in skeleton form but stripped of all real news. The hand of Seyss-Inquart, who sold his soul for this job, is everywhere, and woe to him who crosses his will. He is indeed one of Hitler's *best* Europeans.

His task as viceroy is, of course, more complex in many respects than that of a man like Hans Frank, Nazi governor of Poland. The difference is that Frank can use more direct means, in a country sealed off from the world, to rub out Poles and Jews by the thousands without anyone being the wiser. Hunger and the machine gun can solve problems with amazing rapidity. Every Pole by heredity and nature hates the German, and any Pole alive is and always will be the deadly foe of every German, so why take chances and encourage an increasing birth rate or long life among the Poles? You can hardly expect a man like Frank to see reason in that. If he did, Hitler wouldn't, and tough little Frank is not the man to cross Hitler for the sake of a Pole or a Jew.

Bald-headed and short in build, Frank comes from the legal profession and as a Nazi saw his chance to march into high places in the German machinery of justice. The conquest of Poland and Frank's subsequent appointment as Hitler's viceroy there gave him quite an opportunity to demonstrate the Nazi wisdom of ruling a beaten foe with fairness and justice, but that didn't fool the Poles for a moment. Frank set up his capital in Cracow, instead of shell- and bomb-wrecked Warsaw, and went to work trans-

forming the country into a real adjunct of Hitler's Reich.
He holds forth like the Polish kings of old, and his word is
law. He is boastfully proud of himself, a stickler for court
etiquette, and quick to resent a slight.

Frank will not go back to Warsaw nowadays to take
part in any official ceremonies, unless Hitler is present. All
because he went there for a spring parade of the army in
1941 and found himself up against something he hadn't
looked for. Reeking a bit from the few drinks he had had
during the morning after a light breakfast of ham, sausage,
potatoes, eggs, and coffee—all supplied by the state—Frank
climbed into his huge black Mercedes car and drove with
the air of a Roman conqueror past the Warsaw ruins to the
broad street where the parade was to take place. He stood
up in the car after it drew up at the platform where he was
to stand and for a full minute responded with a Nazi salute
to the volume of *Sieg Heils* coming from the massed Nazi
cordons of S.S. and S.A. troops imported for such occasions.
He was, after all, the unquestioned lord of the land.

We foreign correspondents elbowed forward a bit to get
a better look. Frank snapped his heels to the commanding
general who was to take the review—I believe it was Blaskovitz—and got the routine military salute in return plus an
obvious cold shoulder. The general stood squarely in the
center of the reviewing platform, gazing out over the
crowd, his back to Frank. To anyone watching from the
side lines, the general might as well have shouted at the top
of his voice: "Herr Frank, you are governor but I am
military commander here. I am reviewing the German

Army today, not a bunch of marching Nazi-party hacks. Stand around, if you must, but don't get in my way or too far forward."

I said Blaskovitz might as well have shouted that out loud, but of course he didn't. He merely stood there like a ramrod and raised a monocle to his eye with fine Prussian dignity as the crashing military band came goose-stepping with resounding whacks toward the grandstand and swung aside to play an infantry regiment past. Frank glowered and moved forward to the general's side, his right arm extended in stiff Nazi salute. The general turned ever so slightly, very correctly but firmly waving him a step back, and we could see that he objected to the outstretched hand as interfering with his own military salute.

Frank's face, through our binoculars thirty yards off, was something to see. It was purple and puffed. He appeared to be breathing with difficulty. He swayed a little, sticking his saluting arm very close to the general's shoulder. He could easily have slapped him, but Nazis never slap a general. Once, as the tanks rolled by, the general said something else over his shoulder to Frank, and the Nazi governor's heavy lips moved in reply. The baleful glance he bestowed sideways on the military man revealed enough to know that there had been no compromise, and that the old feud between the German High Command and the Nazi party had not diminished. When the parade was over, Frank briefly extended his arm and without shaking hands, as is customary, walked out on the general. Blaskovitz was very busy talking to officers of his own army who'd come up and conveniently forgot to see the governor of Poland enter his waiting limousine and drive off. There are moments like that in Naziland.

But Frank, on the whole, does well by himself as governor of Poland. Ironically enough, there is said to be more graft and corruption among the S.S. and German administrative groups in his Government General than anywhere else, chiefly due to the millions of Jews from whom money can be extracted in return for the privilege of living a little longer. Yet that can hardly be held against Frank, who delights in inviting foreign correspondents to Cracow for a personal look at the fine job he is doing. He makes a real effort to be convincing, loading the program with important banquets, speeches, teas, and inspection tours. In Cracow, after these exhausting swings through model parts of Nazi Poland, there is a fine hotel to rest up in and the bar is specially equipped to handle official visitors. At night you can find Frank and his immediate assistants there ready to liven up the atmosphere and prove to anyone that they can drink them under the table with slibovitz, cognac, schnapps, or champagne.

The credit for putting these boastful Nazis in their place late last year goes to Alex Small and Charley Lanius, the former an ace correspondent of many years' standing for the Chicago *Tribune* and the latter an N.B.C. man who worked in Berlin. Small and Lanius went down to Cracow on assignment and after the trip was over bumped into Frank, as usual, at the bar of that hotel. The governor, surrounded by three or four henchmen, loudly informed everybody what good fellows these Americans are even if they play with the English. *Ach*, if they could be men as strong as himself and drink all night, there would be more respect for the Americans and maybe they would have to be taken seriously in this war.

The challenge was too obvious and the battle began, as always with much boasting on the part of the Nazis. They had no idea that Small and Lanius had braved many years of hardfisted living in Paris, where visiting firemen from home came in droves before the war expecting to be entertained and shown the sights. You had to evolve a knack of your own and a castiron stomach to boot to live and keep on working.

In Cracow, therefore, the two Americans remembered the Seine and hour after hour stuck to their task. There were small intermissions, and some interruptions when Frank's formerly loudmouthed assistants were dragged or carried off to bed, but Frank carried on and tried to keep a sensible conversation going. Long after midnight he quit waving the bottle and yelling for more, but in the end consented to be led off to his castle with weaving dignity by men of his bodyguard. They didn't like the Americans, and probably figured they were spies who'd gotten the governor drunk. But such is life in Naziland, and among Hitler's viceroys who are creating the New Europe for him.

2

In a sort of class by himself, aloof with the reticence of the native Balt from the shores of the Finnish Gulf, sits

Alfred Rosenberg as the latest of Hitler's appointed viceroys. He plotted and waited longest for his reward, drawing
in the end the biggest slice of all. Soviet Russia, if ever patterned to the Nazi blueprint as dreamed of by Hitler and
Rosenberg far back in 1923, will be then a Nationalist
Russia all the way down from the White Sea along the Ural
Mountains through the Caucasus. He would rule the colos-
sal stretches with an iron hand, inaugurating again the
feudal system of serfs producing and laboring for the
master in Berlin but with never a thought of independent
sovereignty. Rosenberg believes vast Russia and its peasant masses are admirably suited for that sort of robot existence.

I know he worked hard and waited patiently for this
kingdom of his own, nursing all the grievances and fanatic
hatreds against Russia and the Communists cradled in dis-
appointments as far back as his student days in Moscow
before World War I. He sat out the war in Paris and col-
laborated with the then unknown Hitler in Munich as early
as 1921 in the drafting of the weird Nazi political program,
which includes the twenty-five points. When Hitler went
to Landsberg prison for three years, after the abortive 1923
Munich putsch, Rosenberg substituted for him and kept the
Nazi party alive, filling in the weightier parts of *Mein
Kampf* with screaming theories on Nordics and Weltanschauung. He particularly implanted in Hitler's mind and
book the outspoken hatred against all things Polish or Russian and committed the Nazis to the destruction of both.
He organized the anti-Comintern crusade and swore he'd sit

in Moscow someday as lord and master over a Nationalist Russia.

I used to go over to his offices frequently in 1934 and 1935, when Karl Boemer was his press attaché and grooming him for the moment when he should be called on by Hitler and events to take over a post of official rank such as the Foreign Ministry or of Propaganda and Culture. Those ideas went down the river, but Rosenberg remained a busy man behind the scenes in his blue-carpeted office in Berlin's Margaretenstrasse, spinning his counterweb to the Moscow Comintern and conducting the Nazification campaign of youth and German mind. That brought him into conflict with the Church and Christianity as a whole, but never fazed him. He wrote ponderous volumes which brought charges of paganism against him from the four corners of the earth and kept alive in Nazi hearts the will to eradicate the Jews in all Europe.

Rosenberg, strange to say, is almost of the same impersonal nature as Hitler and is one of the few Nazis who trade on simplicity. He wears only the undecorated brown Nazi uniform, drinks sparingly, eats plain food, and lives in a modest villa in the Berlin suburb of Dahlen. His wife is very much a hausfrau, scarcely ever showing up at Nazi or other public functions. There is one daughter, with pigtails. The Rosenbergs never entertain, and he has only his official car. He is soft-spoken, slow of thought, a bad speaker, and reticent to strangers.

His offices in Margaretenstrasse did not change or enlarge until 1941, when he took over a larger building up on the

Knie, to accommodate himself to the new demands on him as dictator of conquered parts in Russia. His chief aides were and are today exclusively Baltic men, tricky and smooth as oil. They talk almost better Russian than German and know the Russians like a book.

On the fourth floor of his offices, in a series of rooms overlooking an inner courtyard, stood an intricate number of powerful radio receiving and sending instruments. Blond young men of Baltic faces sat there day and night listening to every wave carrying Russian words or of Russian origin, unless they themselves were busy sending forth into space thousands of words in Russian aimed for the ears of Soviet masses. Mysterious code messages were picked up and sent by the dozen, for here was the closely guarded and secret Nazi spiderwork of anti-Moscow activity organized by Rosenberg and his young Balts for the eventual overthrow of the Communist regime in Russia.

Busy men sat in adjoining offices with detailed maps of Russian regions on the wall, all marked down in varied colors and specified by pins. These men were directing the underground Nazi activity inside Russia, and the pins represented agents. On the second floor, where Rosenberg sat, you could find maps and blueprints depicting the outline of a future Nationalist Russia. He never let visitors see those. He was wary of foreigners, anyway, and always received them in his study-like office in the presence of Boemer or another of his attachés. He liked to be left alone.

In the eyes of the German public he was less the brains of the Nazi anti-Comintern than the man who promoted and preached Nazism in every form of daily life and activity on the part of the Aryan German. In Catholic regions he was hated more and more because of his pagan crusade and the fact that his evil gospels were drawing the children away from home and Sunday school into Hitler Youth camps with all their anti-Christian programs.

"*Unser Papst!*" some thousands of children, Hitler youths of from ten to fifteen years of age, hailed him in wild enthusiasm as a bunch of us arrived in one of these summer camps with him. "*Heil* Rosenberg, our pope! *Heil! Heil!*" It was a shock to us from outside Germany, but there was no mistaking the teachings and tendencies in those Hitler Youth camps.

I asked some of the boys there later why they hailed Rosenberg as their pope. They replied that he, like the Fuehrer, was their true spiritual leader devoted to and serving the Fatherland, instead of a foreign despot (so the children said) across the frontiers who compelled them to go to Mass and sit through long and weary sermons, thereafter reading (again the children) dull and familiar quotations from the Bible which didn't say the same thing as was told them by their own eighteen-year-old leaders out on picnics and in school assemblies. Only Germans could tell Germans how to live in the Fatherland and grow up to serve it. The Pope in Rome and the priests in the church didn't care about the Fatherland, only about their church. So the boys and the girls welcomed the idea of their own German pope, and who else could it be but Reichsleiter Rosenberg? They were fanatical about that, and if parents at home objected, they could be disregarded because the Hitler Youth leaders told them that loyalty to the Fatherland comes before all, even before church and parents.

I drove with Rosenberg to the Catholic Rhineland one summer on one of his customary tours. I thought it would give me a good opportunity to watch him work at close range and at the same time establish a lot of useful contacts in Rhineland cities. Such contacts could always come in handy, in addition to which the Nazis in Berlin would notice that I was intimate with a big shot and consequently many of them would give me ready ear and therewith tips or information leading to good exclusive stories for New York.

The trip brought me a never-forgotten inside look on the widespread and healthy opposition within Germany to Rosenberg's paganistic and anti-Christian activity and re-assurance that the Nazis must live long before they can re-place any faith with their so-called National Church of Nazi-fed propaganda rituals. The climax came near the famous Dreieck, where the Mosel and the Rhine meet at the foot of the huge Kaiser memorial beyond Coblenz. Here, on a plateau overlooking the beautiful countryside, Rosen-berg was scheduled on a Sunday afternoon during that tour to address some 10,000 gathered from around that vicinity.

He drove up there in the customary Nazi style, preceded by Hitler Youth bands and between brown-shirted cor-dons. But on the plateau, instead of 10,000 heiling throats lined up for him and a welcoming committee of the local

Gauleiter and henchmen, there was nothing and nobody except a decorated grandstand and swastikas lining an empty field. There was consternation in the Rosenberg ranks and I saw a rare red color slowly creeping up over his face, betraying a gathering fury as he guessed the cause of his predicament.

I saw his customary Baltic quiet fade out in a storm of indignant outbursts and adjutants were sent posthaste to Coblenz Gestapo and Nazi-party headquarters. The Gauleiter and half-a-dozen others of high rank, such as the burgomaster of Coblenz, were speedily arrested, despite all protestations that there had been a mistake. They said that Rosenberg, according to their understanding, was to talk at 9 P.M. that evening. Consequently, they had informed the public to march up to the plateau between seven and nine that night.

Rosenberg waived this explanation aside and charged the Nazi Gauleiter with sabotage. Indeed, he made a point of the fact that all concerned with program arrangements were Catholics. I don't know just how innocent or guilty the Gauleiter and his aides were in making that mistake, but I do know that for months afterward one heard whispers and underhand chuckling about the incident in the Rhineland as far as Berlin. Officially, of course, everything was hushed up, as are all such things in Naziland.

Thus, Soviet Russia will get a very thorough and fanatical taskmaster if it is changed perforce into Nationalist Russia. For Rosenberg and his young men work smoothly, persistently, and efficiently. Long experience and many setbacks in the Reich taught them never to take no for an answer, and they don't.

3

A meeker and almost mouselike type is the little man Gustaf Simon sent into Luxemburg by Hitler as his viceroy. Simon was Gauleiter of Trier and is a fanatical Nazi with a mustache like his Fuehrer's. He'd pass for a stockroom clerk and always has a soupbowl haircut but just now he is lording it over 300,000 very independent-minded Luxemburgers. He took their army of two hundred and fifty men and sent them over to Strasburg for training and incorporation into the German police. That chiefly to rob the Luxemburgers of any chance of resistance. The schools he turned into German-language schools and the whole status of the land into part and parcel of the Third Reich. He kicked out the whole administration of the valuable iron mines and replaced it with Germans, whose eyes have been on that highly concentrated iron ore for decades.

"The Grand Duchess fled to America with pockets full of her people's money and a bad conscience," he said to me at a gathering where I had the chance of sizing him up. "The Luxemburgers are glad to be rid of her and the whole French-subsidized system. They are happy to work and be part of the Reich they originally belonged to."

I had several talks with Luxemburgers after the Nazi occupation and annexation. They are a hardheaded peasant nation, small as it is, and will never submit to a foreign yoke. "There is practically a price on Simon's head," the Luxemburgers told me. "And any Luxemburger caught fraternizing with Germans is ostracized and usually gets a bad beating. Girls who slip get a haircut. The hatred is intense, and no farmer strains himself to produce a big crop. It would be unpatriotic. The Grand Duchess is cheered at subversive meetings and nobody for one moment swallows the Nazi propaganda against her or the sugaring over of the annexation."

So much for the Gauleiter from Trier, who is a Hitler viceroy and as such must be regarded as one of the Fuehrer's *best* Europeans. They are all working hard to shape his New Order in Europe, young blood and bold men sent to replace the old graybeards of whom Hitler spoke so disdainfully up in the castle above Nuremberg. There are some others not included here, but all rule with an iron hand and are responsible only to Hitler. He places Europe in their lap, knowing they'll do the job as he wants it done and confident that when the war is over, he will hold the scepter as the Fuehrer of all Europe, aided and idolized by the viceroys he created from the *best* Europeans.

CHAPTER 8

Italy Becomes a German Province

An italian of important position in Berlin came back by air in the fall of 1941 after an extended business trip and visit with relatives in Italy.

Volatile of temperament and proud by nature, he seemed like a changed man when I saw him that night a few hours after arrival. The gray-flecked hair was more disheveled than usual; his monocle wouldn't stay in place, and the spaghetti bolognese he loved so well elicited none of the usual enthusiasm. He drank only a liter of the good chianti I had ordered and morosely ate his share of the native Bel Paese he had brought from home.

I looked around the restaurant and noted that the coast was clear. There were no listening ears or lip-reading eyes within sight of that corner table, so I decided that other things must be weighing on the mind of my Italian friend.

It might be girl trouble, as all bachelors have from time to time, although that could scarcely be the cause for such real gloom. I touched my glass to his and drank a long, sweet pull of the deep red juice from the hills and vineyards of Italy.

"Cheer up, my friend, it can't be as bad as all that," I said to him, and laughed a bit. "Anyway, you Italians sank most of the British fleet in the Mediterranean today again and the Germans sank another batch of convoys on the Atlantic, so everything is lovely. Think of the fun we're having saying what liars they are."

Sirens shrieked forth another air alarm over Berlin but he paid small attention. He smiled a bit, as all of us did back there whenever the Axis announced its invisible victories at sea with time-clock regularity, and gave a deep sigh.

"It is all so very difficult," he said a bit sadly, with a sip at the chianti.

"I am a good Italian, if not a good Fascist, and I love my country with Roman passion for its seven hills. But what am I to do, to say, to think if I go home to my Italy and find only the Germans important there? I land on the airports of my homeland and I am questioned in German and my papers are examined by Germans.

"In Verona, in Genoa, in Brindisi, it is all the same. They tell me at home it is the same all over Italy."

He stroked back his hair and worried his monocle, noting for the first time that most of the others in the restaurant had gone down to the cellar as heavy anti-aircraft fire outside shook the building to its foundation.

"It cuts to the heart," he added. "The Germans sit on all our important airports on the coasts; they have their guns and their key men in our naval ports, in the fortifications except on the Brenner, and even inside the General Staff.

"At home I was told that my brother telephoned to an important section of the General Staff in Rome to invite a staff major, an old friend of the family, to dinner, and he had to give up and try all over again because he was answered in German. My brother knows only a few little words of German, and in any case he was too indignant to continue the attempt.

"You must realize that for a proud Italian family like ourselves, that was bitter medicine to swallow."

Somewhere near by a couple of bombs of larger caliber must have hit at that moment, for the electric light flickered and for some seconds was out. The house we sat in rocked with the force of an earthquake, rattling glasses and plates, and making me wish for the peaceful campus of the University of Missouri. Beyond the blacked-out windows, the deafening crash of guns continued incessantly, and I knew that a score of searchlights were pointing straight above us fingering the sky for British raiders. If police came in now, we'd get into trouble for sitting there instead of going downstairs in accordance with strict regulations.

We looked at each other and said nothing for a while. The bombs had come down and more than likely that wave above was passing on, so that there was no sense in going to the cellar now. Why bother?

"I heard the same guns in Italy," my Italian friend said

suddenly. "The same German *flak* as you hear outside now.

"They have taken us over, or almost. The officers, friends of mine, get red in the face and scowl when I mention the matter. It is strictly forbidden to talk of it, although on some Sundays and holidays the Germans actually parade in the towns.

"They think we enjoy the brass band and will run or march alongside like they do here in Germany. You see, the Germans will never understand us and we will never understand them. They don't like our ways of doing things and we don't like their manners. It is all so difficult.

"The Germans don't say it but their eyes look down on us. They think we're dirty, and not manly or serious enough. Well, we Italians want none of their Teuton regimentation of life, and in our hearts we hate the blond Germans. There has never been an Italian who got along with a German yet. If Hitler had been German instead of Austrian, Mussolini never would have gotten entangled so deeply with the Nazis."

Gunfire still rumbled in the far north of Berlin but around our part of the city silence had set in. I had a spare bottle of chianti on hand to take care of our thirst for the duration of the air raid, when nothing is available. Fire engines had clanged past in reminder of the close shave we had from that brace of bombs and the occasion was worth celebrating. I poured the chianti to the very brim of our glasses.

"In other words," I said, "you are an occupied country.

Don't tell me the Germans also levy the costs of everything on you, as they do in France and all other occupied places?"

"It amounts to the same thing," he said thoughtfully. "Yes, I am told at home that the Germans pay none of the costs of the upkeep or for the food they eat, except what they import for themselves. It all comes out of the Axis war chest.

"I saw German officers—or railway officials—in places like Verona and Milan, evidently in charge of important sections of our railway system. That may be only temporary, or for the purpose of closely aligning our railway organization to theirs in order to bring about a better functioning for war needs."

I could better understand now the weight on his heart, heavy with the unspoken fear of all Italians that some bright morning they will wake up to discover themselves under complete German occupation instead of the present shadow grip on the land by the Nazis.

That could happen several ways and for several reasons. For example, Mussolini might fall victim to his strained heart or the strange bump on his head or finally die of the assassin's bullet. It would blow the lid off the Italian volcano, precipitating in a violent struggle for supremacy the bitter forces in conflict with each other in Italy.

The House of Savoy and its adherents of the upper ranks would soon raise the cry against the rabid old Fascist group and the Fascist machine with which the Duce now holds the country to the whipping post. But Hitler would move first, if only out of military necessity. German troops and planes would appear like magic in Italy the day Mussolini went down, changing within the space of hours the present shadow occupation to a realistic one in numbers and effect. That, at least, was the setup throughout 1941.

Hitler in his recent talks with Mussolini anticipated yet another possibility. It is the dark shadow of fear also lurking unpleasantly in every Italian mind since the Duce foolishly plunged the country into war. That is the likelihood that the powerful Axis foes—and ever more so since America got into the fray—carry out an invasion threat against the European continent by selecting Italy as the outstanding weak spot and hitting there with the might of a rampant tidal wave.

Sicily and the exposed boot of the comparatively narrow mainland are regarded by the German General Staff as vulnerable to any vast and determined enemy expedition bent on conquest.

High German officers I know feel that in case of attack all of Italy ought to be defended and if possible held, at least in its northern parts, in order to maintain a strong barrier into Europe proper. That means that Italy lives today under an uneasy shadow, haunted by fears of becoming the outermost battlefield of a Europe going to ruin and driven to desperation by the inescapable awareness that Hitler's legions will pour over the land the moment an enemy invasion threatens. That is no cheerful prospect for any country.

I saw this evidence on the faces of Italians both in Germany and in Italy and heard them say it. They are dismayed at this infiltration from across the Brenner; they look with deep concern in their eyes at the long trains loaded with Nazi men or guns filing through their lovely land toward secret rendezvous, and they shake their heads at Mussolini.

In 1936, when I escorted Dorothy Kilgallon from the zeppelin in Friedrichshafen to Rome on her race around the world, Italians were definitely against the Duce's line-up with Hitler. They sat in the cafés and the *ristorantes* of Rome and glanced darkly at the German tourists living on cheap lire on the fat of the land.

Down in Abazzia, lovely watering resort of the former Austrian emperors when that coast was still part of the Austro-Hungarian Empire, I saw it come to fisticuffs in a bank where the clerks had orders not to accept German marks.

This conflict of temperaments and human nature came even more to the surface in another form when the Nazi Fuehrer paid a spectacular visit to Italy in 1938. In annexed Italian Tyrol the Germans there rushed to the railway stations to cheer Hitler and shout their displeasure at the Italians; the Italian police in turn arrested hundreds of them and forbade private display of the swastika flag. It was pretty embarrassing to the Fuehrer, and none of us foreign correspondents accompanying the official party courted open trouble by smiling out loud.

In Rome, in Naples, and in Florence the people in shop and office were marched out by the thousands to cheer the visitor in unison with the trained chorus of the Fascist party troops, but time and again Mussolini had to break into the monotonous chant of "Duce, Duce, Duce, Duce!" to point at Hitler and shout: "*Heil* Hitler!"

Then for a few moments my ears made out the clipped reply of the mob: " 'itl-a-i-r, 'itl-a-i-r!" and back again would come the Fascist chant.

Italy by and large didn't care for Hitler, and made him feel it. The only spark of spontaneity came in Florence on his last day of the visit, when he announced from the balcony that South Tyrol, acquired by Italy as spoils of war in 1919, was henceforth permanently written off by him in his book of claims.

They cheered a bit, then, while I was thinking of my interview with him in 1936, when he announced after the Saar had voted its return to the Fatherland that henceforth he had written off in his book of claims all further territorial demands on France. Yet he is master of Alsace-Lorraine today.

2

"I envy you Americans," the chief correspondent for one of the big Tokyo papers said out of a clear sky one night in the Kaiserhof Hotel, where he had his apartment and working office.

Some of us had been invited there for an evening of real Japanese food. They placed an open-flame oil stove on the table and after the fat in the deep iron bowl was sizzling hot, dipped oysters bathed in bread-sauce into it for some seconds. They put a large oyster on your plate and followed the process rapidly with other helpings of oyster, finely cut pieces of steak, or square-cut carrots, all accompanied by big helpings of rice.

All of this, of course, came out of the Japanese Embassy larder and so we had no compunction about eating off the Japs. Their orders were, of course, to get all the information and opinion possible out of us, for they got very little change out of the Germans.

"Yes, I really envy you Americans," the Tokyo man repeated. "You act here and go around almost with the same air as your men in Washington. You can send dispatches which tell something, instead of the cut-and-dried form we have to adhere to."

He glanced a little hesitantly at his countrymen, busy in keeping us eating and showing us how to use the soybean sauce to best advantage. He found what he was looking for, a silent consent that what was said here would not go further.

"Well, I mean that we are just rubber stamps, sending to Tokyo what the Nazis consider the right thing for our people to read and hear.

"Yet they are Europeans, these Nazis. They least of all are qualified to understand us. If I had my way, I'd go back home today, if only to get away from the Nazis and their attitude of infallibility.

"We try to adjust their communiqués to the Japanese way of looking at the world, but it is difficult. Perhaps that explains why our competing newspaper in Tokyo, the *Yomiuri*, day in and day out prints I.N.S. dispatches out of Berlin over its best pages.

"They get a lot of information across that way which Japanese agencies and correspondents cannot touch, and have built up a tremendous circulation. People read your stuff because they know there is something in it, and if *Yomiuri* gets in a jam, it can blame it on you. That is permissible in Japan."

I remember the long face, too, of Kurusu when he signed the Three-Power Pact in Hitler's chancellery in Berlin in September 1940. He scarcely glanced at Hitler or Ribbentrop through that long and weary ceremony of klieg lights and speeches in the overdecorated reception chamber.

We correspondents were hot and uncomfortable; Kurusu was in a state of mental gloom and affixed his signature mechanically. When Hitler finally arose he shook hands perfunctorily with Kurusu, probably sensing the man's state of mind.

Two months later Kurusu was out as Japanese Ambassador in Berlin and the Yankee-hater General Oshima was back in the saddle.

From that day on, Hitler's plot to jump Japan on us and declare an Axis war against America got under way. Kurusu and his American wife and Americanized daughters left Berlin without drums or trumpets. Except, of course, that again the official nicety and sugar-coating for the public benefit came out on top, making everything look as though Kurusu and the switch to Oshima were in no way reflective of the clashing opinions and emotions below the surface.

The Axis, moving into its war against Soviet Russia, characteristically strove at once to give the appearance not only of its own solidarity but of a unified crusade developing under Axis leadership throughout Europe against the common foe in Moscow.

The Axis got away with that for a while, roping in volunteer troops from many nations in Europe, but after the first few months this spontaneous and artificial enthusiasm died down. The war in Russia narrowed down again to what it really is: the battle for survival and supremacy between Hitler and Stalin. All else is secondary.

Axis propaganda still tries hard to varnish over this fact, but few are fooled, either in Italy or in Germany. Least of all in Germany, where letters from officers and men at the front came in with some startlingly plain language toward the end of last October.

Anybody reading those letters could see that the military censors got a wink from high up and got tired of reading and scrutinizing every line from men on the east front. As long as none of this could be published, I heard it said in important Berlin quarters, it was a good safety valve to let the folks at home have some real eye openers once in a while from their menfolk at the front.

I recall the letter in part received by a chic little friend of mine in Berlin from an older brother near Kharkov. He was major in command of a sector around that vital point and had fought his way through many a nasty battle since the beginning of the Russo-German War. Of good family and an officer by profession, he cared not at all for the devious ways of politics. Many a time I heard him rave against the trappings and pageantry of Nazi showmanship or the glamour they threw around foreign visitors and alliances.

His letter, this time, was filled with the hardships of life in Russia; of the dirt and hunger and physical weariness of campaigns they fought in endless territorial spaces, and his greatest grievance was against the Italian troops sent as a grand gesture of Axis co-operation and solidarity by Mussolini.

The bulk of these troops, it appeared, had been assigned to take over and mop up the Kharkov area after its conquest by the Germans. I had seen glowing accounts in the German press of Italian bravery in the face of overwhelming odds, but you get skeptical after the first few years in Naziland. The major's letter justified my suspicion.

"We have had trouble on our hands ever since these Italians with the plumes on their tin helmets came here," the major's letter said.

"*Es sind Hampelmaenner, keine Soldaten.* [Punks they are, not soldiers.] They strut around like peacocks when the sun shines and there is no Russian within miles, but run like mad when a Red plane or any plane comes over. They go around catching and eating all the livestock in sight or whatever they can grab or steal from the villages.

"In the last days we have had more trouble with them. The Russians got through some woods into the villages behind us and at night began raiding the villages, which happened to be held by the Italians. They caught some pretty bad medicine and lost quite a few men before they knew what hit them.

"Now they won't stay in these villages and fight. They are scared stiff, of course, but their officers claim the villages have epidemic and must be evacuated. I have had to sit in on a disciplinary court today to clear up charges by Italian officers that batches of our men have been waylaying Italian soldiers and beating them up in the dark. I don't blame our fellows, who can't stand the scented punks anyway. We keep them apart as much as possible, but everything is so difficult."

That and much more an illuminating glimpse at the real thing behind the polished exterior of the Axis.

It fitted the striking picture of friction and restrained hatreds between Italian and German and vice versa I bumped into in Greece during May of 1941, when I followed the German Army into Athens for its parade there. Arriving in Larissa at 1 A.M., after a grueling drive in heat and dust over the hairpin passes from Salonika, Boemer, Lochner, and I proceeded to the Kommandatur.

It was the only house still intact in that thrice-bombed city, ravaged six months before by a devastating earthquake, and had served also as headquarters for the British Expeditionary Force in Greece.

Boemer had the guard rouse the officers in charge and, as he anticipated, we were promptly invited to stay the night, with apologies for the accommodations, which consisted of a kitchen table and a floor to sleep on.

But there were whole piles of captured tins of English bully beef in a corner of the room, hard but nourishing English army biscuits, scores of bottles of French cognac, Cheshire cheese, and finally eggs from the hens out in the back yard.

It happened to be my birthday, whereupon the German officers lit six candles, and the feast developed into a birthday celebration lasting until 4 A.M. The grain depots a block away caught fire—the Germans said it must have been sabotage—and as the municipal water mains were not functioning, German soldiers were set to work dynamiting the buildings between us and the leaping flames. That all added spectacular fireworks and the resounding crash of explosions and collapsing walls to my birthday celebration. In any case, the German officers in that cracked room of ours were in jovial mood. Laughingly, they told us the reason for it.

"It's the Italians, the fancy little men from over there in Italy," one of the captains chortled, and passed around another bottle of Courvoisier.

"They couldn't get the Greeks down, and when we finally come around and compel them to capitulate, the Italians haven't got an inch of Greek soil to point to.

"*Ach*, and now Mussolini rushes around to pull strings in Berlin and wants to be first to march into Athens. He thinks, I suppose, it will restore his smashed military prestige. So he got Berlin to authorize the transfer through here of a motorized division of his Alpinieri.

"They came in here a couple of days ago hell-bent for

Athens, plumes waving and high officers with terrifically decorated uniforms who'd never heard a shot fired. They had all sorts of impressive documents to get a clear road through to Athens from us.

"*Ja,* we had orders also to give them a clear road"—and here all the officers burst into hearty laughter—"but our real orders were under no circumstances to let those Italians get through to Athens until we are in. *Ach,* it was wonderful.

"We cleared the road of our troops over all the passes from here to Lamia and sent an escorting major along with the Italian officers in the biggest car we could find. We even put an important-sounding horn on the car.

"All went well for ten miles right up to the big pass out of here, but unfortunately there had been an accident or something, and the road from the big curve onward was blocked by a rock slide which wrecked a couple of our heavy old trucks right in the worst spot. We worked hard, but late in the afternoon the Italians decided to come back to Larissa for the night.

"The next day they got held up in another pass, and somehow their petrol supply trucks failed to catch up. We did everything we could to make them feel better and be comfortable and forget the vexing delays, and even showed them our war film under the trees that night.

"Yesterday they finally got going, and they should be in Athens by tomorrow for the parade. We marched in today, you know, and you will be in Athens in plenty of time yourself. You will probably meet the Italians going in. We sit here and laugh, and I guess all our officer corps in the southeast have heard about it now and will be delighted. We cannot stand these Italians."

In Athens I saw German officers and men laughing behind the palms of their hands or inside the cafés when Greeks chased promenading Italian soldiers up and down the avenues in those first days of the occupation. That has changed now, but in those May days the German in Athens was tops and the Italian the despised and hated rear end of the Axis troops in the southeast.

All of which, as I said, is beneath the surface and never comes to the light of day in official attitudes or public expressions. There the pot boils one way, and if the air gets pretty thick underneath or new moves are in the offing, then Hitler and Mussolini can always meet with a grand display of solidarity and throw fresh dust into the eyes of those who would look beyond the outer framework. They set the drums beating and the wheels of the Axis propaganda machinery to turning faster, waving fists at the world and telling each other how good they are.

One thing seems sure: As long as Mussolini sits on the Rome end of the Axis, Hitler will play the game that way, instead of dropping the farcical comedy and calling a spade a spade.

For the sake of an example for others to follow, Hitler is eager to create an impression that the Fuehrer's friendship is golden and inviolable; that he stands by those who have proven trustworthy and deserving, and that he shares burdens and triumphs alike with those who march with him.

Mussolini is the Fuehrer's pet example and display window in that respect, although of course everybody is keenly aware that the Duce by now has no other choice.

He comes to Hitler and goes as commanded. Gone are the days when Mussolini had some initiative of his own, able and hard-jawed enough to make Hitler strike bargains. As, for instance, swapping Austria for Hitler's moral support in Europe on the Abyssinian grab. No, all that is gone, and what remains is a flabby-minded Mussolini, advancing in age and sickly in love with a girl far less than half his age. He is only the Rome echo of his master's voice in Berlin.

I used to see those two in their first get-togethers in the Reich and in Italy, when Mussolini was still a personality to be reckoned with. Springy of step and of roving eye beneath that black Fascist cap of his, Mussolini used to set a fast pace in public reviews—so fast that Hitler sort of loped along with an obvious effort. Down in Munich in 1938, where the Nazis staged a terrific reception for the Duce, you thought of Mutt and Jeff watching that ill-matched pair in the center of their glorified stage.

All that has changed since 1940–41. The two meet as usual, and last autumn, when Mussolini came hopping over to Fuehrer headquarters when summoned, he and Hitler walked by the hour, discussing the big plot of hurling their Jap blitz against us for a follow-up with an Axis war declaration.

Hitler, on those occasions, did the talking. Hitler knows no foreign word, but here again Mussolini accommodated the master by learning his language. He knew some German before he ever met the Fuehrer. After his first meeting with him, however, when Hitler launched into one of his passionate harangues, he realized that he didn't know enough. Since then, by arduous study, he has become fluent in the language. I noticed that the Duce lately even takes pains to adjust his step more in keeping to that of the Fuehrer, whose legs are long in comparison to Mussolini's.

I suppose the two can always find enough subjects of importance to talk about. At such times Hitler becomes an inveterate exponent of everything under the sun, holding forth like the club windbag, which now and then must bore even Mussolini.

He wouldn't dare show that any more than the obedient entourage, but it is known that the Duce's mind is never far from the laughing girl back in Rome. He'd probably like to talk to Hitler about her, or about his favorite subject of sex, yet experience must have taught him by now never to smoke in front of Hitler, or to carry even a decorative gun in his presence or to get intimate and personal unless Hitler himself leads the way.

And that he seldom does, if ever, with those from afar who come to serve him and take orders, such as Mussolini of Fascist Italy, one-time dictator in his own right but now a Faust who sold his soul for a price.

3

The barrier between the fiery temperament of the Latin and the heart of the blond Teutons was never whittled down by the intervening years of political alliance. On the contrary, it seemed to widen to a degree at times amounting to open friction.

Mussolini's rapid drift into the tide of Hitlerism caused cabinet shake-ups in Rome and murmurs around Italy which came echoing to our ears as far away as Berlin, but all observers agreed that things had changed from the 1934 days in Venice, when Hitler and Mussolini had a talk that failed, and that now Hitler was in the saddle and Mussolini running alongside him on foot.

A lot of Italians with axes to grind came back from periodic visits home in those years and blamed the whole Mussolini debacle on the laughing girl of the dull blonde hair with whom he fell deeply in love, from that day on to spend his money and time on her.

They said he bought her a beautiful villa near his in Rome and frequently left the affairs of state in other hands, thinking nothing of keeping the most important visitors waiting while he raced around the countryside in his powerful car with the girl. They spoke of him even bitterly as time went on and Hitler's troops in effect took over their land, cursing the day she caught his eye and the wild passion in his heart.

Be that as it may, Mussolini from 1938 on seemed to be losing his grip and over the next dangerous years made one mistake after another, each one throwing him further into dependence on Hitler.

He miscalculated the war in June 1940 and pounced on France from behind to get in on the kill, although Hitler had expressly asked him to stay neutral and thus hamstring

England in the Mediterranean. Later that year he made the Balkan situation embarrassing for Hitler by suddenly attacking Greece, thinking he could swallow the land in a week or two. When he ran into a wall, Hitler said nothing for months and never lifted a finger to help him, finally to have Mussolini come begging to Berlin early in 1941 for some way out of the impasse. That did the trick, and from then on Mussolini was just another abject puppet to Hitler.

German officers and soldiers moved freely about Italy thereafter, and it was even announced that the German and Italian High Commands in Africa and wherever necessary would function as one. In such cases, as is well known from past experience, the German part of the High Command functions as a law unto itself and all others take orders.

This utter subservience of Fascist Italy to Nazi Germany has hurt the pride of the highborn and lowborn Italian alike. German arrogance, nurtured by the old disdain for races in the warm south and the desertion of Italy to the Allies in 1915, grew apace, and foreign correspondents in Berlin soon enough saw the dog-whipped Italian journalists day by day marching meekly to a conference of their own in the German Foreign Office to take orders from Paul Schmidt's assistant, Braun von Stumm. Schmidt scarcely, if ever, bothered to dignify that handout conference with his portly person.

It brought on moments in the lives of Italians in Berlin when morbid despair overwhelmed them, like the Italian friend who dined with me on the night of that air raid.

They'd swear then that a revolution was sure to come in Italy, bloody and probably futile as it might be, but nevertheless a revolution with guns and knives against the grafting Fascist politicians, the corrupt army circles, and against those in key government posts who gladly turned all secrets and machinery over to Nazi officials for material gain.

They even cursed Mussolini in such moments without looking carefully around, and claimed that the Italian people on the whole have lost faith in him. He is, they vehemently declare, completely washed up, held to Hitler by steel handcuffs politely known as the Berlin-Rome Axis. He is, as Churchill aptly described it in his speech to Congress during the December visit to North America, merely a utensil of Hitler's.

It was no great surprise, therefore, to go past the gaudy red-and-white Italian Embassy across from the Tiergarten last November and suddenly hear an agitated Italian voice shouting in broken German: "Get out of here, get out! Call your dirty police, but get out!"

Those of us passing by paused on the snow-covered sidewalk and watched two husky Italian Embassy porters toss an equally husky and square-headed German out on his ear. He landed in the snow with an enraged howl, while the heavy door with its coat of arms shut tight.

I gathered that the Italian in charge of the visa section was one of those whose cup of bitterness was full to the brim and needed only the right push to spill it out with a vengeance. This German, who stood in characteristic Prussian stubbornness on the sidewalk now and yelled for the police, had marched in arrogantly and laid down a request for an immediate visa to Italy before the Italian official.

It seems he was politely told to take his turn, as others were waiting. He glanced at the menials on the chairs obviously not German and informed the official his business was urgent and his time short. He even produced a Nazi-party pass. The impression he conveyed in displaying it was that he should be handled with deference, as befitting in dealings between the master and the slave. The Italian official, getting madder and madder, ended the acrid argument which ensued by risking career and job and having the obnoxious Nazi tossed out on his ear. On that day and for weeks afterward he was without doubt a very popular man in the embassy and around the Italian colony in Berlin. Those things get around.

There are others like him, symptomatic of dark days to come for Italy. I know from Italians and from Germans, too, that all is not well in the Axis. The factions in disagreement with Mussolini, or those still hoping to extricate Italy from the Nazi morass, are strong in Rome. They have succeeded time and again in putting a monkey wrench in the best-laid Nazi plan, rescuing here and there a bit of their own. The Germans know it, and, although they boil inside, have had to put up with it.

I stood, for example, in Innsbruck in February of 1941, looking at long rows of apartment houses built by the Nazi resettlement organization for repatriated Germans.

Into these barracklike structures, divided into modern

kitchenettes, some 66,000 Germans from the Italian Tyrol had been brought as a result of the Hitler-Mussolini deal two years before arranging the transfer and resettling of nearly 300,000 Germans living at the time under the Italian heel. They shook hands on that deal and called it the grand solution of the only vexing problem between them. That was the political side of it.

On the practical side of it the picture was different. The Nazis who showed us around weren't very happy and roundly damned the Italians, to say nothing about the repatriated Germans themselves. The sore point was that the fine hand of Italian sabotage had nearly brought the resettlement to a standstill, and I doubt if very many came out of Italy in 1941.

"These are all men and their families from factories or handy at odd jobs," the Nazi in charge of the resettlement task told me.

"The Italians haven't let out a single farmer or man on the other side with fields and property. Practically all still over on the other side are the Tyrolean peasantry of fine stock and good herds.

"Under the agreement any German choosing to come across should be reimbursed by the Italian Government for the property left behind and be free to take with him whatever he likes. It is more than coincidence that up to now we have not been able to pry a single one loose from the Italians. Someday the situation will change and then our patience ends."

This Nazi was thinking out loud. At that moment he was

talking out of turn, but in actuality he was reflecting only the truth. Someday, maybe in months or in years, all this will come to the breaking point and bring on the explosion.

Again, take the employment of thousands and thousands of Italian workers in Germany, generally for better wages than they could get in Italy. In the beginning that was hailed as another marvelous Axis project for the furthering of good will and mutual endeavor. Swarthy little men from the Italian south flooded into the Reich to work nine hours per day, specially privileged to send home a major portion of their wages.

On Sundays you could see them walking in groups about the streets of Berlin, a blanketlike headcover extending down over their shoulders in native protection against the fierce southern sun but out of place in Nordic Berlin. They looked at the staring Germans in from the provinces for a day, and the Germans looked at the Italians. The two were as far apart as the poles.

It wasn't long before the Italians, quartered in wooden barracks near their jobs, got homesick for the sun and their own people, which made them cranky and produced nightly fights. First among themselves, then with the Germans doing the bossing.

The upshot was that less and less of the Italian workers have come to the Reich, and those who left as soon as they could after their contracted time was up went home nursing resentment and anger against the iron-handed blond men who couldn't even tell them in their own language what to do. This also had led to fights and misunderstandings. By

the end of 1941 imported French labor represented the bulk
of the 2,000,000 foreign workers in Hitler's Reich.

All this friction beneath the Axis surface detracts nothing
from the glittering official side of the Berlin-Rome tieup or
of its weird Tokyo offshoot.

Once a month you get as foreign correspondent of importance a telephone call from the Foreign Office in Berlin
advising you that an advance copy of the expensively designed publication *Rome-Berlin-Tokyo* awaits your pleasure. They'll even deliver it by official courier if you have
no office boy handy to send over.

The editor in chief is Gesandte Paul Schmidt, the surviving head man in Wilhelmstrasse after Karl Boemer's fall.
He glorifies the Axis and the Three-Power Pact in three
languages in that monthly of his, lavishly enriched with
the finest photographs. Each issue has at least one piece by
either Ribbentrop, Ciano, or perhaps the Japanese Ambassador in Berlin, General Oshima, if not the incumbent
Japanese Foreign Minister.

You never, never, hear or suspect a discordant note in
this official blurb of the Axis. The German newspapers, the
rigidly controlled radio, and the speeches of all tri-power
big shots sound like an eternal love feast and honeymoon
around the earth, even when behind the scenes the affairs
of state go awry.

There must be no scratch or rusty spot allowed to appear
outwardly on the shining Axis, lest this spread to dangerous
size. The dividing forces of the masses at large in the three
countries concerned are far too great to permit as much

as a hint of criticism, an expression of frank opinion, or the ventilation before public eyes of the causes of friction and discord between the three radically different nations and nationalities. By force of circumstances the birth of the Axis therewith signaled the death of any feeble remnant of free press, free speech, or independent thought inside the countries concerned.

As I said before, this strict control weighed heavily on the hearts of most Italians in Berlin. In a different way, it also inflicted itself on the leading Japanese correspondents sent by Tokyo to Hitler's capital since 1940.

Most of them had worked in America, England, or France and knew their way about in European fields, if only on the basis of experience gained by nearly all of us in the prewar Geneva days of disarmament talk and agreements to disagree. They'd cling close to us American correspondents, those Jap boys in Berlin, hiding the East beneath their Western clothes, as if seeking refuge from their allies the Germans.

The Japs were always ill at ease around the Nazis, staring at them with motionless eyes. In all my years in Berlin I never heard a Japanese correspondent ask a question in the press conferences. On trips to the front or elsewhere they'd go to sleep as soon as the car, plane, or train moved, and as soon as they were out in the open, off they'd go with a camera unslung to take pictures. Part of all that, I always felt, was escape from the Germans and from the cast-iron system gripping their Oriental hearts and minds.

CHAPTER 9

Hitler's Plan to Keep His Hold on the German People after Death

---

On a summer day in July 1940, when the evening sun spread its soft golden haze over the Champs-Elysées and made you glad to stand amid all the beauty of Paris, a long gray Mercedes limousine with six wheels turned slowly into the side entrance of the walled courtyard back of the Dôme des Invalides, where Napoleon I sleeps. The spire atop that grandiose dome shone and flashed an evening's farewell to the setting sun; down below in the courtyard, behind the side entrance with its musty barracks, the shadows already cast a sort of gloom over the unswept cobblestones. In the heat-touched air there was just a taint of the gutter and the unremoved garbage can.

Slowly the Mercedes car with its six uniformed men moved forward toward the German officer standing at rigid attention in the main yard back of the dome. There was no other living soul in sight.

The first car was followed by three others somewhat similar in appearance. They, too, were filled with square-jawed men from the Rhine, dressed in varying patterns of field gray, caps at a rakish angle, and black boots in high polish. Those in the two cars behind the first jumped out before the first car had even stopped and rushed up to form a sort of half circle around the one up ahead.

A six-foot adjutant in the first car had sprung to the ground with the agility of a tiger and yanked open the door opposite the driver. Adolf Hitler, wearing a white coat of dustproof gabardine, pushed his right leg slowly to the ground, a little stiff from the long drive into Paris and perhaps again bothered a bit by a twinge of rheumatism, and stood up to stare at the sun-topped edifice above. He preferred to look up at things, like the stars, rather than down into the depths where men work and struggle below the surface. He gazed at the top with a vacant smile, refusing to see the drabness around him. For Hitler, the mighty Fuehrer of the Third Reich and master of armies sweeping over Europe, had come to visit Napoleon.

To Hitler it was a pilgrimage, a dream come true, and a miraculous milestone in a passion which guided at least part of his life. He came here to look at the Napoleon he had followed over the battlefields of Europe step by step through thousands of pages available on the bookstands and even in dusty archives he had ransacked from time to time; he came here to look at the hallowed spot where rests the man whose political ideas for Europe gave Hitler a basic pattern to follow. And here, underneath the great dome with its golden cupola, lay the man by whose military mistakes Hitler swore to profit.

The German officer who greeted Hitler received a perfunctory salute and the mechanical Hitler handshake used for those he doesn't see. The officer led the way up the well-worn concrete steps to a nail-studded wooden door and pushed it open. Hitler stepped inside, walked quickly through the vaulted antechamber into the great rotunda under the dome, as if he knew his way in the dark. A dozen of his men and guards were scarcely able to follow him through the narrow doors at that pace, and before they had even reached the antechamber, Hitler stood at the marble balustrade and looked down into the pit at the sarcophagus inside of which Napoleon I sleeps.

He didn't salute; his cap with the golden swastika eagle stayed on his head; he just stood there with hands on the balustrade and mouth slightly open. Around him men keenly aware of his mood and temper tiptoed, like children afraid of a spanking, to the balustrade and also looked down, saying nothing and most of them far from impressed by what they saw below. To the half-dozen gunmen of the quick eye and hard muscles in that company sworn to the daily task of guarding the Nazi Fuehrer with their very lives, this was just another tomb or museum or something they had seen in many cities and capitals of Europe. Their job at the moment was to keep from sneezing, coughing, or breathing too hard. They touched the flaps of their gun holsters to make sure the guns were easy to reach, and their bright little eyes roved around the rotunda to the darker corners and around the pillars in the church beyond, all a matter of duty and habit to them from long and constant practice. They never opened their mouths or talked to the Fuehrer, unless perchance he threw a word or two at the nearest one. Then it was usually without looking to see which of the six constantly with him happened to catch that command to bring him a glass of water or perhaps to call this or that adjutant.

I guess it was a full minute before the Fuehrer broke that strange silence which laid a cold hand on your heart there under the Dôme des Invalides that dying day in July. Four or five of us from Berlin had been taken there a little bit earlier on our pledged word of silence on what we would see, a method used many times by the Nazis as the surest way of forestalling a leak to the outside world about an incident or event they are not anxious to have published at the time. In this case Hitler was to make his formal visit to Paris some days later, when the Nazi propaganda machine intended to go to work and make the most of it. On this day the Fuehrer had come in his own right and on a pilgrimage dear to his heart.

We stood opposite the tomb and waited, keenly watching the Nazi dictator in the fading light of day. He was lost in thought, with that faraway expression again creeping over his face. He folded his arms and murmured something we could not hear; his lips moved, as if he were talking to himself, and once or twice he shook his head. Then he came out of the trance as suddenly as it had begun, and he leaned forward on the balustrade to stare more fixedly into the pit.

"Napoleon, *mein lieber*, they have made a bad mistake," the guttural voice of the Fuehrer said suddenly out of the void. It startled me, standing there across from a live war lord and above a dead emperor. What was he talking about? He had sounded a bit cynical and slightly amused, or was I mistaken? He was turning to his Press Chief, Otto Dietrich, to tap him on the arm. But he was talking to all before him.

"*Ja*, it is a big mistake they have made," Hitler repeated, and pointed into the pit. "They have put him down into a hole. People must look down at a coffin far below them. Their eyes cannot come close and really grasp what they are looking for.

"They should look up at Napoleon, feeling small by the very size of the monument or sarcophagus above their heads. You do not impress people if you walk in a street and they are on top of a building. They must look at something above them; you must be the stage and the center of attraction above the level of all eyes. Then the mind reaches out and fastens itself upon the object or the person. It is all a matter of common psychology. The effect of Napoleon and his hold on the nation would have been much greater if people could come and actually touch the stone he sleeps in by reaching their arm up and perhaps by standing on tiptoe. This way, I must assume that the thousands who have come here before me look into their guidebook and go away without remembering more about it than about the next place. Their minds failed to grasp the greatness of Napoleon, and Napoleon down there in that pit failed to touch their hearts and effect his mission after death of keeping alive the spirit and tradition of a great epoch."

Hitler began to walk slowly around the balustrade, pausing once more at the glass door leading into the church with its tattered flags of Napoleon's wars in Europe, to look almost carelessly into the pit from the opposite side of where he had stood before. I could not help but feel that a sort of disdain had replaced the man's former intentness.

"I shall never make such a mistake," Hitler said suddenly. "I know how to keep my hold on people after I have passed on. I shall be the Fuehrer they look up at and go home to talk of and remember. My life shall not end in the mere form of death. It will, on the contrary, begin then."

2

Hitler left the Dôme des Invalides, as I later found out, determined to carry out among the first things after the war the great plan for his life after death. I knew that in years gone by he had gone on the assumption that death would not find him a very old man; he used to work out blueprints for terrific construction projects in Germany by the pile, throwing millions of men into the jobs and billions of marks. He was in a hurry then, racing his monuments against the Reaper and always saying to people that the great things he would leave undone would never be finished by those coming after him. He was firmly convinced that the furious pace and the epochal age in which he lived and moved (he really is convinced he is the motivating force and the molder of that age) would terminate soon after his death, swinging the world by nature and inclination into a long span of digestive process marked by a sort of quiet inactivity. People in his "thousand-year Reich" would build monuments to him and go around to touch and look at the things he had built, he thought. He said as much on that glorified visit of his to Rome in 1938, adding that a thousand years hence the greatness and not the ruins of his own time must intrigue the people of those faraway days. For, believe it or not, that is how the mind of this man Hitler projects itself without a blush over the centuries.

This grasp of the Nazis for everything that assures them the distant future and the never-mentioned fear right down in the bottom of their hearts that after Hitler might come the deluge to sweep them away, hold the key to their tireless efforts through all available means to foster and create around Hitler not only the sacred aura of infallibility but also a state of mind and attitude toward him approaching the mystic.

They want people to sit in their homes in the deep valleys and villages of the Fatherland and talk in awed tones of the Fuehrer sent to them in their darkest days like a gift from heaven. To them, a short salute from that right arm of his should be taken as a blessing from the altar; there can be no question of the Fuehrer's wisdom, of his holy inspiration.

He and Goebbels want it that way, and after awhile it just about got that way in the provinces around Germany.

Without batting an eye, Hitler himself called on God and Divine Providence in many a public speech, achieving at times a tone which made you think of cathedrals and solemn moments. He was playing on the minds of his Germans, striving to create the mystic, and pounding home to them that he is a Fuehrer with a divine mission. To the propaganda-massaged mind of the common man and woman in Germany who are isolated from the world and living in a hard little shell built around them by the Nazis, this was a potion of magic which held them spellbound. Hitler knows that and every once in awhile puts it on pretty thick. Then he goes back to his chancellery for the night, refreshed from the effort and glowing with a self-satisfied fervor.

Thus it has come about that inside Germany today, as a foreign correspondent, you may take an attitude against the Nazis on many things and at times even risk your personal safety with sharp criticism and exposure of something which might have happened or is going on in the land. But you must never, either by act or word of mouth or in a dispatch, say or suggest anything which might be a slur or a reflection on the office and the person of the Fuehrer. He is above all earthly things. He is in a class all by himself, "untouchable and infallible." After eight years covering him in Berlin, you begin to understand what Hitler means when he says that the next Fuehrer will inherit a thousand-year Reich to steer on its course but never again to rebuild and create from the bottom up. And after eight years there you know just why there is only one boss in Naziland today—Hitler. All others are secondary and easy to replace, even Goering as his designated successor. The distance downward between Hitler and the next ranker in Naziland —which happens to be Goering—is as immeasurable as the distances of space. In short, Hitler lives, breathes, plans, and commands in a world all by himself. The others really don't count.

I should say that the war thus far has given him a boost in his efforts to nail the German mind to the temple of mysticism. The Nazis themselves, drunk or sober, will tell you at length that Hitler will live after death. They have steeped their own mind in this fanatical conception and conviction, and are never weary of playing this chord on the hearts of all Germans. They get results, and I believe that after awhile Hitler and Goebbels and Rosenberg will have molded the minds of a large part of the German people to accept the drug in this magic cup.

So it comes about that Hitler, if his Third Reich should outlast the war, might reach the point where he can prepare on this earth the material means of keeping his grip after death on the hearts and minds of men. The plans for it are all made, and the blueprint lies in the vault of the Fuehrer House in Munich. In fact, the plans are a change of those from some years back, when they bored and drilled up through the throat of an alpine peak to build the solitary Eagle's Nest for Hitler high above the clouds of his mountain chalet in Berchtesgaden.

I was up there once, in this fantastic engineer's feat of

stone, steel, and glass. The idea back of it was to have a mausoleum here for Hitler after death, embedded in the clouds above, ever beyond the reach of the ordinary man but always there to look at from the valley far below.

They say it was built without Hitler's knowledge by a favorite architect who later died. It was intended as a great surprise to the Fuehrer from those of his close devotees and from that grotesque circle of Nazis clinging around him like blindfolded apostles. They believed and preached his divine inspiration and mission, convinced that his hold on the German people after death would grow to enormous proportions, drawing them to him as Mohammed draws the pilgrimages to Mecca. So they built the Eagle's Nest atop the highest peak in Berchtesgaden and presented it to him in the initial form of a teahouse and secluded place to get away from the world for a few hours.

It was a spectacular and a grandiose idea, perfectly in line with the thunderous and mystic chords of Wagner's mighty *Götterdämmerung* come true. Hitler the mighty, like Siegfried and the Teuton masters celebrated in the operas he loved so passionately, would come after death to his throne above the permanent snows and symbolically his spirit could go forth. It had that immortal touch of Wagner, or so they thought. That was some years ago, before Hitler had his mind clearly made up on that point. I happened to know that he was pleased as a child when he first went up to that lair of the gods. They chiseled and dynamited a hairpin road out of the mountain cliffs across from Berchtesgaden, blasting and smoothing a road wide enough to let a powerful car negotiate its way up there through the whistling wind and cutting bursts of snow. There was no other traffic, of course, for only the Fuehrer and occasionally some invited guests were taken to Eagle's Nest. Then it was all arranged by telephone with the adjutants who went ahead of the party and got the place warmed. On many days of the year one cannot go at all owing to the bad weather.

Coming in the car from Hitler's house above Berchtesgaden, you are already several thousand feet up, but the road by car to the base of the peak clocks up about ten miles on your speedometer. An occasional glimpse around hairpin turns downward gives you the shivers. Even on a clear day the wind whistles and screams deafeningly, but the road is built so that its full force cannot hit the car and menace its equilibrium.

Suddenly, after a turn straight toward the towering peak over your head, you see a brass-studded door before you. Inside your breast you get a funny feeling, and all the childhood tales of dungeons and dwarfs come flooding into your mind. There is an inclination to pinch yourself to make sure you are not having a bad dream. Slowly the fantastic becomes reality, and in speechless amazement you see that brass-studded door slide apart to let you go straight into the heart of the mountain peak. The car moves forward into an eerie tunnel, dimly lit by iron torches of electric light with just a reddish tint, enough in itself to convince you that you have definitely gone mad. Then another surprise awaits. It is a comfortable elevator, upholstered in

expensive red leather and done in polished brass. Up you
go through the throat of the Bavarian peak for nearly three
hundred feet, to emerge in a burst of light that dazzles
momentarily. You are in Hitler's Eagle's Nest, thousands
of feet above prosaic mankind, gazing at what originally
was intended as the crypt of the first German Fuehrer after
his death. It looks at first glance like a winter garden, a
pleasant tearoom enclosed in glass.

Look down on the east side and you find a sheer drop
of the cliff three thousand feet down; on the other side the
shoulder of the mountain proper, where the road comes up,
is hundreds of feet below. If clouds do not interfere, your
eyes are treated to a panoramic view of the Bavarian and
Austrian Alps such as only those who have stood on the
peaks of the Zug Spitze or the Gross-Glockner can visual-
ize. It is majestic and perhaps somewhat terrifying. There
are the inevitable flowers all over the room, with Bavarian
wood stoves of porcelain and pretty designs giving off a
reassuring warmth. Through a curtained glass door can be
seen another smaller room with a couch and desk, reserved
for the Fuehrer if he wishes to spend some hours here and
work. But it is difficult to stay there more than one night,
for cooking and other essentials such as running water are
not easy to have at such a height. Consequently, Hitler goes
there only once in a great while in the afternoon, and in
fact since the war has hardly visited it at all. As in so many
other cases, he seems to have lost interest, probably to a
large extent because his mind is filled with another plan for
himself for life after death.

3

Perhaps I found out by chance on that day at Napoleon's
tomb why Hitler has abandoned the idea of using the
Eagle's Nest as his last resting place after death. The Fuehrer
felt that up at the Eagle's Nest he was far removed from
the personal touch essential to the success of his plan; up at
the Eagle's Nest there could be no crowds coming in future
pilgrimage from the far corners of the earth to stare at him
in silent awe and perhaps touch the crypt before them.
His plan needs constant emotion and a play on hysteric
mass minds, and the more he can arrange the means and
ways of achieving this after he dies, the more surely he is
assured of his goal. At least that is how he looks at it, and
that is the line he is working on.

People don't know it yet, or at least the secret remains
that of a few dozen around him. It is this blueprint in the
Fuehrer House in Munich, carefully drawn to meet every
condition, that this man Hitler believes will fasten that
mystic hold of his on the people within Germany after he
dies. This blueprint, if ever it materializes, visualizes a
great square in Munich on the spot where the city's present
central railway station is located. All these tracks, all these
rambling low buildings of the station, and scores of big
hotels and buildings immediately facing it vanish from
sight on that blueprint. From the huge square emerging
here would unfold also an avenue of majestic proportions
leading straight through the city to the historic street and
square down which he and his brown-shirted Nazis walked

in 1923, to meet a blast of machine-gunfire and therewith the end for another ten years of their beer-hall *putsch*. On that blueprint it is to be an avenue with an arch such as only the Caesars dreamed of. Hundreds of houses which would have to be razed on either side never offered its draughtsman a moment's qualm of conscience. As Hitler designed it with that ever-busy pencil of his, a great squat and square mausoleum is to rise in the exact center of that Munich square, forming the basic mantle of a gigantic square column to rise some seven hundred feet into the air. On top of that column is to stand a great Nazi eagle holding the swastika in its claws. The spread of the wings, according to the specifications on that blueprint, from one tip to the other would measure two hundred and twenty-five feet. Columns and pillars, like the Roman temples of old, would provide the chief architectural relief to the eye in the vast structure of the mausoleum. Inside, and thus actually inside the hollow column above, the sarcophagus of Fuehrer I of the Third Reich would stand on a high pedestal. It would be a masterly work of German stone and artisanship, simple in its exterior design but impressive to the eye. Here, amid the eagles and flags and wreaths of Nazidom, guarded day and night by steel-helmeted men who marched with him or the sons who come after them, Hitler could lie and keep his hold on the masses. As far as I know, he had not yet definitely decided whether it would serve his purpose best to follow the method of Lenin in Red Square in Moscow and give the pilgrims to the shrine a glimpse of himself through a glass aperture. There are many around him—he consults, or used to, with astrologers and psychologists alike on this point—who are inclined to believe that mystery and the unseen are more powerful than the opposite. One school of thought in the Reich, for example, is convinced that the actual sight of Lenin's body under its glass case in Moscow detracted from the mystic effect desired and secured largely a physical reaction. This school feels strongly, too, that with a glass aperture the crowd filing past naturally would stare only through the glass and fail to get into the spirit of its surroundings. In fact, they say, the average man or woman in his eager and excited state of mind at seeing Fuehrer Hitler through the glass probably would never notice or glance at anything else.

Be that as it may, an important role would naturally be played by the spectacular decoration surrounding the tomb. There is an idea for the moment of huge torches burning in an eternal flame of red fire, the smoke being drawn off through special air filters but nevertheless offering just a touch of incense.

The soft blue light always filtering upon the tomb of old Emperor William I in Berlin—so famous and effective that tourists from all over the world used to make a beeline for it—also has come into consideration. There would be a specially soundproof floor, carefully designed to deaden the footfalls of the passing crowd and thus to preserve the glorified silence.

Leading into and away from the shrine itself would be the doors into the various antechambers comprising in part the museums and exhibition rooms of the things held most sacred to Nazidom. There could be seen, in one section of the structure, all the uniforms and personal things used by the Fuehrer in life. The boots, the hats, the caps, the shoes. In a special glass case the iron cross he won in World War I, and perhaps the Nazi-party button he originally put on as Party Member Number 7 back there in the roaring days of Munich of the Buergerbrauekeller and street fights with Communists. Another case no doubt would show the Fuehrer's pen-and-ink sketches and the water colors drawn by him in the lean and hungry days before the World War I and later in the trenches, sold for a pittance until he came to power, when the price for each of them went sky high and the Nazis combed out all art shops and attics in the hope of raking up every last one of them. Those and the designs for his highways and Nazi edifices now standing around all over Germany as laid down on paper by him will all be in a glass case in that exhibition room. The idea would be to let the visitor see for himself the Fuehrer as he was in private life and as the leader, always stressing the simplicity and the miracle of this man. It would be effective preparation on the mental side and indelibly stamp into the mind that here in the shrine next door lay more than just an ordinary mortal. It would be a privilege to the wandering pilgrim to come near him, even as it was in life. All this and much more is contained in that locked-up blueprint in Munich, where Hitler always has felt more at home than in Berlin. His Brown House of early days still stands there as it did a decade ago; alongside it, facing the great Koenigsplatz, he has changed everything by building the temples to his sixteen dead killed in the *putsch* of 1923 and also the Fuehrer House, a lavish edifice now used by him for official receptions and as headquarters down south of the Nazi party.

In Munich also Hitler still has that private little apartment of his over a former garage in one of the side streets. That is where he lived when money was short and times were uncertain. He drank beer then and ate dry bread with sausage, and even that much was frequently sent to him as a gift by friends who knew that his gaunt cheeks were not from internal illness or overeating. The Bavarian furniture and fittings inside that little apartment remain the same today as they were then; it is one of those sentimental things about Hitler which no power and no glory in the world can change. He has his moments, and at such times he likes to relax. It doesn't last long and it only happens when a few privileged cronies of his old days are around. Then he talks freely and sometimes even tells a joke.

Hitler clings to Munich like a desperate man in love with the wife he is losing. That is the whole irony of it, for the saying goes in Germany that Black Bavaria harbors more Nazi-haters and Hitler foes per square inch than all the rest of the Reich combined. The hotbed of this anti-Nazism is without question Munich itself, where the stolid Bavarian of largely Catholic faith and the more liberal-minded artist and student class of people like to take life easy and shake hands under the table against the Nazis.

Perhaps more has happened or almost happened to Hitler in attempts on his life in Munich than anywhere else; for example, the bomb blast of 1939 in the beer cellar or the shots from windows as he drove through the streets not many years ago. Even the trains he arrived on have had accidents in the Munich railway station, but his luck has held out. Despite it all, Hitler has that fatal love for Bavaria and particularly for Munich, perhaps because it is close to his own Austria, and therefore he has chosen to lie after death in the midst of that city to keep his mystic hold on the Germans. That is, if his luck holds out and the war he is fighting doesn't end with him in flight and his Third Reich in ruins.

CHAPTER 10

Catholics and Jews in the Third Reich

Oɴᴇ ɴɪɢʜᴛ in the winter of 1938 the Nazi party staged a *Bier Abend* (beer evening) in the Kaiserhof Hotel in Berlin for a batch of us foreign correspondents.

That meant the guzzling of much Pilsener and heavy trays of sandwiches, all for the sake of rubbing elbows with some of the brown-shirted Reichleiters and maybe a few Gauleiters and smaller fry in the land. I knew from weary experience it meant also a heavy dose of Nazi propaganda, always squeezed in like the uninvited guest between the "ifs" and the "ahs."

But an American newspaperman in Berlin like myself, head of a news agency hungry for news and operating in flashes of seconds and minutes, could no more refrain from showing up at a party like that *Bier Abend* than he could go off for a week end. That is, unless he cared to risk getting scooped by the opposition.

So I climbed into a tuxedo as requested on the invitation —very formal and officious looking as all Nazi invitations— and wangled a taxi for the Kaiserhof Hotel. The Kaiserhof stands on a far corner across from the Wilhelmsplatz, and from its bar and restaurant you get a fine view of the balcony of the Reich chancellery on which Hitler appears like a "gift from heaven" to his people for a public show whenever the occasion calls for a little heiling.

The hotel itself is a sort of an incognito Hitler chancellery, closely allied to his moves and to the Berlin history of the Nazi party. All the big shots from the government go there with regularity, sometimes even transacting important state business on the glass-topped tables of the bar or in the grillroom with its high red-leather chairs and its checkered tablecloths.

The Nazis had requisitioned the famous Yellow Room, done in silk tapestry alternated with white marble. Huge chandeliers gave the added touch of official solemnity, and here in this medley of old-fashioned glass and glory the Nazis staged many an ornate banquet to important guests from within or without the land.

I checked my hat and coat and fixed my tie again before moving into the brightly lighted reception chamber, where smoke from free cigars and the smell of stale beer soon moistened the hardiest brow.

The gilded bust of Hitler, the speakers' rostrum decorated with pine branches and flowers, and the usual Nazi flags were categorically in evidence, with German cameramen in Nazi uniform running around busily as always to photograph the little fuehrers and the foreign correspondents. The Nazis always laid stress on such pictures for some reason.

I shook hands with the presiding Nazi functionary who headed the receiving line and greeted my colleagues. In those days before the war Berlin counted a large corps of foreign correspondents, hailing from something like forty different lands. Most of them were aces in their line, fast-stepping and quick as lightning to grasp the situation as it arose.

The flashy ones were gone by 1938, pushed out by the demand for hard facts and objective reporting without much trimmings. The survivors were the real thing, trained and seasoned enough to face any sudden demand on them, and it was a real pleasure to know them and be of their crowd.

I caught the eye of Jimmy Holburn, crafty Scotsman and chief Berlin correspondent at that time for the London *Times*. We always worked hand in hand, swapping the good and the bad.

Jimmy was at a corner table talking to a scarred, round-faced Nazi. I identified him as Party Fanatic Bormann, the deputy of Rudolf Hess and earmarked around town as an intriguer and bootlicker, with a long knife out for his immediate chief. He liked to be taken seriously and considered of first-rank importance, which meant that after half-a-dozen beers mixed with schnapps he'd probably shoot his mouth off and spill some low-down for future background. I knew the type.

Jimmy was quick to introduce me, if only to share the burden of talking to a screwball like this Bormann. I had met him at the Nazi party congresses in Nuremberg and on other occasions, but Bormann only remembered people bigger than himself or those who could do him favors. I sat down and drank beer, listening to Jimmy and Bormann argue the delicate subject of religious freedom within the Nazi state.

Holburn, rolling German words with a Scotch burr, boldly reminded the little Nazi that the Catholic Church had persevered through thick and thin for a couple of thousand years, as had the Jews, and a mere puff of persecution could hardly be expected to conquer it.

In fact, Holburn pointed out, the Nazi drive against the Church so far had merely served to strengthen it, as could be seen in the Rhineland or Bavaria.

Bormann's piggish little eyes, reddened a bit and moistened by the smoke and drink, began to pop out. He was a man of savage temper, raised in the gutter and dragged to the top by a pair of handy fists. His personal history was one of those you never read about in official obituaries; they give you a doctored and polished version and call him a self-made man.

Naturally, he was violently loyal to Hitler, even before he met him, like the wardheeler to his political boss. He also became very loyal, in due time, to the great powers above him like Himmler and Ribbentrop. They were worth cultivating.

I listened to the flood of Nazi phrases and contentions

on the Church and the Jews, all of which amounted to
the same thing. This Bormann was merely repeating what
men like Rosenberg had written down. He even beat on the
table with his heavy fist, shaking our plates and glasses.

"I repeat, you are wrong in your papers and stories when
you say we Nazis persecute the Church.

"*Ja, ja,* it is all wrong. The Jews we exterminate, or will
soon, but the Church is free in our Fatherland. I tell you
now we will rid Germany of every Jew, from the first to
the last, and if I had my way they'd all be dead or gone
by now.

"But the Church, Evangelical or Catholic, we do not
touch. Only those of its priests and bishops who try to use
the pulpit for political agitation or the Sunday school as
a back door to politics.

"We need no secret organizations or societies like the
Masons and the Heidelberg clubs, so we did away with
them. Why should they be permitted to sit behind their
closed doors and prescribe to millions of our people how to
live and act?

"We Nazis fought the Communists and the fat-bellied
politicians in this land for fifteen years and smashed the
Jews, and we don't intend to have the pulpit or the crazy
student in Bonn stab us in the back. Every German can go
to church if he wants to, but every church has got to remember that the Fatherland comes first and before all. I
mean that Peter's penny shouldn't have to go to Rome, and
it doesn't any more in this land because of financial restrictions.

"But there are still hundreds and thousands of our people who put the Vatican first and the Fatherland second. That has got to stop."

Bormann swung a schnapps and beer in quick succession to his lips and the heavy glass came back to the table with a crash.

"That has got to stop," he said again after wiping his mouth with the back of his hand.

"I for one shall never rest until the last Jew is gone and until all churches in Germany serve the Fatherland and God instead of some outside power. A lot of us feel the same way.

"Why, we fought the Communist down to kick Moscow out of Berlin, so to say. We Nazis do not intend to have a foreign power ruling in the Fatherland with an unseen hand, such as Moscow was doing. Well, then, what else is the Vatican but a foreign power telling some thirty million Germans how to act and to be loyal first and foremost to the Vatican?

"I tell you we won't have it!"

Bormann was getting loud, spurred on by schnapps and beer. "What is the Vatican but a foreign power ruling through its religious hold on the masses?" he ranted now. "Why should we let a foreign despot in Rome tell us what to do any more than the Bolshevist in Moscow. Either the Catholic Church in Germany stops that or we will. I can be a bad enemy."

That was in 1938, when little Nazi Bormann was still small fry. But two and one half years later, when Bormann already had laid claim to an adjutant and large car in the best style of Nazi big shots, his immediate superior Rudolf Hess conveniently got out of his way by flying to Scotland to woo peace without Hitler's consent.

Bormann had prepared his ground well and in fact thought he had Hess on the run anyhow. Ribbentrop and Himmler were backing him, in return for favors done.

The appointment from Hitler as successor to Hess came without surprise, and in some quarters not very friendly to Bormann it was said that he got out the new uniform with its high-ranking stripes he'd been secretly admiring himself in and walked the length of Unter den Linden to shake hands with any gaping provincial who cared to recognize and idolize him.

Bormann moved into the office of Hess across the hall from his own so fast that his own secretary didn't find him for some hours after trying to locate him all over town.

The girl did not know of his appointment until the official announcement came out much later, when it occurred to her to look into Hess's office and there she found Bormann sitting in solitude of his own grandness, feet on the desk, staring at himself in the mirror on the wall. Yes, the little Nazi Bormann of street fights and unpaid bills had become Big-Shot Bormann.

This daydreaming and glory stupor didn't last long, for soon enough the roughhousing hand of Bormann came to be felt. He kept his nose clean with Ribbentrop and offered to play ball with Himmler, the Gestapo man. Both of them had it in for the Catholics and the Jews, resentful in their inner hearts against the restraining forces which blocked every move of importance against them up to now.

"We can clean out the Jews and straighten the Catholic Church entirely our way during the war," Bormann argued. "After the war the old handicaps and consideration of public opinion inside and outside Germany will again stand in the way. We must do it now, while our hands are free."

2

The first to feel the whip was the Catholic Church, and soon after the Hitler attack on Russia Catholics all over the Reich heard with dismay and some incredulity that the wild ones among the Nazis again seemed to have gained the upper hand.

Men shook their heads and preferred to believe that Hitler knew nothing of it. They had sons and brothers at the front, some had already died, and it just didn't make sense to say that the Nazis in the midst of war would revive old bitternesses and frictions by lashing at the 30,000,000 Catholics in the Greater Reich.

But that is what the mouth-frothing Nazis, led by Bormann and backed by Himmler, were doing. These rabid old-timers of the beer halls and street fights were feeling their oats again now that their Fuehrer had tackled the Red foe, and to them it was a go-ahead signal to square accounts with the Catholic Church and the Jews, inherent enemies of the Nazis.

In the minds and in the pockets of men like Bormann,

Himmler, and scores of important Nazi pivots like Wagner of Bavaria, reclined that dormant plan to rid Germany of every Jew and mold the Catholic faith and in fact all faiths to the standards and ideologies of Nazism.

This plan, known as part of the Nazi program to every Hitler youth and rabble-rouser of the brown-shirted ranks, was planted in Nazi minds and pockets long years ago by that "Thinker" and pseudo-philosopher from the Baltics, Reichsleiter Alfred Rosenberg, author of ponderous volumes and tutor in a sense of the early Hitlerian mind.

It was Rosenberg who kept the Nazi party breathing when Hitler went to jail in Landsberg for three years after the abortive Munich beer-hall *putsch* of 1923; it was the same reticent and dry-of-speech Rosenberg who fathered and partly wrote the thoughts and ideas which crowded the pages of Hitler's *Mein Kampf*.

He originated the notorious Nazi phrase of *Blut und Boden* (blood and soil) and into the volumes of his many books penned the iron-clad Nazi theory that the Fatherland and the State come before all; that the Church of Rome is but an evil influence and power playing darkly on the hearts and minds of mankind, that Christianity itself is but the means to an end.

This and other bloodcurdling theories, wrapped into language and expressions so confusing that in many places there is no head or tail, except in those books and chapters of Rosenberg dealing with the subject of Jews and the Catholic Church.

His ideas and plans in that respect are perfectly clear and

have long been the adopted Nazi policy. With regard to the Jews, Rosenberg simply preaches and promotes the utter extermination of Jewry; he wants the head of every Jew within grasp. The first eight years of Nazi rule showed them to be pretty faithful to this doctrine.

As for both Catholic and Protestant faiths, Rosenberg demands and propagates the National Church of Greater Germany, allied in thought and principle and unified with the Nazi regime in methods of furthering the power and dominance of the Reich.

The Catholic Church above all, under this Rosenberg plan and Nazi program, must cut all connection with the Vatican and its world-wide clerical machinery; the Catholic Church must become within Greater Germany a church where people go to pray to God (if they must) but not carry on "mysterious rites secretive to the non-Catholic" and outside every control by official machinery.

The Rosenberg plan and therewith the Nazi mind brooks no interference by outside forces. If there is to be any church at all and the people insist on going there instead of to the speeches and rallies useful to the Fatherland, then that church must be on the side of the State and not against it.

The Pope outside the German borders, so Rosenberg has said, must no longer have connection or contact with the Catholic Church within the Reich; he sees no reason why the bishops of the Fatherland should not elect their own German pope.

The priests under his plan should be priests without pulpits, that is, the gospel could be read if need be but the task of preaching to the congregation would fall to the *Reichsredner*. These sanctioned speakers from the pulpits in churches would be appointees of the Nazi regime, trained and steeped in the doctrines of Nazism.

Hitler Youth camps and summer excursions would replace the Sunday school, which has been one of Rosenberg's chief targets as the weapon used by the Church to catch them young. He has striven with might and main over the past years to lure the children away with temptations like free trips and picnics, coercing through party machinery those parents stubbornly clinging to the Sunday school.

"Give me ten years and no boy or girl in the Reich will as much as remember what the Sunday school was, let alone attend it," he asserted to me back in 1935.

Rosenberg lost no opportunity to impress on Nazi minds the importance of Nazifying the children while young. His plan eliminates the convent and cloister as evil influences; it places the Fatherland and Fuehrer before the altar and God, leaving the latter as a sort of tolerated commodity to be called on for effect whenever the occasion warrants it.

On the whole, if the church of any faith is to function at all under the Rosenberg plan, it would do so only as an instrument of the State and as a national means to an end like, for instance, the compulsory Labor Service. Without much Christianity.

This, then, was the fountain of inspiration from which hard men of ambition like Bormann and Himmler drank great draughts and over the years saturated their minds with its poison.

When the time and opportunity came to Bormann to vent his hatred against the Jews and Catholics he did so with a furious passion, rousing all of his ilk in brown uniform to the task in hand and urging them to devote all energies and resources to the disciplining and "adjustment" of the Catholic Church.

He found ready help in the heartless machinery of Himmler's Gestapo, and it was whispered into his ears that out in Fuehrer headquarters they were too busy to worry about Catholics and Jews. The setup, as far as Bormann was concerned, was perfect.

In the early weeks of July 1941 the great Catholic areas of the Rhineland, Bavaria, Westphalia, former Austria, and Sudetenland among others found themselves in the throes of a new Nazi wave of oppression, featured chiefly by the wholesale closing down of convents and cloisters.

Uniformed men of the S.S. and non-uniformed men of the Gestapo swarmed into towns and villages, rudely dispossessing nuns and priests alike and driving them into the streets without notice.

Catholic orders of all kinds were disbanded; German families going to Mass on Sunday had to file past glaring S.S. muscle-men at the door of the church; the cloisters and convents were turned into dormitories for Germans brought back from abroad.

Those Catholics who contributed heavily to the Church or refused to be intimidated by ordinary means were subjected to the fine process of terrorism by telephone calls at all hours of the night or became targets for poisonous letters with threats. A lot of those under pressure cracked under the strain and stayed away from church in the end.

In Poland the churches were temporarily closed, with the exception of Cracow; in Innsbruck of former Austria the drunken Gauleiter Andreas Hofer forbade further religious processions.

Roadside shrines with pictures or statuettes of Christ were stripped; in the heart of Innsbruck city a beautiful bouquet of roses appeared regularly, as if by magic, in the empty shrine in the square, a silent but bold protest against the fanaticism of Hofer. The Gauleiter, drunk or sober, raged at the insult and posted guards at the empty shrine, but not only did the bouquet appear each day but similar ones decorated shrines all over the city, placed there by mysterious hands.

A switch in guards and the dire threats by Hofer changed nothing; people stood in obvious lines before church doors to attend Sunday services despite the Gestapo.

3

Bormann soon had his hands full. Mighty voices from the pulpits of the Reich thundered their warnings, and pastoral letters of the aged and suffering Cardinal Faulhaber in Munich and Prince Conrad Preysing, Bishop of Berlin, spread the tide of indignation throughout the land.

But an even doughtier warrior of the Church arose to the forefront and led the battle against the Nazis with hitherto unprecedented vigor. That was Count August Clemens von Galen, bishop of the ancient Westphalian town of Münster.

He had watched with heavy heart as his beloved city and flock suffered terribly under the hail of British bombs which began on the memorable night of July 6, 1941, continuing incessantly for some time, after which Münster could be classified as practically in ruins. It was up to the end of 1941 one of the worst blitzed cities in Germany.

On July 12, according to a letter which Bishop Count Galen sent to me and to Louis Lochner of the Associated Press in Berlin, the Gestapo descended on cloisters and convents in Münster and various church orders to confiscate all in favor of Nazi district leaders. They claimed the buildings were needed to house families left homeless by the bombings.

The bishop enclosed a copy of the telegram of protest he had sent to Hitler's chancellery, in which he pointed out that German men and women had been thrown into the street and even banished from town despite the fact that their relatives were fighting at the front. He said he had gotten a curt reply advising him that his telegram had been turned over to Himmler "for further investigation."

Bishop Galen knew what that meant and was ready to face it. He dispatched another long telegram to Hitler direct, voicing sharp protests against wanton acts of violence toward his flock at a time when bombs were tearing hearts apart, and warned Hitler against the consequences of such continued high-handedness by the Gestapo.

Then he entered the majestic cathedral of Gothic beauty and preached a stirring sermon to his silent but unflinching congregation. The six-foot bishop, standing in full regalia of High Mass on the altar beneath the eternal flame, spoke straight to their hearts from there instead of ascending the elevated rostrum. His quick eye had picked up at a glance the uniformed S.S. pair sitting in the pews a few steps down the aisle. He had been made aware, too, of angry men who accosted the churchgoers outside and in some cases "accidentally" kicked shins or stepped on touchy corns. He knew he was facing the answer to his telegrams.

He preached of the sufferings of men that Sunday; of the tribulations of mankind, and of the unfailing comfort and mercy of God. He recalled to their minds the persecutions and the patience of Christ; the blindness of men dazzled by power and glory of days gone by and of our days, and the storms they unleashed.

He talked of the Rock of St. Peter; of the sacredness of the family; of the home, and of the child and its immortal place in the heart of Christ.

Bishop Galen, tirelessly active against the creeping poison spread among the young by the blandishments and seductions of Rosenberg, then lashed the dark forces seeking to undermine the authority of parents and the innocent minds of children.

He reminded friend and foe inside that cathedral that Christ was the special protector and the eternal Savior of the young in particular, so demonstrated by Him on earth even two thousand years ago. And woe to those who harmed the body or mind of the child, or sought with false gospels to lead it astray from its Shepherd.

It was at this point, as people who were there told me, that the S.S. man of Himmler's Gestapo and his companion stood up and both stamped into the middle of the broad aisle. They clicked their heels for all to hear, raised right arms above the level of their eyes in Nazi salute, and both said loudly: "*Heil* Hitler!"

The congregation sat in stony silence. They tell me that Prince von Galen, German patriot and able servant of God, looked with quiet tolerance at the two in the aisle facing him and waited for them to speak. The expression on his face clearly said: "My poor friends, why must you wait so long to muster the courage to carry out your orders? Please proceed."

But they did not march forward to arrest him. They had slightly different orders. The one who had stood up first stared straight before him and shouted:

"You preach here in a language of hidden meanings, aimed to stir the minds of these Germans against the government. You talk of home and the family and children and call on us to follow the example of one who is told of as a man without a family of his own—a bachelor wandering from one place to the next but never settled long enough to establish a home and learn to know it. And what could he know of children?"

It was typical Nazi language and an accurate reflection of Rosenberg's utterances. The crudeness and callousness of

Nazi sneers in the face of Christianity were amply contained in the S.S. man's words and tone.

The bishop on the altar gazed for just a moment at the heckler before him and a slow hint of amusement and sarcasm spread over his face. He raised the finger of his right hand and wagged it solemnly in protest.

"I will not have the Fuehrer insulted in this house of God or hear slanders against him," he declared as gravely as though pronouncing the benediction.

There were sudden snickers among the congregation; they tell me you could almost hear the cheering, although actually, of course, nobody cheered aloud. But the blow hit home, and the S.S. men paled visibly at the verbal boomerang.

There was no comeback possible, even if their minds had been agile enough to grasp for one, and in any case it was dangerous to trifle with parallels on Christ and the Fuehrer. They were on somewhat thin ice there. So they swallowed hard and clicked heels again with another "*Heil Hitler!*"

"You will hear from us," the one who had done the talking said, and both swung about and marched down the aisle and out with clanking heels. Bishop Galen went on with his sermon, finishing later the reading of Mass without any outward sign of agitation. Afterward he put on his bishop's mantle and purple biretta and went over to his residence, easy of conscience but firm of heart.

The Gestapo were waiting in his study. They wanted to

take him away, but outside there was clamor and shouting for the Bishop of Münster. Hundreds of the faithful had sensed the menace and boldly crowded the street in front of the bishopry in defiance of the combined threats of police and Nazi storm troops. Vociferously they shouted for their bishop, threatening disorders if he failed to appear.

The Gestapo men were in a quandary and shifted the burden of responsibility by putting quick calls through to Gestapo headquarters in Berlin.

Ten minutes later all but two of them left, and the bishop stepped to the open window to bless his flock. He told them to go home and not to worry about him, as he would remain in their midst. He did not tell them that from that day on he would be shadowed and escorted wherever he went, under house arrest and subject to all sorts of fine annoyances in which the Gestapo excels.

But the battle he fought was not fought entirely in vain. The forces unleashed by him and equally courageous men of the Church and outside of it swelled the pressure to such proportions that Hitler had to give ear and in the end unbend to forestall what began to look like a serious inner rift on the home front.

He danced around Fuehrer headquarters with fury but finally told Himmler and Bormann to lay off, therewith suspending for the present the Nazi onslaught against the Catholic Church.

But those of us who know our Berlin and the wild men in the Nazi party are not fooled. Nor have the undaunted bishops of Germany been fooled by the letup.

It is nothing but a truce, a breathing space to the next move, for in the minds and pockets of these Nazis rests like an embedded rock that Rosenberg plan for a National Church of Greater Germany, be it Protestant or Catholic, but stripped under all circumstances of outside ramifications and of the gospels and preachings injurious to Nazism and its doctrines. There can be no compromise or halfway solution here.

Bormann naturally was sore of heart when the brake was slapped on his crusade against the Catholic Church, although there was some consolation in the fact that no high command came for the reopening of the Catholic orders and convents he had closed, or the restoration of that property to the rightful owners.

Nor was there any indication that his drive against the Jews would be interfered with. He sat in the Kaiserhof Hotel bar and drank great gulps of champagne, mulling the whole thing over in his head.

Yes, the Catholics had stopped him again, but the Jews hadn't a ghost of a chance. Himmler and he had agreed— and Himmler's sharp-faced assistant Heydrich was in on it —that the Jew must be torn up by the root and wiped from the face of the Reich.

The Catholic campaign and other urgent tasks inside the Nazi party had kept him pretty busy all summer, but now was the time to get going. The head of every Jew must roll in the sand, one way or another.

The first essential step was to prepare the public mind and arouse antagonism against every Jew.

I remember well the days of late summer in Berlin, when propaganda slogans from all sides shrieked suddenly that the Jew was the enemy of all Germany.

Worried and trembling, Jewish friends and acquaintances came in the black-out to the foreign correspondents and inquired in frightened voices as to what was in the wind. They had suddenly been ordered to give up roomy apartments or move on short notice into crowded quarters assigned to them with other Jewish families.

Later they couldn't even go out after 8 P.M. They had to register themselves and every stitch they owned anew and in itemized detail with the police.

4

Bormann was busy again with the full support of Himmler and the whole-hearted sanction of all the fanatical Nazis.

We knew that the plight of the Jews in Poland was terrible beyond description, a living hell ruled by corrupt and grafting S.S. overseers and dealers in death, who sold the Jew his lease on existence and life day by day for money and valuables he could offer, but once penniless they'd drop him like a hot brick and soon he was just another on the condemned list.

The mortality rate in the ghettos of Poland stands high and is climbing steadily. For men like Bormann it cannot climb fast enough.

Men of his kind foisted on the German Army the supposition that every Communist is a Jew and every Jew a

Communist, consequently the backbone of Stalin's war machine.

Every inch of the scorched red earth in Russia was played up in the eyes of German soldiers by tireless propaganda as resting on the shoulders of Jews alone, inspired by Jews around Stalin and transformed into a policy by the "half-caste Jew" Stalin.

Therefore, it was possible last fall to read on front pages of German newspapers indicative revelations like those in a clipping from a leading Nazi newspaper in Berlin which I brought with me. Signed by Nazi War Correspondent Kurt Kraenzlein, it says in part:

"It is but natural to find the Jew in occupied regions the friend of Bolshevism and the most dangerous single influence on public opinion. It was the Jews alone who carried out Stalin's orders to destroy barracks, public buildings, factories, and storehouses.

"In many cases they plundered towns and villages before leaving, or buried available supplies. The smoky black walls and windows of Russia often are not from the effect of shell or bomb but solely the work of the firebrand Jew. The Jew, and before all the Jewess, is the foremost ally of our foe.

"Against this dark enemy behind our lines, frequently part and parcel of the criminal element, German authorities proceed with iron hand. In all towns of Russia, Jews are being assigned their own reserved section. Day by day they are being evacuated from the villages.

"Everywhere they are commandeered for productive

work. Acts against the safety of the German Army or local population are summarily punished. The ghettoing and death penalty do not solve the Jew problem in Russia any more than up to now it has in the Reich, but much can be done as time goes on, when circumstances and the New Order in Europe will contribute much to the final liquidation of Jews on the European continent."

I reprint this extract of Nazi propaganda against the Jews to give a better understanding of the background and the causes of events that happened. As is customary in the Hitler way of doing things, the German Army goes in and occupies a country by force of arms, but on its heels to subdue and "adjust" it comes the dreaded S.S. and Gestapo of Heinrich Himmler. They carry a black list, too, and every name thereon is hunted down for the reckoning.

As in all occupied lands after the conquest, the Jew was the chief target and victim in Russia. Not only did the S.S. go on a rampage there but the mob was incited wherever possible to have a field day against the Jews.

Thus it stands in the records of Bormann and Himmler in Berlin that by the end of October 58,000 Jews had been slaughtered in the Riga area alone. The S.S. had turned the machine guns and population loose at the same time and made short shrift of the Jews around there. Similar shocking casualty figures come daily to your ears in Berlin from people who have been there.

Down as far as the Black Sea, whither I sent my American assistant in Berlin, Hugo Speck, last October, the guns are blazing away at the Jews under Nazi guidance. In the naval shipyard city of Nikolayev, where the Rumanians took over after the Germans drove the Soviets out, more than 4,000 Jews were killed in one day. In the smaller port of Otchav, Speck and a Danish colleague saw a boy of fourteen lugging a heavy-looking rifle, obviously with eyes open for a target to shoot at. He spoke French, or enough to carry on a conversation.

"What are you shooting at?" Speck asked.

"Jews," the Rumanian lad replied. "I get five lei for every one I kill. On this stick in my hand I have thirty-four notches, each made by a policeman I show the dead Jew to. When I have fifty, then I get an extra bonus. It is only three o'clock in the afternoon and it will not be dark for three hours. I may get the fifty."

Farther up the street the two correspondents saw the untended bodies of several Jews, pushed aside into the gutter until they could be hauled away. That is the lot of the Jews in New Order Europe today.

Perhaps, in his carpeted office in Berlin, Bormann dreamed of liquidating the less than 300,000 remaining Jews in the Greater Reich as speedily and systematically.

Therefore, every Jew first of all had to be exposed to the mob, branded, and identified beyond all possibility of mistake. He did this by pushing through an edict compelling every Jew—man, woman, or child—to wear over the heart on overcoat or blouse a Star of David of yellow cloth two inches across. Then with Joe Goebbels' aid he put over a propaganda campaign calling on the German people to take note of the many Jews still in their midst.

This didn't faze the downtrodden Jews so much; in fact, they kept their chins up and went almost proudly about their business. I saw a German officer step up to an old gentleman with a Star of David in the Tiergarten and salute him, with apologies for the Fatherland.

But the mob and the narrow-minded and prejudiced little German striving to be 500 per cent Nazi when any superior of his is looking went out of the way to annoy the Jews.

The Nazis, to assuage the offended and anxious section of the public mind, spread the word through school and beer hall that the Star of David was fixed on Jews because in America President Roosevelt had compelled every German to wear the swastika in his coat lapel. That was a typical trick of slick Joe Goebbels.

Bormann's outfit, aided by the Gestapo, went further step by step and organized a fine terrorization campaign against the Jews. The night telephone call, the knock on the door, and the sudden arrest of some member of the Jewish family blanched faces and revived suicides by the score. It had happened before, but never on such a large scale.

The most diabolical of all was the black-bordered death notice that came through the regular mails to hundreds of Jews in Berlin. I saw dozens of these cards, printed in staid black type with crossed palm branches at the bottom. It read:

"You are instructed herewith to deliver your useless person at 3 P.M. tomorrow to the ground back of Lichtenberg cemetery, equipped with spade or shovel, to dig the hole in which you will lie with other Jews after liquidation of your carcass free of cost."

In Berlin alone that devilish little card produced scores of deaths from heart shock or suicide. Jews came around to us with blanched faces, in the depths of despair, fully cognizant by now of the sworn oaths of Bormann that before the end of 1941 not a single Jew would be left inside Germany. The lid was off; Bormann was riding high and the Gestapo and S.S. pounced like packs of hungry wolves on the Jews.

One dark night in the black-out I walked past the big synagogue on Fasanen Strasse. It had been gutted by flames after the Nazis set fire to it in their mad outburst of violence against the Jews in November of 1938. Only the walls remained in mute testimony of the crime.

I saw large motor trucks drawn up there, and thought it might be one of the mobile anti-aircraft batteries getting located for a night's raid. But I heard sobbing and moans in the dark, and harsh voices commanding people to move fast. I slowed down and even walked back, trying to catch the meaning of it all. I had stumbled by chance, as it turned out from subsequent developments, on the first of the systematic hauls of Jews from their homes for assembly in synagogues and transport next day to bleak ghettos in Galicia.

Bormann's method of liquidating the Jews was as thorough as it was inhumane. Night after night, beginning around 11 P.M., flying squadrons of Gestapo in motor trucks would spread over the city and knock or ring peremptorily at addresses of Jews on their list.

The terrified members of that Jewish family, five or seventy years old as the case might be, were told then and there by their sinister visitors to get out of bed and within one hour be ready to leave with not more than thirty pounds of clothing and personal possessions in hand, in addition to not more than ten marks apiece.

The wailing and weeping availed nothing; those who died of fright or by their own hand in the space of that hour were carted away along with the living. The Gestapo always turned out the lights after their victims had gone down the stairs into those waiting trucks, and carefully pasted a printed slip over the door outside leading into the apartment saying:

"Closed and sealed by the Secret State Police."

The motor trucks, when filled to capacity, proceeded with doused blue headlights to one of the several big synagogues of Berlin, there to unload their cargo of agonized human beings with muttered oaths and commands. The synagogue in Fasanen Strasse, roofless and windowless, received about five hundred nightly. Some of the others got more.

Next morning, or even two days later, when pneumonia and sheer misery had ravaged the weak and the old and reduced the survivors by an appreciable percentage, the S.S. loaded them again on trucks, and off they went on the long ride to Poland.

Many more died on those cold trips; scores died within

a short time after being dumped into miserable little villages located on the barren stretches of Galicia earmarked by the Nazis as Ghettoland.

S.S. rifles, of course, greatly helped the mortality rate.

In Berlin, the Spree Canal had to be dragged every morning for its haul of bodies, to prevent epidemic. They were all bodies of Jews.

I knew a very cultured Jewish family who in 1935 owned a great Berlin department store. Man and wife had gradually been pushed down the ladder to a two-room apartment.

When the Gestapo came on the inevitable night, she sat in front of her boudoir mirror, ready for bed and in beautiful silk pajamas. She had a drink of excellent Martell on her dressing table and rings on her fingers.

She smiled when the Gestapo entered and told the man in the doorway of the bedroom to come in. She told him over her shoulder she was alone, all alone, because her husband at the moment was hanging dead out there in the bathroom. She drank her Martell and, very nicely, before there could be any roughhousing or interfering, she shot herself straight through the heart with a beautiful little revolver.

She died as she was born, a lady.

The Gestapo men who had to do the dirty work of gathering the Jews in at night complained that so many of those on the list were not to be found. Apparently they slept away from home, desperately hoping to stall off the black fate another day. So Bormann dispatched advance notices to the victims days ahead, telling them just when their turn would come and to be on hand. That caused more suicides.

The Nazis were angry by the end of October when they had to admit to themselves that the job of tearing some 300,000 human beings away from the land is not easy.

I found out from one of the Gestapo that Himmler and Bormann were raising Cain in early November because the records showed that only 86,000 Jews had been taken away from Berlin to Poland up to then. Twice as many remained. When I left some weeks later, the raids on Jews were continued with renewed vigor.

The Nazis touched no foreign Jew up to then, except those in occupied lands. But I heard from very good source that the foreign Jew will be "regulated" in Germany in 1942.

When America and Germany went to war, the last loophole of escape for the Jew was closed. But even before that the blow had fallen. On the night of November 5, at 9 P.M., the usual special train carrying émigrés away from the Reich stood on the tracks of Friedrichstrasse Bahnhof waiting for the signal to move off.

The émigrés without exception were Jews, who had secured permission to enter foreign lands after years of waiting. Many had been on the list of the American Embassy, waiting their turn. When it came and the final German and foreign papers were in hand, they sold everything except the clothes on their backs and kept ten marks in cash after paying off all tickets and incidentals.

The Germans had regularly provided a special train for transport of these outcasts to Lisbon. As they put it, they were glad to get rid of them. The Jews on those trains could hardly restrain tears of joy, and from an abyss of despair climbed into a new paradise of life mile by mile as the train left Hitler's land behind.

But that special train on the night of November 5 never did get the go signal. At 9:10 P.M. S.S. men in steel helmets and plain-clothes Gestapo men appeared in swarms on the platform and rudely commanded all to get off that train. They were told to take only a bundle of personal possessions and leave everything else behind.

Then, amid the wailing and shouting, they were marched downstairs to the inevitable trucks. Two men dashed past the guards before they could fire and sprang to death in front of an electric train just coming in on the other side of the platform.

That was the last special train scheduled to leave for Lisbon.

In the Berlin newspapers during November you could read long advertisements by official auctioneers. They offered scores and scores of auctions in furniture and clothes, all confiscated from apartments of Jews gone to Poland.

There was a mad rush on the part of the Nazis to get at these coveted goods, and wives of Nazi officials even pulled each other's hair at these auctions. In the party offices they distributed the empty apartments among themselves and patted themselves on the back for a job well done.

Thus Bormann the little Nazi of a few years ago and

of the ominous prophecies became Big-Shot Bormann with favors to give.

He can stand in front of his mirror now and say to himself that thousands of Nazis are grateful to him for crushing the Jew and bestowing on his friends the wonderful apartments and furniture offered for a song.

CHAPTER 11

Hitler's Battle of Wits with Stalin

LATE IN DECEMBER OF 1940, when wind laden with snow swept the bleak fields of East Prussia, the hardbitten farmers of the land in the areas closest to Russia scratched their heads and went around to the local branch house of the Nazi party to ask why they shouldn't prepare their fields for spring planting. They showed the official circular they had received through the mails that day advising them that spring planting would have to be dispensed with; many of those living in the immediate vicinities of the frontier in succeeding weeks were even told to move with livestock and bodily possessions to points inland. Questions by the worried farmers were answered by local Nazi-party administrators with gruff reminders that orders are orders neither to be questioned nor disobeyed.

It wasn't much comfort, and the farmers were made even more miserable by the sudden ruthless requisitioning of all available draught horses. That hit home hard, for in East Prussia the farmer and his horse are one and inseparable. The horse does the work in those wind-swept open fields and never bogs down during the rainy spells. It is a part of the family.

Other orders, equally mystifying, came from time to time, leaving the impression after awhile that the area in which they lived was being transformed into a military operations zone. They began to hear over the grapevine, as did· all of us foreign correspondents in Berlin, that in the areas of former Poland now bordering that of the Soviets the situation was much worse. There the Germans didn't bother to instruct and compensate people for their removal from house and home or for the loss of spring planting: they simply marched the Poles out of those villages and towns to already crowded places in Galicia and let it go at that. That is the way the Nazis do things where Poles are concerned.

I remember well the gnarled little woman from East Prussia who came to relatives in Berlin just after New Year, weeping bitterly at the cruelty and injustice of having to vacate the house and the patch of ground she lived on. Without explanation, but at least with some compensation. *"Der gute Hans ist weg. Eingezogen."* And she cried some more. I sympathized politely with host and hostess and their troubled visitor. *"Ja,* Hans was a good worker. He never made trouble in the fields or the barn and the veterinary told me he is the finest horse in the country. Now he has to go out and pull cannons."

I felt somewhat less sympathetic, disinclined to feel sorry to the point of tears for a horse drafted into the army. Our hostess, the visitor's sister-in-law, apparently looked at it the same way and made an added explanation for my benefit:

"What made it so hard for her is that her only son was called to the military a few days earlier," she said. "He ran the farm, didn't he, Gretchen?"

The tearful visitor looked up, trying to stem her grief, to focus her mind on the conversation going on around her. "*Ja,* my son was called too. I have a letter from him, and all is well. But I cannot bring myself to write him that Hans is gone. It is terrible." She wiped her eyes with a moist handkerchief. "Last week," she added, "they brought many bus loads of men and trucks of supplies to the village. Out in the fields and woods they are building and digging like crazy men. We could not visit our own fields to measure the snowfall. All is forbidden, with soldiers standing everywhere like policemen. I think they heard of our Hans and came to get him for the work."

I perked up my ears and looked out of the window, away from the host and hostess, as if I hadn't heard or taken notice. They were Germans of the middle class, none too bright but straightforward and honest. The woman from East Prussia had babbled forth something in the presence of a foreigner which could have brought the Gestapo down on their heads. They apparently didn't notice, and I felt relieved. Rumors had come from time to time of vast activity on the eastern borders, where Hitler was said to have ordered his construction master-at-all-tasks Major-General Fritz Todt, now dead, to complete him an eastern wall of fortifications as solid as the Siegfried Line. Thousands upon thousands of labor service men going out on trains and by bus toward the east, I now knew for certain, were engaged in large-scale military activity of some sort on the Russo-German frontier. This woman had seen it, not just heard the rumor.

I can look back now and understand the urgent necessity of keeping all they did secret in those months preceding the attack on Russia. None knew at that time of the startling decision Hitler had announced to his inner circle on December 15, when he summoned them to hear that the time for a showdown with Soviet Russia had come. From that day on the wheels began to function. In effect, the Nazis and Hitler's armies basically were ready and waiting to take on Russia at the first opportunity, but it required some months to assemble the vast war machine in all its aspects and with all its striking power. Hitler gave his generals orders for the attack to take place on April 20, 1941, but Moscow learned of the intended attack and pulled the coup against him in Yugoslavia, which forced him to march through the southeast first and postpone the Russian invasion to June 22.

All moves against Russia, massive in scale, were to be carried out until the zero hour under the mantle of friendship with Moscow as properly established in the Amity Pact of 1939 and the subsequent trade deals. In fact, Hitler reinforced his orders that everything and anything dealing with Russia inside Germany or going out of Germany must be couched in the nicest vein. He made speeches lauding Stalin and Russia, reaffirming that the Reich and the Soviet republics had buried the hatchet and never again would be foolishly at each other's throats. We foreign correspondents were constantly warned against falling for dark rumors floating around town that all was not well. The late Ralph Barnes, an American colleague working out of Berlin for a New York paper at the time, was summarily ordered to leave Germany because he wrote a story suggesting that the Hitler-Stalin friendship was not what it was cracked up to be. The Nazis would hear none of that, and rapped the knuckles of any Nazi foolishly reverting to old battle songs against Bolshevists in alcoholic moments.

"There is no reason why National Socialist Germany and Soviet Russia should not get along," the glib-tongued spokesmen of the Wilhelmstrasse were coached to say. "We Nazis have our Weltanschauung, and it stands in the record of many Fuehrer speeches that Nazism is not for export across the borders. Communism no longer exists in Germany and will never come again. We have nothing to fear from Moscow any longer, and what Moscow does in the outside world does not concern us. We are interested in making trade deals with Russia and mutually benefiting by the exchange of goods or raw materials. We both are realists."

That and much more was said to keep up the deceptive front and hide from the eyes of the world in general, and Moscow in particular, any suggestion of the deep treachery being prepared behind the scenes. Hitler was playing his favorite game of lulling the next victim to sleep with large doses of security propaganda, preparing at the same time for the moment when the knockout potion would come. He sent whole corps of economic and technical experts to Moscow to give advice and even sign trade deals amounting to billions of marks; he delivered machinery and manufactured goods by the trainload in return for wheat and oil, declining to listen when tales came to his ears from suspicious and enraged key men of his Economic Ministry about the obvious double-crossing and sabotaging in Russian deliveries.

Hitler was playing his game of bluffing Stalin quietly, confidently, never for a moment doubting that he would catch Stalin unaware and smash him and the Red Army long before he could be ready to make a real stand. It goes without saying that when the Russo-German Pact of August 1939 was signed, Hitler and Stalin both, in their innermost hearts, fully understood that they were merely marking time against each other. They spied on each other at every opportunity, careful at all times to do so under the guise of military and economic co-operation.

They exchanged not only fine goods and raw materials along with serious-minded experts but also crack military key men. German officers from the General Staff were assigned to Moscow as military attachés, and Stalin retaliated by planting in Berlin a dozen of his best from the Red Army. The Japs and the Italians watched the festivities in Berlin and the picnics between the German and Red military with growing dismay and with some foreboding.

From their standpoint this wasn't so good, although on the whole it was remarkable how little concern seemed to be felt either in Rome or Tokyo. A whole staff of Red Army officers came with the powerful new Moscow Ambassador Dekanozov; in Moscow on the railway station platform Stalin embraced the German military chargé and told him before all that everything was hunky-dory and never again would Russia and Germany revert to the knife to please the capitalistic democracies. No, never again, and Stalin slapped the beaming German major heartily on the back. That was after Matsuoka had come through from Berlin and Rome and had just been given an official farewell at the Moscow railway station by Stalin. Molotov and a whole trainload of his entourage had just returned to the Kremlin from Hitler's capital, too, with a special freight car hooked on to carry all the goods they had purchased in Germany. The Germans had stood aghast as the Soviets swept like a tornado through the huge Berlin department stores, emptying even the display shelves, and therewith giving the Nazis some of the medicine they'd been giving the occupied lands. It was a real cleanout, and they say that even today Stalin is going around wearing the warm underwear Molotov brought him from Berlin along with the shaving outfit of silver.

2

So the comedy of make-believe went on through the early months of 1941, although beneath the surface the Molotov visit to Berlin produced a stalemate.

Hitler took the visit as a sign that Stalin was eager to please and keep on good terms and therefore thought nothing of the sour smile Molotov wore on the platform of Goerlitzer Banhof the day he left. Hitler may have thought that Molotov slept badly on account of the nuisance raid the R.A.F. had staged on Berlin the night before for the visitor's benefit.

Stalin must have been laughing into his mustache in the early months of 1941. He had Hitler fooled, and he knew it. Hitler himself spent a lot of hours inside that Berlin chancellery in those early months of 1941, laughing up his sleeve at Stalin. He thought he had Stalin fooled, and if suspicion of his sincerity and intentions was increasing week by week, it didn't matter much because Hitler was sure of his case.

All intelligence reports from the Military Espionage in the German High Command had agreed with his fifth column inside Russia that the Red Army would crack after the first blitz thunderbolts hit home. A long report on his desk stressed the internal confusion in the land and its deadening effect on the machinery of the Red Army. The consensus of opinion in the heavily sealed secret documents which he received was that Soviet Russia could be whipped by the German Army in about six weeks; much stress was laid then on the probability of an early blowup within Russia and Stalin's fall once he became entangled in a foreign war and the sins of his past rose up against him. It was felt that Red Army leadership, nursing grievous wounds from the killings of its best brains by G.P.U.

squads on Stalin's orders, would rise to the opportunity for revenge and turn the machine guns loose against the Communists and their hair-trigger troops.

"In fact," Hitler was told by a Balkan diplomat stooging for him in Moscow, "it is the assured opinion here that the Soviet military inner circle is pressing Stalin to change course in his relations with Germany and make a firm stand against any German demands in relation to the Balkans or Finland. We are deducing from this and other tendencies we observe here in Moscow that the Red Army inner circle intends to get rid of Stalin and the ruling Communist ring at any price, and are willing to go to the extent of suffering military defeat at the hands of Germany as their best chance of overthrowing Stalin and his regime."

Hitler, if he was skeptical, nevertheless placed that report beside the others, which included the weighty documents of 1940 summarizing the effects and causes of the Soviet debacle in Finland and the ridiculous display made by the Red Army in taking over the part of Poland donated by him to Stalin as the first reward for signing on the dotted line in 1939. It had taken the Red Army a couple of weeks to reach that demarcation line, more than six days behind schedule. German officers sent across the line to size up the Red Army in action came back with flea-bitten skins and a look in their eyes which spoke of contempt and disdain for armed mobs of the sort they had seen.

The Red Army, they said, had no discipline whatever and was nothing more than a traveling mob of conscripts officered by men who didn't know what a wrist watch was for and who were hounded and dogged by political commissars who held the power of life and death over everybody.

Why, the officers said, with a touch of the Prussian abhorrence for anything contrary to military form, they had seen women in the ranks carrying rifles just like soldiers or driving trucks and even tanks. It was difficult to understand, this Red Army of Stalin's, except of course that his blood purge had robbed the top of all coherence and efficiency.

Hitler filed those reports away for future reference, in the same file as the opinion on the Russian Air Force brought back from Russia the year before by Charles Lindbergh. The American had not been much impressed by what he had seen, particularly after a good look at the Luftwaffe and its intricate and vast ground and technical network.

Hitler held his own counsel and when the Soviets successively swallowed the Baltic States he issued circular instructions to the German Army and the Nazi party silencing all outspoken criticism, although that couldn't entirely shut off the beer-hall storm and fury sweeping over the land. All the sugar-coating spread on the Russian snatch of the Baltics could not silence the popular indignation, and that murmuring tide reached almost dangerous proportions when Stalin attacked Finland. That was a country particularly close to German hearts, for Finnish and German officers had fought side by side for the same cause in the troubled days of World War I when Finland broke away from Mother Russia to resume an ancient independence.

Nevertheless, Hitler commanded silence on the subject in Germany. In the press conference at the Foreign Office, where Finnish journalists asked nasty questions along with other Scandinavians, youthful Paul Schmidt, as Ribbentrop's mouthpiece, delivered himself one day of a pompous oration:

"If Russia feels herself menaced at a vital point of entry, then it is but natural that she should find ways and means of guarding herself. We are neutral bystanders and do not see reason to interfere or intercede if Russia considers it vital to her security to have control over all points leading into and out of the Finnish Gulf."

That, in a nutshell, was the official policy of the Reich toward the 1940 war in Finland. But every Russian defeat or setback started off the popping of a million champagne corks all over Europe and particularly in Berlin.

Hitler sat back in his chancellery and read every item from the Russo-Finnish War with care, wearing, as he does on occasions, his horn-rimmed spectacles. All reports agreed with previous observation that the Red Army was a colossus without real striking power or military leadership. It was an exceptionally bad winter, of course, but even that couldn't excuse the sort of debacle transpiring on the snowfields of Finland. The Red Army, he concluded in the end, would be no threat in the rear during the coming attack on the west. By next year, with Stalin floundering in lost military prestige and happy to have no quarrels to worry about with Berlin, the road to Moscow would be appreciably easier. All it needed was time and patience.

Thus it came about that Hitler along with the German General Staff and the Finns became victims of the greatest hoax in military history.

I have heard high German officers frankly confess to it, and in Finland and around the Ladoga front I again heard crack Finnish generals and officers corroborate the fact that Stalin fooled everybody with diabolical cleverness in Finland at the price of enormous sacrifices. He achieved the impossible of hiding from outside eyes the amazing strength and titan equipment of his Red Army. He kept it under cover for the supreme test, offering the world only glimpses of a second-rate war machine.

If there is one thing the Nazi invasion of Russia accomplished beyond doubt, it was the penetration of Russia's inner secret. In the last twenty years, as the Germans soon found out, the Stalin regime had built up a war industry and war machine never before equaled in history. That was the whole secret of Soviet Russia, and to avoid its exposure strangers were never allowed to rove freely around the land. Intourist arranged for all visits of the ordinary tourist from the outside; the G.P.U. and silence cloaked everything else.

In Russia, as is now clear, Lindbergh in his 1938 visit there was shown everything of ordinary interest but nothing of vital importance which could serve as a signpost to the real air power in hand. Stalin sent the Red Army into his share of Poland with careful instructions—as German and

Finnish officers have since heard from Soviet officers taken prisoners—to use only raw recruits with secondary equipment.

In Finland, during 1940, reserve troops of secondary units, gathered together from everywhere inside Russia, were thrown into the battle, supported by tanks and guns taken from second-rate stock in the arsenals. Only a few of the newer types later were tested out, as has now become known. It was all part of the Stalin game, for the vast space of Russia easily swallowed the real Red Army and air force.

3

We foreign correspondents sat amid the usual political maelstrom of Berlin at the beginning of 1941 and kept ears and eyes alert to see where the next blitz would strike. People came around by the dozen to sell us exclusive tips, most of which tried to convey the impression that Hitler and Stalin were cooking up a military pact actively bringing Russia either into the Three-Power Pact of the Axis or at the very least opening the transit road for his troops through Russia down into the Middle East. It was one of those Nazi ruses you smell out only by intuition and after years of experience.

One day a German woman of aristocratic family called me for tea, as she was wont to do occasionally. She was very much puzzled and when I got there showed me a letter from her husband, the titled Count von ——, an officer of high standing in the German Army.

I looked at the postmark and marveled. It was from Tiflis,

far down in Georgia, the town where Stalin came from in his youth. The German officer simply said in his letter not to worry and that all was well, although he might be out of touch for a while.

There was no other explanation, except that on the surface it bolstered rumors of German troop movements through Russia toward the Turkish border. Was there a deal on after all between Hitler and Stalin, as everybody seemed to think? I looked at that postmark again and wondered. Something warned me to go easy.

That was only the beginning, for in successive weeks after that letter it became a common tale to hear of German soldiers who wrote their families of the vastness of space they were marching through in Russia. In several cases, as I remember, those letters gave graphic descriptions of the dust and the food, the flies, and the waterless stretches.

"Three weeks we have marched," a young shavetail wrote to his girl friend in Berlin, who promptly showed the letter around to all her friends. "Three long, dreary weeks and the end is not in sight. We have just crossed the Volga and are going south. You mustn't tell anyone. There is a proverb in this land which says: 'The sky is high and Russia is big; the czar is far away.' They will say that, czar and all in it. So you can imagine what a strange country it is. But my men are standing the strain well."

I went to the Taverne of evenings to drink champagne and eat lobster to avoid the use of food tickets, and mulled the situation over in my head.

It seemed strange, this whole business of German troops

in Russia. For instance, how come army censorship was letting the men get through such important information in letters to families or relatives and girl friends dead sure to gossip?

By coincidence, too, German families well acquainted with us foreign correspondents seemed to be recipients of those letters. Was there a catch to it, or did I detect by instinct the fine hand of Goebbels in the background?

I called on my good Russian friends who acted as correspondents in Berlin for the official Soviet News Agency Tass and sounded them out on the whole thing. They knew me pretty well and were always willing to talk if sure there were no strange dictaphones or Nazi ears around to eavesdrop. They could make no head or tail of these German letters.

Late one night I was asked to step over to the Russian Embassy on Unter den Linden to have a chat. Dekanozov, the Ambassador and a key man in the Stalin regime, through the Tass man who interpreted, swore up and down that not a single German soldier was inside Russia, except for the military attachés in Moscow.

I went back to the Taverne that night and sat out a long air raid, drinking schnapps with beer for a chaser while the guns roared outside and occasional shocks like an earthquake informed us that somewhere in that part of town a heavy bomb had blasted holes into property and lives.

Willy of the Taverne and I shot dice until nearly dawn to kill time. By morning I went home, convinced within myself that Goebbels and his propaganda machine were hard at work spinning a new web of camouflage to hide something nasty going on behind the scenes. A plain military order to officer or soldier could easily bring him to pen the desired letter, with the desired postmark stamped on in government printing shops. Military silence and secrecy would accomplish the rest.

There were other symptoms to back up the suspicion that Hitler was playing the old game again of throwing up a smoke screen to hide his real hand. He'd done that before his sweep to the Channel, preluding it for weeks at a time with scare propaganda of war about to burst over the Mediterranean. Obviously, he desperately wanted us to believe that he and Stalin were marching in step, while preparing in actuality something entirely different on one spot of the map or another. The question was where.

It came to my ears through the grapevine about that time that out in East Prussia and around Poland all prisoners of war were being removed from the camps there to places farther west. Nearly a million men of all nationalities were being evacuated, obviously to make room for new customers.

The main camps, I heard about the same time, were also being enlarged to nearly twice the present capacity. Thousands of carpenters aided by war prisoners were working day and night building new camps, and by early May I heard that accommodations for three million war prisoners stood ready in the east.

That was something worth keeping in mind, and I was

careful to make no mention of the knowledge gained. The heat of this sort of information is enough to burn your fingers in Naziland, unless you know how to watch your step.

Other evidence of big things brewing came progressively to our ears, like the ominous signs of a blood-soaked spring ahead. Thousands of horses throughout Germany and the occupied lands were quietly being commandeered into the army, recalled to their place in the sun. In the west there had been little use for them, as tanks took care of all needs. But on the long and roadless steppes in the east they would be enormously useful, as would the picturesque cavalry of old.

I watched the long columns of them again clomping through the avenues of Berlin, tail on tail and led by a few soldiers, as I had seen in the first days of war when Hitler blitzed Poland.

One day, as I stood outside the Adlon vainly trying to hail a rare taxi, a clattering and scraping of steel on stone drew my attention to the corner of Wilhelmstrasse and Unter den Linden.

A column of Panzers were roaring through the red lights, paying no attention to the police or the traffic. They were squat, square-nosed affairs, strikingly devoid of the usual round turret. A formidable new type, obviously, with something like a three-inch cannon projecting from the flat-topped center.

The tanks must have weighed about twenty tons each and anybody could see they were built to take it on the rough through walls and wood. A total switch in design from those used out west against the British and French. I made a mental note of the incident.

Back in my office on the fourth floor of Dorotheenstrasse I had troubles of my own. The military was pulling in men for service at terrific pace, taking peg legs and hunchbacks in the rush. There had never been anything like it, and exemptions were practically impossible to secure.

Like all American press outfits in Berlin, the office routine was handled by seasoned Germans who had worked for us anywhere from fifteen to twenty years. Some of the office boys had grown up with International News Service, so to say, and knew no other way of making a livelihood. They banked on me, their immediate chief, and sought refuge and comfort from the hard Nazi hand in the protection and influence I was able now and then to exert through contacts.

At the start of the war the names of every one of them came up for military service, like those of millions of other Germans. I rushed around to the Wilhelmstrasse and in due time secured exemptions on the ground that they were doing highly specialized work and that their drafting into the army would cripple an American news agency.

That worked, although from time to time in the next two years the calling card of one or another came up again and I'd have to go through the same process of indignant protestation.

Early in January the military refused to hear of exemptions. The American situation by that time was of no help and so I lost two of our men. Three months later I sat in my office and faced the prospect of losing two more of the staff. It looked bad, and all around town the same story could be heard. Even skilled men in war factories were being placed into active service.

Everything pointed to an unprecedented move afoot, calling for millions of new men. And yet the Nazis refused to change tune on Russia, doggedly maintaining silence on all questions in that connection.

4

In April, Hitler struck at Yugoslavia, and his armies marched clear through to the Mediterranean.

A dozen of the seasoned correspondents among us were invited as usual to follow the German Army and with one-time Big-Shot Karl Boemer in charge we moved out of Berlin in half-a-dozen army cars and a supply truck to start on the hardest trip I had made under war conditions up to that time.

Ten days later we drove into Athens, hot and weary but rich in experience and material. In a famous restaurant on a side street, under the shadow of the majestic Acropolis and amid the noise of an overcrowded place, I heard German officers of the line speculate, over the wine and Turkish coffee that night, on the amazing order in hand from head-quarters to turn right around and report for duty at un-named points.

They had heard hints of where they would go but weren't sure. Some mentioned Adrianople; others spoke of the Turkish border. In any case, they were not going back west.

A week later our party was driving back through Macedonia and Yugoslavia en route to Berlin. The shooting in Greece had scarcely died down yet here we met the crack units of the German Army marching north again, hardly pausing for a night's rest. The Panzers, the motor trucks, and the motorized infantry were everywhere. They clogged passes and filled the roads. Huge dust clouds in the May heat stood like milestones over the mountainous landscape. It was terrific.

Back in Berlin the old silence prevailed, although the Nazi tempers were getting an edge on over questions and rumors relating to Russia and things in the wind.

The dispatch of heavy German troop detachments to Finland, secretive and delicate as the subject was around the Wilhelmstrasse in those warm May days, nevertheless was the talk at every beer table. From Finnish sources we knew that those German troops moving into the woods of Finland were heavily equipped for war.

Furthermore, all windy explanations by the Nazis of needing enormous supplies for their troops in the southeast could not allay suspicions from growing when it became known that railway and road traffic going east was jamming aside all normal movement.

We foreign correspondents looked at each other and said nothing. To have mentioned anything in dispatches would have brought swift retributions on our head.

Then one day late in May the first little crack of light

pierced the mantle of camouflage hiding the huge moves behind the scene. *Pravda* in Moscow had issued another of those communiqués deftly showing the rapier underneath the surface in Hitler-Stalin relations. It was one of those communiqués worded with skill and tact, printed and commented on by *Pravda* in such a way that the really deep meaning could only be gotten by reading the full text.

I placed a question for comment before Paul Schmidt at the Foreign Office press conference and got a vapid answer. The Moscow piece had been more or less a warning and challenge to the Nazis, but they turned it aside by presenting a distorted version.

I tried then to pin Schmidt down by quoting a direct paragraph from *Pravda*, whereupon he branded it sharply as differing from his own version and testily closed the conference. That was a favorite trick of his when cornered, a perfect imitation of his lord and master, Ribbentrop.

For that day, as many times before and after, I was of course in the official doghouse. The Nazis hate to be put on the spot, and despite the indirect censorship and rigidly controlled opinion in Naziland, the Foreign Office press conference was a world sounding board and a sizzling hot spot. You had to know your stuff and mind your p's and q's there.

My version of the Moscow communiqué had come from the I.N.S. Moscow office and there was no reason to question it. Schmidt's was obviously a doctored text to suit the Wilhelmstrasse policy. Anybody could put two and two together then and figure out that sparks were flying behind the scene and that all was not well between Moscow and Berlin, however much the Nazis tried to put a pleasant face on it.

I was rising slowly from the green-covered conference table when the blond and genial little Russian correspondent of Tass tapped me on the shoulder and asked me to wait. When nearly everybody except a Swedish and a Turkish correspondent were gone, he pulled out a printed paper and from the Russian translated for us the Moscow communiqué as issued by his government the night before. It fully corroborated my version.

But a red-haired little Foreign Office clerk watched us with baleful eyes and next day Schmidt came storming into the press conference to announce peremptorily that anyone hereafter busying himself with the distribution or acquisition inside the Foreign Office of literature or communiqués from a foreign capital would be dealt with as a foreign agent.

He looked straight at the Tass man and advised him to stick to newspaper activity, and in fact that it might be a good idea for all European correspondents to remember that Americans directly or indirectly were the listening post for England. He added that Tass men were not specially privileged for activities outside their profession and if they didn't see their way clear to such working conditions in Berlin, they had better leave.

It was the first open hint of the claw, the first slight dropping of the Nazi mask in connection with Russia.

We said nothing and went about our business, accustomed to such temperamental storms. But all of us knew that there was more to it than that; the Russians from that day on began to watch all moves in Berlin closely and above their embassy the constant black chimney smoke told a familiar tale of burning documents.

I knew that weeks before the orders had gone out that Soviet military attachés were to be treated with the same courtesy as always but be shown nothing. Hitler stayed at headquarters and became suddenly inaccessible to all but the Italians and the Japs.

On Saturday night, June 21, many of the foreign correspondents were invited to an official shindig at Paul Schmidt's political club on Fasanen Strasse. I knew the night would not pass without a world sensation; old experience and an intuitive nose in addition to inside tips had told me pretty definitely that Hitler's latest move was ready.

So I went and found among those present the worried correspondents of Tass. They looked at me and I looked at them, thinking for just a split second I must be wrong. But sure enough, they had received invitations, as if nothing out of the ordinary was to happen. They drank their champagne with studious indifference, one eye on Schmidt in the far corner of the big and festive room.

At midnight on the stroke they, the three men from Moscow, were asked by one of Schmidt's henchmen to come up to his office on the second floor, adjoining the bar. I knew the Gestapo was waiting for them, and they knew it too. I turned to Emil Rasche, the only man in the Foreign Office without a uniform and the congenial friend of the correspondents, and told him I'd like to go home and get some rest.

He winked encouragingly. "*Ja, mon cher*, I will telephone you at home as soon as anything develops," he added, and shook hands.

Driving in the official car past the Soviet Embassy some ten minutes later, I satisfied a last bit of uncertainty when I found half-a-dozen police outside. The war was on, if not yet the actual shooting.

I called the office and, as might have been expected, all telephone and radio communication in and out of Germany was cut. There was nothing to do but go home and snatch a few hours' sleep in readiness for the great Hitler attack on Soviet Russia, an event Hitler and his Nazis had been preparing and planning for years.

It was to be the fulfillment of a task, a mission, and perhaps the end of World War II. Hitler was sure of himself; he had planned and prepared for months under cover. He was sure he had Stalin fooled; that the Red Army was hollow; that Russia would blow up from the inside, and that in six weeks he would enter Moscow in triumph.

The phone in my Berlin apartment rang at 3:20 A.M. on June 22, 1941. It was Herr Rasche of the Foreign Office to summon me to a special conference in the Wilhelmstrasse set for 6 A.M. I thanked him as on other similar occasions and hung up.

Hitler and Stalin had quit bluffing and playing fox; the war between them was on.

CHAPTER 12

An Interview with Hitler a Month before He Declared War on the United States

---

Hᴉᴛʟᴇʀ is afraid.

He is afraid of Franklin Delano Roosevelt.

He is afraid of the might and power of the United States.

He is afraid—perhaps most of all—that the crest of his wave has passed; that he may be visiting upon Germany and the world the unparalleled catastrophe that he long ago promised would be the only alternative to a Nazi victory.

But he does not say so.

I saw him scarcely a month before he declared war on the United States, and talked to him at length. It was not until the interview had long proceeded past the stage of bombast and boasting that I was able to sense the fear that is nibbling upon his strange mystic soul, keeping him awake at night.

But as a shield to these innermost feelings he shouted:

"I will outlast your President Roosevelt; I will also outlast this crazy man Churchill. I can afford to wait and take my time to win this war my own way."

Beneath that close-clipped little mustache the pursed lips of this man Hitler parted for just the fraction of a second, reflecting a pin point of Russian sun in that upper gold tooth of his. His eyes of watery blue looked at me with a vacant expression, lost in thoughts far away from that spot known to the world as the Fuehrer headquarters. He stood there amid the parklike scene, hands folded behind his back and the great coat of rubberized field gray nearly touching his boots.

I stood on the beaten path of hard sand already slightly edged with snow and waited. The Fuehrer was doing the talking; I knew from previous experience that this was no time to interrupt him.

"I am Fuehrer of a Reich that will last for a thousand years to come," he said suddenly, as if coming out of a distant mental space. His hands sprang into gesticulate action and his gray suède glove slapped the empty palm of his ungloved hand.

"No power on earth can shake the German Reich now. Divine Providence has willed it that I carry through the fulfillment of a Germanic task.

"Roosevelt and Churchill are passing phases of a world in upheaval and a social revolution. They don't seem to know it yet. I do. They are sitting over there in their plutocratic little world, surrounded and enslaved by everything proved obsolete in the last decade. The moneybags and Jews run the show behind the scenes; a parliamentary circus tramples on what is left in rights and privileges of their people. I have my people behind me and they have faith in me, their Fuehrer.

"But can Churchill say anything like that with any degree of certainty? For the time being he has whipped England into a state of obedience and what you people over there would call popularity. He is using this as political capital and eating off it like the man on pension.

"Someday, when the time comes and my armies strike more bitter blows against the vulnerable spots of the British Empire, then Mr. Churchill will suddenly find himself a man without political capital.

"History has shown that a British prime minister's life in office is of pretty short duration. Three or four years is a long time for a man in 10 Downing Street. The fortunes of war make it even harder, for not even Churchill can hold at bay indefinitely criticism and opposition in face of constant military blunders and reverses. I have seen three changes in 10 Downing Street precede Herr Churchill's premiership since I came to power. There will be more before this war is over."

Hitler stamped nervously with the polished right boot, a familiar habit of his and hard on the carpets. Back in the Café Louvre in Vienna, before the Anschluss and Gestapo put an end to this fascinating hotbed of rumor, gossip, and international journalism over the coffee cups, they had nicknamed him "Teppichfresser" because of that little habit of stamping or boot-pawing the carpet in nervous or thoughtful moments. Literally translated, it means chewing the carpet, and the term went easily around the world.

We walked with a loose stride toward the little lake amid the birch and pine woods, scarcely aware of the birds still chirping in the wintry sun. It isn't always easy to walk with Hitler; it is an unwritten rule that you keep in step no matter what the pace. Hitler is an erratic walker, falling at one moment into a slow lope caused probably by the twinge of rheumatism periodically bothering his right leg; the next moment, on the urge of a sudden torrent of speech, he changes to a light and almost dainty quickstep, turning slightly sidewise to talk while slapping the palm of the left hand with his glove. Curiously enough, he never looks back over his shoulder.

I stepped along with him, keeping just a fraction of a pace behind. Some years before, when I had first met and interviewed the Nazi Fuehrer high up in his Bavarian alpine chalet in Berchtesgaden, I had learned from brief instructions preceding the interview to keep my hands in plain sight. Even here in the open woods it would be a *faux pas* to put your hands in your pocket in company of the Fuehrer. He might get nervous, and if not his lynx-eyed bodyguard and uniformed shadows would definitely dislike your attitude. Even his field marshals and generals scarcely do otherwise, and by common consent they leave their service sidearms behind when around the Fuehrer.

We came to a turn in the path leading back to Fuehrer headquarters. On the sun bench alongside the lake's edge a squirrel was busily gathering supplies for winter. Hitler slowed up and motioned to me to look. He reached into the pocket of his coat and brought forth a paper bag of hazelnuts. Quietly, and with a half-smile on his pinkish face, he walked forward toward the squirrel, holding some nuts in the open palm of his right hand. The bushy-tailed little fellow looked with bright eyes at the man and his nuts, and waited to be coaxed. Then, with a quick jump, it ran up his coat and climbed into his hand, calmly to gather the nuts in its paws and sit there chattering. The Fuehrer and master of nearly all of Europe was pleased as Punch. He chuckled and talked to the little animal, forgetful of the world around him and the thousands fighting and dying at his command far out there on the Russian steppes.

"*Ja*, if the world would only mind its own business like this little squirrel," he said suddenly and brushed bushy-tail aside. We resumed a slower walk, and the half-dozen S.S. guards and yes men always around him moved forward at appropriate distance behind us.

"It gathers in food to live and keeps itself busy in the business of getting it all its life. That was all I wanted to do before the madmen made me change my plans and fight for the existence of Germany. I had plans and work for my people for fifty years to come, and didn't need a war to stay in office like the Daladiers and Chamberlains. And, for that matter, Herr Roosevelt of America."

My ears picked up a slight edge of annoyance in the voice of the Fuehrer when he mentioned Roosevelt. I looked at him out of the corner of my eye and saw his brow pucker beneath the visored cap with just a slight frown. Instinctively I felt that we had touched a sore spot, easy to guess and easy to irritate into a mental outburst. He was inwardly bitter and vindictive against the man he obviously considered his greatest political and personal foe, a man at the head of a state more powerful and more resourceful in a different way than his own, and therefore to him a direct menace and danger. I felt intuitively that just for that second an icy chill had crept between us. It struck me suddenly, with unmistakable clarity, that I had stumbled on a secret locked within the Fuehrer's breast, a secret he would never let out and which he may never admit having.

Mighty Hitler of the Nazi Reich and the New Order Europe basically and by instinct *fears* President Franklin D. Roosevelt of the United States of America, and no chest-pounding in public or boisterous talk of invincibility and unshakable faith in Divine Providence and victory can alter that fact.

I got a fleeting glimpse deep into his heart on that day of early November 1941, if not the secret plan in his mind for Japan's attack on us as the first step of desperate vengeance and expression of that very fear I discovered.

I repeat, Hitler down in the bottom of his heart is afraid of Roosevelt and as long as some years ago knew that he had met his match. He declared his own war on us in the wake of Japan's attack scarcely a month after I discovered his secret, proving beyond doubt that he is wildly grasping for safety by rushing into the fray in the hope of catching us before we are ready.

Like a tiger at bay, he wants to spring and land the
knockout blow to paralyze the power of the man and the
land he fears more than anything else in the world. His
sixth sense has told him that death and destruction of himself and his Nazi Reich lie at the end of the path if he fails
to thwart his mighty enemy across the Atlantic before
the next year of war has passed.

After that, it will be a downhill grade for the Fuehrer
and his cohorts, swept along by that tidal wave of overwhelming power and resources mobilized into action
against him by America and Roosevelt.

2

"*Ja,* Herr Roosevelt—and his Jews!"

The now-scowling Hitler added this as an afterthought.
He seemed to be talking to himself, forgetful of the American at his side, and brooding over the man he hated.

"He wants to run the world and rob us all of a place in
the sun. He says he wants to save England but he means he
wants to be ruler and heir of the British Empire.

"I first saw this some years ago, when Roosevelt began
his undeclared war on me through speeches, boycotts, and
political intriguing in all chancelleries of Europe. Every
time I reached forth my hand he slapped it down. When I
began to show him that meddling in European affairs was
not so easy and might be dangerous, he lost all control of
himself and began his campaign of vilification.

"With his Bullitts and Biddles he pushed Europe into the
war against me, not to save and preserve the obsolete

democracies, but to despoil the youth and the strength of the nations of the world in order to enslave them in plans of his own.

"I have realized all this long ago and I knew, too, that the sabotage of Munich was arranged as much if not more in your Washington than in London. All that year before the war I saw the hand of Roosevelt in everything over here that went on, and it seemed at times that even the British were merely acting as the tools of another man.

"When the war came, I felt that peace and common sense were not yet lost and therefore stood back time and again blinded by Roosevelt and his golden calf. He wanted the war to go on and bring misery and destruction to the German people."

A cold rain mixed with a bit of sleet had begun despite the patches of sunlight peering out of fast-driving clouds. We reached the glass door leading into the central house of Fuehrer headquarters that looked not unlike a comfortable hunting lodge. Inside the small hall with its mounted deer heads, flunkies with booted black pants and white coats without ornament took our things and deferentially stepped aside. So did everybody else around that house, giving you the uncomfortable feeling that none but the Fuehrer should be heard or seen, lest perhaps a blitz of unrestrained temper and authority hit the man nearest this volcano. That has happened time and again, coming and going with the destructive and startling force of a whirlwind.

Hitler walked into the plainly furnished reception room with its little round table surrounded by easy chairs and a sofa. The whole was the familiar reproduction in miniature of Hitler's personal style in reception rooms and chancelleries, at Munich and Berlin and Berchtesgaden, all slightly on the stiff side with a restrained reach for the dignified.

A fire of split logs blazed cheerily on the hearth. A shepherd dog with a swastika collar strolled lazily up to Hitler and nuzzled his hand. He stroked the head, motioning me to sit down opposite. Others like his unimaginative Press Chief Otto Dietrich and Chief Interpreter Schmidt also came around to sit there and listen in silent obedience.

By no stretch of the imagination could one call a party like this a gay or inspiring occasion. A taste of the formidable, mixed with suspense and the uneasy feeling of something unreal, pervaded the room. It seemed very warm around there suddenly, and on the back of my neck I felt the slight moisture of perspiration. Yet I do not perspire easily.

The Fuehrer looked at a message held before him on a tablet by one of his military adjutants. Without glancing at the man who had brought the message, he scribbled on the pad and pushed it away. He sat forward again and held his hands between his knees.

There was a moment of hesitation as his eyes came to rest straight upon me, striving, no doubt, for a split second to identify again this mortal before him.

"I know how to wait," the nervous mouth said suddenly with a quick draw of breath. "*Ja*, and I *can* wait. I waited three years for Austria, and at the end of that time, despite all the mischief and opposition against me by paid political criminals and elements in and outside of Europe, I got back Austria without firing a shot.

"When the time came, I marched in with flying colors and drums beating. Where was all that big talk then? Where is Starhemberg? Where is Schuschnigg now? The world has forgotten them, and today Austria is as much part of the Third Reich as Sudetenland.

"I know my people and I know war. If we must fight for a decision as to who will survive in Europe, then I as a soldier from the trenches of the World War know how to fight that war. Over here we will come out on top, and no Stalin or Churchill or Roosevelt can alter that fact."

He began rubbing his knees in growing agitation. It was not necessary to bait him on with questions; on the contrary, it would have interfered with his thoughts. In any case, I was there more or less by "royal" command without being clearly aware of the purpose.

I was due to leave Berlin for America within a few days, after eight years in Berlin as chief central European correspondent for International News Service.

I was not even to publish what was said, except for some doctored propaganda I wouldn't take, although I knew that within a few days Hitler was to hold his annual speech before the Nazi-party vets in the traditional Munich beer cellar.

Perhaps, after the many talks and some interviews I have had alone and with others before and during the war, he wanted to get something off his chest. Keeping in mind that even at that moment this master of Naziland had in his pocket the zero hour he had fixed for Japan's attack on us and the subsequent declaration of war against America on the part of the Axis, I would make a guess and say that he had a bad conscience. Without knowing it, I was a sort of father-confessor to him. He was groping for a way to justify himself before the deed.

"As I said, political storms and military setbacks one of these days will sweep Churchill away the same as it swept away the Daladiers, Reynauds, Chamberlains, and eventually the Stalins." The right boot dug into the carpet again, this time almost viciously.

"*Ja*, I can wait. I can wait years but Churchill can't. One of these days he will be gone, and even if I have not landed with my army on the island, where is England then? They don't know why they are fighting the war, and the aristocrats as well as the underfed classes are being crushed in more ways than one by the burden of war.

"Perhaps then, if I wanted to, I could strike a deal with the British Empire within twenty-four hours and settle the war over here. Where would Herr Roosevelt be then? My armies would be in all vital spots of the Continent, and inside from the Channel to the Urals we could be busy building up our New Europe, independent of overseas and feeding itself without worry about the wheat or the coffee going to rot in Canada or South America.

"I could sit here behind my guns for the next twenty years and let America do what it will.

"But the next twenty years will not be twenty years of

Roosevelt. I am young and healthy. Roosevelt is not. He is, furthermore, a president already sitting in office for the third time in violation of all political tradition and customs of his land. In a few years he must once again face the voters to keep the office or get out. He practically had to get into a war with me to keep going until now.

"He and I are at war, and even if he goes into his White House for a fourth term, I will still be here. If not I personally, then the next Fuehrer. Germany will not go down before Roosevelt, and I can wait until he is gone.

"Then we shall see what is what in the two hemispheres."

3

Hitler talked on, scarcely pausing for breath. Inside his peculiar mind he was then and there already at grips with Roosevelt, mentally grasping for the throat of his deadly foe and tearing him to bits in an inborn rage over wrongs and grievances he believes he has suffered at the hands of the man with the smile in Washington.

I sat there listening to this tirade of bitterness rooted in fear; he gave the impression of a man who had had victory in his grasp only to have it torn out of his hands again by the elusive foe who haunted his dreams.

Hitler repeated much of what had been said often and which since has become superseded through the declaration of war between America and Germany. He declared that American ships of any kind coming under the range of torpedo tubes or German guns en route to England would be sent to the bottom. His U-boats, he said, were equal to the task of enforcing that blockade against the combined sea power of England and America, and his planes and surface craft would drive rivets into that steel net on the Atlantic around England.

From his side of the military viewpoint, he argued, there was nothing to fear from America.

"Long ago," Hitler said, "I saw America inevitably being led into this war. There is a limit to everything, and people playing with dynamite are going to get hurt.

"I have told the German people day in and day out for more than a year now that they must be prepared to face America at war. I felt it my responsibility to keep our people mentally and morally prepared for all such eventualities. I also took all the military precautions essential to the safety of our position over here.

"Today I have a clear conscience and feel sure that, come what may, America from the military standpoint can do nothing to hurt us on this continent. Her entry into this war will cost many a brave U-boat or naval or Luftwaffe German his life.

"We may be compelled by American aggression over here to undertake new tasks to defend ourselves. Whatever that is, we shall not be afraid to do it and meet the enemy man to man."

He caught himself suddenly, peering fixedly at the dog, and said: "There is more than one way of fighting America. I can let Herr Roosevelt in for a few surprises. It's all a matter of how you do it.

"Of course I cannot walk across the Atlantic and

America, from the standpoint of invasion, might as well be up on the moon, but, on the other hand, the same goes for Herr Roosevelt. He has lots of ships at his disposal to bring an expedition over here for an attack on us or to occupy some undefended islands this side of the Atlantic, but I hold the coasts of Europe and I am ready any time he wants to come over here with one million or five million to fight it out once and for all.

"We Germans know we are fighting for our very existence, be that in Africa or on the Don. We Nazis also have a cause to fight for and nobody can rob us of the ideals and principles we fought for over the past twenty years.

"Do you think for one moment that any single German outside of an idiot or two ever wants to go back to the days of hunger, starvation, revolution, and Bolshevism inside our land?

"There can be no choice, even if they wanted it.

"Stalin and his Red armies are practically smashed, sitting over there beyond the mud and snow hoping against hope that England and America will save them from the final reckoning. There have been minor setbacks through climate, transportation, and other circumstances, but these difficulties all will fade away when the time comes to resume the grand-scale operations we have now suspended.

"Stalin can go sit behind his Urals and talk as he wants to; he will then no longer be a factor in this world. Bolshevism will never again be permitted to gain a foothold on this continent. Russia no longer will be just a vast armament factory exploited and dedicated solely to the task of generating sufficient military power behind a curtain of silence to carry through the Moscow dream of world revolution.

"There will never again be a Red army of fantastically armed millions. These untold resources and raw materials and wealth of the land will be turned to a new task by me: I intend in the shortest time possible to turn Russia into the European breadbasket, the factory, and the industrial nerve center. There is no limit to its possibilities, and we know how to make the most of the opportunity."

Outside it was getting dark, although it was scarcely five o'clock. Fidgety attendants and adjutants were sufficient proof that I could soon go, down through the path to the spur of railway track with the little station especially built near Fuehrer headquarters to receive visitors from the outside world. They come and go all day long, handled with care or politely given their bill of fare as served on the New Order program of Hitler's Europe.

Here, in that very same room of the fireplace and round table, Hitler plotted his revenge against the man in Washington he fears. Here, in the very chair I sat in, sat time and again Japanese Ambassador in Berlin General Oshima, Yankee hater Number One and in a way the father of the revived anti-Comintern pact.

In this room Hitler and Oshima, in company of Champagne King and Foreign Minister Ribbentrop, put their heads together repeatedly to hatch out in long and weary sessions the exact details of the plot against America.

The political consent and agreements between the governments of Tokyo and Rome for such a policy undoubtedly were the first essential. That is shown by the fact that Mussolini during the late summer and fall twice came all the way from the seven hills to Fuehrer headquarters in Russia. Even then, I doubt if today either Oshima or Mussolini could identify the exact location of Fuehrer headquarters. You never ask Hitler any questions like that any more than you get down to brass tacks about his girl friends. You can do that with Mussolini and he'll talk by the hour of love and lovers, but never Hitler.

Knowing the ways and methods of Hitler after all these years, I could easily imagine the process and procedure arrived at in weaving to perfection Hitler's twofold move against the United States.

As far back as the forging of the Three-Power Pact in Berlin he laid the groundwork for his war of revenge and desperation against Roosevelt. From that basic political agreement of September 1940 the wily Fuehrer was able to spin his web of intrigue and world war.

He was beginning to lay his guns for Russia, and in strictest confidence was able therewith to assuage both Mussolini and Hirohito. He told them to be patient and keep in mind that Nazi Germany in its conception would always remain the mortal foe of Bolshevist Russia. But they must bide their time and do nothing prematurely.

It explains the strange self-assurance of both Italy and Japan during the trying six months that followed, interspersed with rumors of trouble underneath the surface between Berlin, Tokyo, and Rome. Actually, this was a false front deliberately manufactured by the propaganda machines of the three countries to hide from the Anglo-Saxon world and from Soviet Russia the deeply laid plot that was brewing.

Once set on this course, Hitler rid himself in Berlin of the pro-American Japanese Ambassador Kurusu, who had replaced Oshima in the latter's downfall after the signing of the Hitler-Stalin deal in August of 1939. Early in 1941 he maneuvered the reappointment as Japanese Ambassador to Berlin of General Oshima, and from that time on the Fuehrer had a free hand to chart the course of his Machiavellian plot. It was not definite at first whether this radical resort to war against America would become necessary after a blitz defeat of Russia. In fact, Oshima was convinced that America was bluffing and would back down before Japanese demands if behind those demands in the Far East stood Hitler and Mussolini as victors unparalleled on the battle front of Russia.

The failure subsequently by the German armies to secure that blitz decision over Stalin in 1941 seriously upset the applecart for the tripartite plotters and there remained only the single choice of tackling America before it had an inkling of what was up. Several changes in Tokyo governments had to be made to oust all timid factions, and Mussolini engaged in some internal head-knocking of his own before the tripartite regimes stood ready to face the zero hour Hitler so cleverly and ruthlessly had set.

It remained then for all concerned to map out in the last and finest detail the military coup aimed to knock out both the American and British spearheads of defense in the Pacific.

I can imagine that day after day in this room where I sat Hitler expounded the absolute need for secrecy and surprise.

An Italian mission from the General Staff and a group of high officers from the general staff from Tokyo soon met in the finely shielded remoteness of Fuehrer headquarters.

Of course it goes without saying that Hitler in his scheming of this giant plot had not overlooked the importance of correlating German and Japanese efforts in the Far East itself.

That would have been a vital error. He needed a good machine of intrigue out in Tokyo and Shanghai. He set out to build himself one to suit, based on battle-scarred and six-foot Major-General Ott, his ambassador in Tokyo. Ott is a powerful and influential man in Tokyo, who helped train Japanese troops and officers before the first shot was fired in Manchukuo. Some say Ott knows more about Japan and her politics than the rapidly changing foreign ministers there.

Hitler appointed him in charge of the job of swinging Japan against America. He sent as able assistant Heinrich Stahmer, who sold the Japs the Three-Power Pact. Stahmer was given the official title of Ambassador to the Nanking regime. But in actuality Stahmer was to smooth the way behind the scenes for Japan's complete immersion in the war, and Stahmer always has done a thorough job of all assigned to him. He is not unlike Von Papen in this respect, although much younger.

A bright young man named Helmuth Wohlthat, renegade protégé of Hjalmar Schacht of the high collar and orthodox financial principles, was dispatched to the Far East to negotiate and shape into line the economic "New Order" of the Pacific.

In Shanghai, Kurt Meisinger operated, a retired colonel and former Gestapo chief in Warsaw. He had his fingers in the pie throughout the Far East and to him fell the task of keeping Ott on the right path. Hitler also sent Fritz Wiedemann to Tientsin after his return from San Francisco as Consul-General there and told him to push the war in the Far East all he could.

Hans Borchers, the former Consul-General in New York, was sent as aide to Stahmer, in addition to which scores and scores of Nazi agents sailed or filtered away to the Far East, spreading even through Thailand and all vital points of the Orient.

The center of Nazi intrigue and pressure for war in the Pacific remained Tokyo, but Shanghai became the beehive of Nazi propaganda activity and machinery. Here the ever-busy Baron von Puttkammer was assigned by Hitler to ride the saddle, and ride it he does. He has drawn to him a score of Nazi brain-trusters for the control and utilization of radio, press, and café. All of it part of that Hitler machinery operating against America and the British Empire in the Far East, such as the springing of the Japanese attack on Pearl Harbor and the Philippines.

There before the maps of the Pacific and Far East, Hitler's pencil drew a circle around the spot identified as Pearl Harbor in Hawaii. He drew similar circles around tiny dots of the Midways, Wake Island, and Guam, denoting the Philippines with a cross for occupation by Japan.

My guess is that the Dutch East Indies, Singapore, and Australia were treated similarly. Each and every pencil mark called for action at a given moment by the Japanese fleet and air force. The consultations over details with the German General Staff and the Japanese military must have been long and lengthy, guided always by the Hitler plan.

Then, after the initial attack, Hitler and Mussolini were to come in with a moral boost for Japan by declaring war on the United States.

The military operations of the Axis against America came in for the same precision, leaving nothing to chance or in favor of British-American co-operation. No doubt the weight of the Axis blow was to be against the British Empire and against America in the Atlantic and Africa, keeping both so busy that out in the Pacific Japan faced an enemy worried by a two-front war. It took a lot of painstaking preparation, but once the time was set and the signal given those who sat in this room before me shook hands and considered it a job well done.

I left that place with the feeling that something was in the air. Actually, I had come to it as close as anyone outside of the plot could possibly have come to it. The war is on now, and my hunch that I would never again set foot in this house is now confirmed.

There was in my mind not so much at that time the things that Hitler said but rather the things that he had said in the years gone by in private and intimate circles. That was before the war, when he was still building up his armies and blitz machine. Without knowing for sure whether he would master even a part of Europe.

In those days he was hoping to find a way to smash Communist Russia but, failing that, as he frequently stated, he would go down on the smoking ruins of Europe and leave no stone upon the other. He has repeated that same assertion since World War II got under way, and it is more than an assumption on my part to say that Hitler is fanatic and fatalist enough to carry out not only personally, but for Europe, the verdict he himself pronounced at the beginning of this war before the German Reichstag. He put on his uniform of field gray, named those to succeed him in case of death, and declared that he would come out of this war the victor alive or the vanquished dead. He meant also that he would come out of the war complete master of Europe or go down under the greatest shambles of blood and ruins and scorched earth ever to blot out a civilized continent.

Thus, as darkness covered the woods and the train in which I traveled back to Berlin, I left a man committed to win or to die in this war.

With a shock I realized that down in his heart is gnawing intuition that the crest of the wave for him has passed. He may have heard that astrologers are saying that the eighth year of his favorable sign in the heavens is the last. It is a worrisome thing, sufficient to keep him awake and in a restless mood for many hours of the night.

He paces the floor or reads a book, trying to keep down the uneasiness in his mind and in his heart symbolized and personalized ruthlessly and mercilessly by the face of the smiling man he fears, the man who sits in the White House far out across the Atlantic—the man who keeps him awake sometimes until the break of dawn.

DATE DUE

GAYLORD			PRINTED IN U.S.A.